WITHDRAWN

Lope de Vega Carpio

Desire's Experience Transformed: a Representative
Anthology of Lope de Vega's Lyric Poetry

translated into English verse
by

Carl W. Cobb

Lope de Vega Carpio

Desire's Experience Transformed: a Representative
Anthology of Lope de Vega's Lyric Poetry

translated into English verse
by

Carl W. Cobb

Spanish Literature Publications Company
York, South Carolina
1991

Library of Congress Catalog Card Number 91-60466

ISBN 0-938972-18-9

Printed in the United States of America

This book must be for Emily
In sign of your appeal;
You, presence bright, our loves unite,
Dear Emily Jane Beal.

Grandmother Jane Dreams a Sonnet
for Emily Jane on Her First Birthday

You safely here, your mother said to me
You would be christened Emily Jane Beal.
Into my heart I felt a rapture steal,
And thus began our wondrous intimacy.

I cared for you those first days lovingly,
Your little being relearning how to feel
In acts that were each moment true and real,
Yet acts re-lived from deepest memory.

Grandmother, mother, daughter makes a bond
Where immemorial emotions flow,
A bond to last our lives and even beyond.

I hope to dream you, hold you, help you grow,
To see you, Emily with Jane, respond:
May God on you, on us, his grace bestow.

Sonnet for Lope in Two Languages

Just Lope de Vega . . . from the Mountain though,
You with those nineteen towers on your crest;
"As good as Lope's," late they called the best:
It's strange nobody's called you "don," you know.

In rhyming verse eight hundred plays or so,
Some sixteen hundred sonnets, and the rest;
All Spain mourned you, your "dying well" expressed,
Then soon your bones did to the boneyard throw.

You had the courtly faith, yet practiced life;
Poor Friar, worse priest, but Christian humbly real,
As "greatest sinner" you yourself did cite.

Desire kept you in strife, domestic strife,
Yet you upheld Spain's Golden Age ideal:
The image of a perfect gentle knight.

Lope de Vega, escudo de Montaña
que diecinueve torres relucía;
"bueno como de Lope," se decía:
que no te hayan llamado "Don" extraña.

Ochocientas comedias fue tu hazaña,
sonetos milseiscientos de poesía;
tu "bien morir" lloró la patria pía,
y al osario tus huesos dio España.

Con fe cortés, la vida practicabas,
mal Frey y cura, Cristiano bien sincero;
de "el mayor pecador" te condenabas.

Visión tenías de Español entero
(mientras con tu Deseo te embrollabas):
la imagen de un perfecto caballero.

Contents

Preface

Even while still polishing the translations of the sonnets and ballads of Quevedo, I foolishly turned to the lyric poetry of Lope de Vega, with the modest fires of inspiration still glowing. Outside scattered examples of some religious sonnets and anthology pieces, such as those translated by Longfellow, Lope was there as a challenge to translate, the goal again a representative anthology. The simple question in beginning such a task remains, is the repeated effort of finding the modest inspiration and employing the technical resources to recreate each poem with its multiple problems worth it? With Quevedo it was, given the variety and thrust of his poetry in three contrasting areas, the courtly love with Neoplatonic vision, the satirical-grotesque, and the Stoic-Christian. With Lope de Vega the effort has been well worth it, although there has been a bit of ice with the fire. It is of course not Lope's fault that of the important Golden Age poets he has been singled out for his simplicity and directness of expression. Even in his sonnets there is often an elegant simplicity closer to natural speech. Now just this quality is the terror of the translator, especially since English is monosyllabic and syntactically much different from Spanish. In addition, the translator, who needs to penetrate every phrase and relation, soon discovers in Lope forced syntax and ambiguity of meaning. Unlike the critic, the poor translator must decide on the meaning of every phrase. With Lope a certain haste is expected; he himself declared that he had written a three-act play, in completely rhyming form, in twenty-four hours.

A larger problem for the contemporary translator of Lope de Vega involves his stance as a Renaissance poet and his cultivation of the poetic modes and themes of this period. (And of course why should he not?) In our age the poet is generally in anguish in the sub-realism of an insufficient world, sometimes with a faith in the "people." Above all he must be "serious," even grim, in certain ways which have gradually been delimited. Now Lope de Vega had (in Vossler's phrase) a "lust for poetry"; on the basis of a slim conceit he could spin out a near-perfect sonnet, ending it with a powerful line of resolution or surprise. Lope suffers in his poetry, but not seriously enough for us. Whereas Quevedo would scream in his anguish, Lope even keeps the chaos of his love under poetic control. Whereas Quevedo in struggle with his ideal dares to express its counter face in the grotesque, Lope only brings the courtly ideal down a little nearer to the human. Only in his religious poetry does Lope touch extremes, and his extreme of personal sin and abject repentance are not much in fashion in our century. Thus, while both Góngora and Quevedo (since Unamuno's time) have almost become cult figures, Lope has enjoyed a modest revival, with emphasis upon the strong human note in both his religious and late love poetry. In working toward this meaningful and representative anthology of Lope de Vega's lyric poetry, I have kept constantly in mind that here is a man of his age and for all ages, a man and his poetry. A man he was with his *deseo*, or desire. With that excess of desire he wrote perhaps as many as a thousand plays, all in verse form. From what was left over he wrote his lyric poetry. Lope de Vega is a great poet of Renaissance stance, who while still believing in the two ideals of his age, the Neoplatonic and the religious, transformed his rich and turbulent experience into a poetry which still touches the ideal, but moves ever closer to the real and the human.

    In seeking a text to translate, I have gone from Lope's original volumes, the *Rimas* (*Rhymes*), the *Rimas sacras* (*Sacred Rhymes*) and the *Rimas humanas y divinas* (*Rhymes Human and Divine*) to the various anthologies with modern editing and back. In a few cases I have had to modernize the text of the original volumes, since my choice has not been anthologized. I have utilized basically the *Poesías líricas* of the Coleccíon Austral, the older anthology of Sainz de Robles, and the recent one edited by José M. Blecua, *Lírica* (Madrid, 1981). Perhaps I should be but I am not much of a student of textual variations. In most cases I am translating anthology pieces which have been before us for years. In identifying the originals from the books of poetry, I have used Lope's Roman numerals for the *Rhymes* and *Sacred Rhymes*; since the *Rhymes Human and Divine* are not numbered, I have counted them and given them an Arabic number for identification. The poems scattered between these books are identified by the volumes in which they appeared.

    In translating Lope's sonnets and ballads (by far his most

prevalent forms), I have continued to use the Petrarchan form of the sonnet and the standard form of the English ballad. After passing 300 sonnets in this form I no longer whine at having to put his effortless (and sometimes sloppy) octaves in double-quadruple rhyme, with his having a rhyming advantage. In English, while Shakespeare chose not to struggle with Petrarchan form, Milton, Elizabeth Browning, Dante Rossetti, especially Wordsworth (who left 535), and Edna St. Vincent Millay in our century proved that the Petrarchan sonnet is possible in English. By his later years Lope was consistently using the double-triple rhyme (cdc, dcd) in the sestet; after a few successes with this form I attempted it more and more. By now I sometimes wake up composing pentameters. It has been a special pleasure and a challenge to translate Lope's fine concluding lines, there being many of them. Interestingly, Lope's sonnets often have the classical structure, that is, with the problem or the metaphorical example in the octave, the resolution or the main theme in the sestet. As for the ballads, I have continued to use the standard 4-3 form in English (a form that comes down to Auden), with rhyme on the even lines, a form somewhat different from but historically comparable to the Spanish ballad form which utilizes octasyllables with continuing assonance on the even lines. In English, assonance and imperfect rhyme are ineffective unless used very sparingly. In both languages the meter and the rhyme—the sound, the rhythm, the music—are essential to the ballad.

Lope's sonnets (like Quevedo's) offer a particular problem of grammar to the translator: the use of two patterns for the pronoun *you*, without his making a clear distinction between the two. (During these same years Shakespeare in his sonnets used both *thou* and *you* without a clear difference in meaning.) Surely Lope must have *intimately felt* that either *vos* or *tú* was more real to him; apparently poetic tradition was stronger than personal feeling with him. In any case with both the Lady and with Jesus (or God) he uses these two forms. Although language is a prime vehicle for prejudice in many other ways, our democratizing age tends to demand one second person pronoun; yet we can argue it is no particular virtue to have one pronoun for you. When I began, then, to show this variety I cast a few sonnets in the *thou* form, which is still understandable in English. As I continued to re-read my sonnets, however, especially the series to Jesus, I decided that the two forms seriously upset the continuity of feeling and I went back and put them all in the *you* form.

With this solid volume of a representative selection of Lope de Vega's lyric poetry, along with a companion volume of Quevedo's lyric poetry already published, I bring to a close a satisfying project I believe unique in English. Although the previously mentioned poets proved that the Petrarchan sonnet can be written in English, no translator has dared to meet this form head on in English in sonnet after sonnet. Of course the contemporary translators can convince themselves that since unrhymed, unmetrical, common prosaic prose is our form of poetic expression, one can best capture the "spirit" in such a lack of form. I have observed (and I speak in lightness) that when the contemporary translators declare that they are going for the "spirit" of a poem, we can expect all spirit and no form. I continue to say no against terrible odds. The literary community, the defenders of liberal arts, have always been more of sheep than even teenagers. Surprisingly, while "structure" has been the rage, traditional form has all but disappeared as a subject. The youth especially will not even consider form. This is puzzling when we consider that for youth traditional music does not exist, but that music has been reduced to a single, stultifying, simplistic, ear-destroying beat—or *form*! It is encouraging to report that in 1990 a voice or two arose questioning the free verse tide. Bruce Bawer in *The New Criterion* (November, 1990) discusses his failure when he set out to lead a poetry workshop dedicated to the sonnet, for the students would not and could not take form seriously. He goes on to discuss at length a solid book by Timothy Steele, *Missing Measures* (1990), which traces the "revolt against meter" in the modern period, pursuing the theme all the way back to the Greeks and Aristotle. Among the major 20th century Spanish poets it is instructive that Jiménez, Lorca, and Guillén all three worked their way toward individualized free verse in mid-career, then all three returned to traditional forms, even the sonnet. In very traditional forms, then, I offer this volume dedicated to Lope to go with the one dedicated to Quevedo, and I shall not return to the Spanish Golden Age poets, since both St. John of the Cross and even the Baroque Góngora have been adequately translated. Instead I am already in loving struggle with both Lorca and Jorge Guillén, whose poetry in modernized traditional forms offers a daunting challenge.

(The author wishes to acknowledge the generous grant from the Graduate School, represented by Dr. C. W. Minkel, and the College of Liberal Arts, represented by Dean Lorman Ratner, of the University of Tennessee, Knoxville, toward the publication of this volume.)

Introduction

Years ago in preparing a talk for a general Liberal Arts program on Lope de Vega, I was firmly struck by the idea that he is a stunning example of a man who pursued rich and turbulent experience to the fullest, then transformed (not merely recorded) that experience into poetry. With further reading I could see that I had re-invented the wheel. Years ago Montesinos declared: "There is no other great Spanish poet whose biography reveals to us in such an instinctive way this process of transformation of the flowers of life, avidly enjoyed, into the honey of eternal art."[1] The important Lope scholar Entrambasaguas entitled his long biography *Vivir y crear de Lope de Vega*, the very title joining his living and his creating. Finally, Blecua in his recent Introduction to his anthology of Lope's poetry declares in his opening sentence: "No Spanish poet has transmitted his agitated existence into so many very beautiful poems as Lope de Vega."[2] Prate how we will as critics, we would all like to see the poet live fully and completely, at the same time transforming (not merely recording) those vital experiences into books of poetry. Extreme in everything, Lope is at times too close to the experience; yet he himself was aware that his facility in poetry was such that he could do it automatically, without fresh experience.

Certainly Lope de Vega (1562-1635) crammed a great deal of domestic experience into his (for the times) long life. It takes a whole page to list and identify the thirteen women who touched his life (some very briefly!) and the sixteen children which followed. Beginning with an unknown woman he called "Marfisa" in 1579, the parade continued until 1632, three years before he died. The most turbulent relation is surely that with Elena Osorio (Filis and later Dorotea), beginning around 1583, the only one in which Lope was losing, and thus it brought out the worst and the best in him. Still embroiled with Elena, Lope met Isabel de Urbina (Belisa) from a good family, charmed and seduced her, was forced to marry her; in exile from Madrid, they enjoyed a home for six years until Isabel died in child-birth. Around 1595 Lope met Juana de Guardo, daughter of a well-to-do butcher in Madrid, who became his wife of duty until 1615, and Lope served her faithfully in his way. Around 1598 he met Micaela de Luján (Camila Lucinda), already married with children; for a time Lope established two households for his two families. After a favorite son died in 1612 and Juana followed in 1613, Lope suffered a severe religious crisis, ultimately becoming a priest with cassock and title from Rome. Finally, at about 55 he met Marta de Nevares (Amaryllis), waited until her husband died, then moved her into his household; she started going blind some years later, then went mad, finally died in 1632. Lope was then left with only a favorite daughter, Antonia Clara, who herself was stolen from Lope's house by a Don Juan. All this domestic living by a man who at the same time was writing 800 plays, six epic poems, 1600 sonnets, in all perhaps two million lines of poetry! And it is only fair to add that Lope lived, suffered with, and idealized these women (except for Juana). Indeed, whereas Garcilaso de la Vega, Herrera, and Quevedo exalted an ideal they barely knew, Lope idealized the very women, in some cases even illiterate, who were producing his children and cooking his meals.

Since Lope consistently and insistently transformed the details of his life into poetry, we have jotted down this dizzyingly brief biography. The study of Lope's poetry, despite the intensification in scholarship since World War II, has proceeded piecemeal and in general toward his emphasis upon the popular. In fact, as late as 1981 Blecua's bibliography does not list a single book which attempts to synthesize his poetry. As early as the 1930's however, Montesinos in his editorship of Lope's poetry established in his introduction the outline of his extended production. Although Lope began early and continued to produce quantities of poetry throughout his life, it is possible to organize that poetry generally according to specific books and cycles, with the addition of certain groups of poems in their proper place. Chronologically and poetically his poetry begins with two loose cycles of ballads which became very popular: the Moorish and the pastoral ballads. Lope's second and perhaps most typical book he called starkly *Rimas* (*Rhymes*, 1602), a volume of modified Neoplatonic love, along with other Renaissance themes. This little book (of 200 sonnets!) was sneaked into a larger volume between two Renaissance epics, the second one on Sir Francis Drake. (As was still the case with Shakespeare, it was not yet proper to publish personal lyric poetry). His second important volume is called *Rimas sacras* (*Sacred Rhymes*, 1614), a collection of personal and general religious poetry in sonnet, ballad, and other forms. The religious and the love poetry of his mature years is generally scattered in books of varied content. For example, his continuation with the ballad form, now polished to perfection in poems of prudence relating to his own existence, appears in the important work *La Dorotea* (1632). His writing of songs and poems (and even sonnets) in the plays, continues throughout his career. His final important book (especially for our age) is *Rimas humanas y divinas* (*Rhymes Human and Divine*, 1634), supposedly by his *alter ego* Tomé de Burguillos. These *Rhymes* are much more human than divine. From this ample collection we have made a selection, including anthology pieces, but going beyond, a selection we trust representative of Lope de Vega's achievement as a lyric poet.

Surely it is proper to begin with the series of Moorish ballads, since generally they all relate to Lope's first cataclysmic love, a relation "have" but ultimately "have not"—at first Lope enjoyed her favors, then her family intervened. Although a Renaissance poet to the core and thus a defender of the Italian forms, Lope early and late utilized the traditional ballad form of the *Romancero*, the great collection of anonymous historical ballads relating to early Spanish heroes such as the Cid. Along with Góngora and Quevedo, Lope is responsible for elevating this humble form to the respectable position it has held ever since. The Moorish ballad, related to the chivalric novel and the Renaissance epic, but especially to the traditional Frontier Ballads, presents the noble, heroic, courtly world of the Moors in Spain, *from their viewpoint*. Thus Lope utilizes this literary world as a kind of giant metaphor for the specific amorous experiences of his own life. These experiences, often tawdry on his part, are transformed almost beyond recognition in the ballads—and why not?

Among the Moorish ballads, we are beginning with two in an elegant vein, poems which sustain the heroic and yet emphasize the amorous. In "The Almoralife most renowned," Lope's protagonist projects a nobly heroic pose worthy of Richard Lovelace. His Almoralife (in Arabic, the minister who collected the King's taxes), he of the "lance most feared," is on his way down to the sea to win one of the King's wars. The first third of the ballad is given to a physical description of this heroic figure. But the renowned warrior is also courtly lover: separating himself from his subordinates, he takes out a portrait of his Filisalva (that is Phyllis, the names vary) and laments to it that she is angry with him because he has to leave her. As a point of honor he must first go to battle; therefore he begs her to send him his soul now living in her so that he can conquer. Although his love is important, in the last stanza he rejoins his subordinates and they begin to speak of "arms and battles." A companion piece in this subtle aesthetic elegance is "Go saddle the colt of silver gray." In dramatic fashion, the protagonist (here Azarque) calls for his subordinates to bring him all the tools of his heroic trade: the coat of mail, the shield, the plumed helmet. But this protagonist is also a poet: it takes a stanza to describe the helmet's plumes. Moreover, he also wants his medallion on which is the famous scene of Adonis—the words below say, "He dies." The protagonist of course sees himself in the "grace and fate" of Adonis and he cannot resist a monologue to Adalifa, urging her to be constant. She should study his portrait in which his eyes are "open" (not like Adonis's), eyes which have shed tears for her. But battle and duty call:

> Though willingness him conquers not,
>   To conquer parts of Moor:
> His honor and his effort make
>   His promises secure.

For Góngora, who was a clod in feeling but a giant in verbal dexterity, this was too much, and he produced a burlesque version of this ballad which rivalled Lope's, the first line beginning, "Go saddle my ass of silver gray." In our age, it is difficult to take Lope's poem as "serious."

In a pair of ballads, which became very popular (in part because they have popular touches), Zaida and Zaide haggle over the problems and dangers of their relationship. The opening line "Mira, Zaide, que te aviso" is from the old ballads. Of course even courtly love was a truancy (in Otis Green's phrase); here Lope pushes toward domestic squabble. Although Zaide is confessed to be noble and heroic, the lass Zaida warns him not to prowl before her door, endangering her existence; because of his big mouth she dismisses him with the well known adage, "One who such does, such pays." Zaide in his ballad responds to her point by point, arguing that he talks a lot to assuage his woes, and ends by quoting her her own adage. In another ballad, "In prison cell Adulce lies," the protagonist lies in prison, not because of his vicious conduct but because of "unjust enemies." (Behind all this is the fact that Lope's rage-induced conduct landed him in jail.) Here in jail at the grille he touchingly remembers "another grille" when his Aja was in his embrace. Although he protests his undying love, when his page brings him a letter from Adalifa (clearly another love) offering "condolence for his ills," Adulce declares defiantly "What matters it / If Aja my end wills?"

Apparently by general consent the jewel of the Moorish ballads is "The star of Venus now comes out." The ballad begins in the wider world of nature and not with just any star, but with Venus, that of lover and the evening. Indeed, it is a time of portent when "that old enemy of day / Outspreads her thick, black gown." The protagonist is a "mighty Moor . . . in anger." The world is still wide, for this Moor, having left Medina-Sidonia, is speeding across southern Spain on the plains of Jerez, down to where the Guadalete flows into the "sea of Spain." The Guadalete is of course where Rodrigo the Visigoth met his fate in 711. That very night his "cruel lady," abandoning him "Because they hint he's poor," is to wed a "dull Moor" who is both rich and powerful. In the protagonist's language of conceit with the Lady, "You leave a poor man very rich / And rich one poor you choose." For twelve angry stanzas the protagonist calls down curses upon the Lady and her life with the rival. In fact, he hopes that she will arrive on the battlefield where the rival is "fighting Christians" just in time "to see him dead." This furious monologue to the Lady ended, the mighty Moor arrives at Jerez in the middle of the night. The final action is swift:

> Before the bridegroom he stood up
> In stirrups him to view,
> And hurled his trusty lance at him,
> And pierced him through and through.

This ending evokes the primitive note of the old ballads. Interestingly also, here is Freudian wish-fulfilment with a vengeance.

The extensive section of pastoral ballads also reveals the imagination of Lope de Vega in transforming turbulent, domestic, and even tawdry details into artistic poems. The pastoral is of course an ancient tradition going back to Theocritus, a surprising tradition which indicates how man, bored in the countryside, will congregate in the city and fight to defend it; then he will soon yearn for the pastoral and sweet nature. In his pastoral ballads, which follow the popular pastoral novel still being written by Lope and Cervantes, the world of the shepherd becomes the world of the noble, with heavy emphasis upon the amorous. In these ballads Lope has gone behind courtly love: while indeed the love is yearning and suffering, its effects include jealousy of a rival husband, jealousy between ladies, and even the inclusion of children. As may be expected, in general Lope's hero is the wronged one. There are two distinct but overlapping experiences, first with Phyllis, the unattainable love, then with Belisa, who became wife.

Certainly these ballads are artificial in the original sense of the word, and specifically charming, imaginative, and artistic. Perhaps the most artistic of the ballads is "The trunk with river weeds adorned," in which Belardo (the general protagonist of the series) sees two loving turtledoves in a deciduous poplar down by the Tagus River. Angry since his own love is unrequited, he picks up a stone and scatters the lovers. But the pair alights in a "verdant pine," the evergreen symbolizing the permanence of their love. Thus, Belardo, in *redondillas* (the quatrains in *abba* of the plays) philosophizes that true lovers cannot be separated: therefore he can hope to be rejoined with Phyllis forever! Charmingly imaginative is "Along the famous river banks," in which Belardo, whose love for Phyllis has seemed hopeless for many reasons, sees himself riding like a Knight to Phyllis's village, there where the Jarama joins the Tagus, to be wed with appropriate pastoral ceremonies. Even the father-in-law is cooperative. Here Lope uses a ballad form somewhat like the English song, for after each two stanzas a refrain in a different meter is repeated: "How blest that shepherd who redeems / Such pleasant end for all his hopes and dreams." Even playful is the ballad "Dear Phyllis contemplating was"; here the poet can reassert his recently shattered superiority. Alone at night Phyllis sees a fragile moth immolating itself because of its (or her) love of the light; Phyllis seizes upon the example, takes up a sewing knife, and declares to the absent and disdainful Belardo, "Here was Troy!" As a timorous woman, however, she must first prove the pain, and when she pricks a finger the sight of one drop of blood causes her to forget the whole matter. In "Within the grip of fever harsh," Belardo projects himself upon his deathbed, the victim of an "amorous accident." In his bequests, since he has few goods, he focuses upon the parts of his body, especially his eyes and heart, the latter to be burned and the ashes scattered in the ocean. Ever a poet, Belardo asks that his letters and papers serve as a shroud. Perhaps surprisingly, given the turbulence of this experience, the ballads relating only to Phyllis show more imagination than venom.

The series relating to Belisa, however, begins with a ballad imaginative, dramatic, and stunning, perhaps the most powerful in the whole collection. This one has a real title: "Ballad of Lope de Vega When He Was Going to England." The time is around June, 1588, the place Lisbon; the poet imagines that Belisa has followed him there where he is ready to depart with the Armada for "Engeland." (Sonnet LXIII from the *Rhymes* uses the might of the Armada as a metaphor for the poet's love.) Belisa, the speaker in the poem, although weeping "tender tears," is in a rage as the refrain lines indicate: "Go off, cruel one, there is someone / In whom I can avenge the wrong you've done." Deft lines explain the refrain: "I don't just have your steely sword / And the wrong I did myself;" and there remains a "portrait of Aeneas" beneath her heart. The "steely sword" is of course phallic; the "wrong" her sin in permitting its entry. Belisa, beside herself, wildly declares that she will kill herself so as to kill the child; then she suddenly reverses herself: she will wait to see the child, then kill him if he resembles the father. Then she changes again: she cannot wait, for the child will be a viper which will destroy her very womb. At this the signal comes for the ships of the Armada to hoist sail. In desperation Belisa cries "Wait!", but then she prays to God that Belardo never return. Surely in total context this is one of Lope's greatest poems.

One of the most sparkling ballads (and one always popular) is "Belardo was a gardener," in which Belardo, in fact in exile in Valencia, is struggling in a new role to earn a living. But what details here! As a "gardener" in Valencia's "garden-spot," this incurable romantic in addition to planting flowers of his own "hopes," plans to grow specific plants for women of all ages and types: clover for the girls, sweet basil for the married women more than thirty, and thistles for the prudish. Then in mid-ballad, since the noble Belardo is now a rustic, he makes of his courtly clothes a scarecrow in the garden. In a changed form (the Spanish hexasyllable) he addresses the scarecrow, in passing revealing biographical details. Once on a balcony in his town (Madrid) he saw a lass and things happened quickly: "She let herself be tricked, I married her." This summarizes Belisa's story. But the incorrigible Lope will not stop here: he reveals that the lass who reigned as queen in his Troy one time (Phyllis) was infuriated and destroyed all his things (even his papers) in a bonfire. Here then is life as backdrop, but life transformed into poetry by Lope's grace and imagination.

Yet Lope the eternally amorous can surprise us with a theme. As a Renaissance poet, he is always alert to themes which revive the past, especially that past which teaches lessons. (Contemporary man generally considers himself beyond lessons.) In "Now looking at the ashes cold," Belardo, although still near Valencia, has visited the ancient Roman ruins of Saguntum alone. Throughout the ballad, then, he is speaking of the ruined city, lamenting of course how the "fleeting time" has laid it low. Gradually he compares himself to the ruins: as an "exile" he has come to this locality as to his "center true." Belardo, still blaming someone else for his misfortunes, exaggeratedly declares that his life is "spent." In fact, he was barely thirty.

Lope's maudlin immoderation shows at its worst in "Now welling with the saddest tears." These tears are Belardo's, who is trying to convince Belisa that her "mortal jealousy" has been the "unjust" cause of their problems. In a sweeping refrain Belardo attempts to reassure her, to cure that jealousy: "The Lord doom me to weeping evermore / If I don't Phyllis hate and you adore." Then Belardo, assuming that this is not enough, in the rest of the ballad envokes a succession of catastrophes to befall him if his refrain is not true. The last stanza is almost heroic: "Let water fail in all my wells, / My hut away be blown, / Burn my supply of unthreshed grain, / The earth gulp me alone." Although this ballad is brilliantly executed, only Lope in his passionate ingenuousness would dare so tacky a theme.

The ballad which closes the rich but turbulent amorous experience with Phyllis and with Belisa is "When all the scrub-oaks, lofty oaks." Truly "pastoral" is this ballad, since more than half of it exalts the rebirth of nature in the spring, when the trees, the plants, the flowers flaunt bright colors and the kids and the lambs play in the meadows. This long introduction, however, is prelude to a terrible contrast. In this "anticipated happy time" Albano (who is Belardo disguised further) "weeps alone, his sadness grows." The reason becomes clear in the final section of the ballad: Albano is remembering that exactly "one year ago" his Belisa died. What he recalls specifically is his dedication during her illness. "I served you sick for one whole year / Would it a thousand were!" But at least Belisa has left him as guard of her "flock," the "sweet treasure wonderful" of a daughter, in whose countenance he could see her portrait. Then as a final blow, the daughter, perhaps for his sins, followed in her mother's footsteps to heaven and "Albano weeps alone, his sadness grows."

In these two series of ballads, then, Lope as Renaissance poet recreates the pastoral manner going back to Theocritus, and the Moorish going back to the Spanish Frontier Ballads. But Lope does not merely "imitate" past traditions; he utilizes them as vehicles in which to transform his own experience into poetry. While Belardo and Phyllis and Belisa almost become figures in their own right, they serve more importantly as metaphors for the lyric poet and his particular experience. This technique comes down to Federico García Lorca in the 20th century, for in his famous *Romancero gitano*, his gypsy figures in the ballads serve as a kind of metaphor for the poet's own aims.

Lope de Vega's second major effort in lyric poetry is a collection of 200 sonnets ultimately called simply *Rhymes*. As we mentioned, in Lope's time there was still a hesitancy in publishing lyric poetry—such was beneath nobles, and epics were still the rage. (Let us recall that Shakespeare's sonnets were saved freakishly.) Thus in 1602 Lope published his collected sonnets sandwiched between the new epic poem *The Beauty of Angélica*, which Lope swore he wrote on shipboard with the Armada, and the *Dragontea* on Sir Francis Drake, both in impressive royal octaves. From the beginning this extensive collection of sonnets, correctly called *Rhymes* in generality, is Lopesque in both its strengths and weaknesses. At the time biographically Lope was deep into domesticity with his lawful wife Doña Juana; at the same time he was also deep into domesticity with Micaela de Luján, who as Camila Lucinda was also serving as his Petrarchan Lady. For Lope the *Rhymes* is a grab bag of sonnets touching more than a decade.

Very generally the *Rhymes* is a Petrarchan Songbook *in vita* only, but the book also contains many other diverse elements. Included are some fine pastoral sonnets relating to Phyllis (Elena Osorio), and a group which echo the classical theme of the destruction of Troy, with Lope pressing the conceit that Elena's real name was of course Helen. A significant number of sonnets were taken from his plays; as Lope himself defined the Golden Age comedy, the expectant lover could properly utter a sonnet. A significant number are typical Renaissance sonnets in which a great noble (such as the Duke of Osuna) is exalted, either in heroism or in death. A significant number also are reworkings of classical or Biblical themes. Finally, certain sonnets also reveal the beginning of *desengaño*, or Christian disillusionment, but Lope in his Renaissance poetry is generally upbeat, and not much given to resignation or to lingering tragedy.

From the initial sonnet of the book, marked "Primero," the mature poet (around 35) knows what he is about, for the poem emphasizes the two halves of his existence. These sonnets, he says, are "Verses of my love, conceits set free. . . . " The first half is in this initial phrase, "Verses of my love"; thus the 200 sonnets which follow spring from his love, his passion, his desire. As the sonnet continues these verses are his "children"; children "engendered in the soul" to frame his cares, "offspring" of his senses, finally "foundlings" wandering in the wider world. From the first also his verses are "conceits set free." Very early the critic Montesinos established the conceit as the base of Lope's poetry. This verbal kind of play, taken seriously poetically, ruled the Renaissance; even Shakespeare almost said, "Aye, I eye eye!" In our age, we *know* this is silly; the ragged, whining grimness of our age is of course serious. While it seems that this love expressed in conceits is his whole existence, the conclusion of the sonnet provides the other half. In Vossler's phrase Lope had a "lust" for poetry; late in life he could declare that "loving and making verses is one thing."[3] But this contradictory figure also finally insists that he is even more poet than lover: "They have not found in me any licentious passion outside natural love in which I, like the nightingale, have more voice than flesh."[4] While for Lope "Love's remedy" is "to want to conquer love" (Sonnet III), nevertheless, clearly his unending production proves he was more poet than lover. Thus this half of his existence prevails at the end of this Capstone sonnet: to his verses, if that "enchanting asp" (the Lady) will not receive them, he tells them, "In your own center you will come to rest."

In general Lope is bedazzled by the great Petrarchan tradition, especially as it was developed by Garcilaso de la Vega and Herrera in Spain. His love poetry, however, truly springs from his incurably amorous nature. In a sonnet (LXVI) to Lupercio Leonardo, when this friend apparently chides him for his constant amorous theme, Lope declares that for him to write is to live, and challenges the friend: "Then you see to it I my love don't feel, / And I'll see to it that my pen not write." To express this all consuming love, in Sonnet IV Lope sets out in Petrarchan fashion to focus upon the time and place of his being smitten; it was, he tells us, on the eve of Mary's Assumption (August 14), "When Love for that first time to me showed clear / Lucinda's lovely eyes in her sun's diadem." Here still in Lope is the "optics of the eyes." In Sonnet VII the poet identifies, though very generally, the scene of this love.

> These are the willows, this as fountain shows,
> The wooded hillocks these, and this the shore
> Where of my sun I saw that day before
> The lovely eyes, the brow in sweet repose.

Sonnets to Lucinda are scattered throughout the *Rhymes*, but never with sufficient concentration to develop an accumulation of subtle emotions.

As Montesinos very early emphasized, in Lope the general conceit is often the base of his poetry, and a number of sparkling examples relate to Lucinda. In "To a Tempest" (XIII), for thirteen lines a storm with lightning bolts buries the Guadarrama mountains in snow, the rainbow drinks the sea, taking the water to the Poles and returning it as rain, so that "earth and sea and sky embrace," and Phoebus himself disappears; but just when it seems the very harmony of the universe is threatened, "Lucinda appeared, and all became serene." In Sonnet LXLIX, the very heavens will change course, confusion will assume form, the immortal soul will belong to death, the humors of mankind will settle into sweet accord, he tells the lady, "Before I stop adoring your bright eyes." In Sonnet CLXXIV there is a little story of thirteen lines which tells how Lucinda while feeding her pet songbird lets him escape from the cage, in tears she warns the bird of dangers outside the cage and assures him that she loves his song. The little bird heard her compassionately and "to his ancient prison took his wings"; for "So much can do a woman when she cries." Sonnet CLXX is a syntactical delight, a "not so much, not so many" pattern. Not so much honey has Attica, so many flowers Spring, more eyes the firmament, more birds the wind, says the poet, "Than for Lucinda I breathe sighs in vain." It was Petrarch himself who established the "breathing of sighs" as a pervading theme; here Lope develops his own particular conceit in a structured sonnet. For our age, alas, the sigh is out of fashion; a mere sigh cannot measure up to our anguish.

In a significant number of sonnets from the *Rhymes* the poet focusses upon his own feelings (X, XLIV, LXI, LXX, XCVII, CXXVI, CLXIX, CLXI), the usual ones being frustration and suffering, sometimes (in Petrarchan fashion) to the point of death. Perhaps the most striking of these is Sonnet CLXIX, in which the first three stanzas list a profusion of jumbled military debris and effects—unshackled irons, old driftwood, dented helmets, and even jail, combat, Argel. Then the poet drives home the comparison in the final tercet: "And thus my verses scattered everywhere, / The sea of my torments, my love in chains, / And in my feelings mortal war and strife." Generally Lope does not dwell upon passive suffering as a good Petrarchan should. In Sonnet CLXI, which is classically structured, he projects in the octave a "deluded child" who has trusted in an untried string with his pet bird, which escapes when it breaks, leaving the boy in tears. In the sestet the poet equates this with his love, suspended by a "single hair"; when the wind took both bird and glory away, the poet is left with only the cord, which he says ruefully, "I perforce around my neck should wear." While earlier poets such as Garcilaso and Herrera remain humbly serious (or even abject) toward their love, Lope de Vega in general displays lightness along with a touch of will. This is not to say that he did not take the Neoplatonic ideal seriously. In Sonnet XLVIII, another with classical structure, the poet focusses upon the shepherd, then the pilgrim, then the animals, then even the plants, and all of these can find simple rest for the night. Only the poet cannot close his eyes in sleep; as he concludes, "For these eyes of the soul remain on high."

As a Renaissance poet Lope de Vega confidently reworks the classical and Biblical themes alive in his time. Since by chance (or was it fate?) his first tumultuous love (which ended in ruins) involved an Elena (or Helen), Lope gleefully exploited the theme of Troy in a number of sonnets in the *Rhymes*, surprisingly never playing with the name itself. In Sonnet XXXV the poet utilizes Troy in flames and smoke in a general way: after presenting a scene of people fleeing a Xanthus flowing with blood, a wall falling in the octave, in the sestet this conflagration feeds an "extraneous fire." This extraneous fire of course involves Helen, the "fierce occasion" of all this catastrophe, who now "Sleeps in the arms of her Greek conqueror." More nimble and personal is Sonnet CXXIII: the "Troy" that is his soul has fallen into "Earth's mire," but despite the soul's struggle and distress he still cannot quite say, "Here was Troy," for the soul is immortal, the fire of his love eternal. In Sonnet II of the whole book (strangely given this high position) Lope returns to the Anthony-Cleopatra theme in which Cleopatra challenges Anthony to prove his love by melting in wine two priceless pearls. Anthony indeed melts one, but saves the second. That pearl remained without equal, the poet says in the last line, until that day "Lucinda fair, when you the world first braved."

Surely Lope's outstanding example of the personal and literary utilization of a Biblical theme important in the Renaissance is Sonnet V, which develops the Jacob-Rachel theme. As a scholar, Erdman in his book on some of Lope's poems mainly from within the tradition gets a whole chapter out of this single sonnet. As Erdman explains, Jacob became a model of the faithful lover in the Renaissance, and at the symbolic level Leah became the woman of this earth, Rachel the ideal. Ultimately, then, Leah is this life, Rachel the eternal one. In the classical structure of Lope's sonnet, Jacob serves seven years for Leah, then Rachel "fills his sighs" for seven more, but at least he can look forward to a solution to his problem. The poor poet, however, to "suffering disposed," "waits for Rachel in the other life / And Leah has forever here in this!" The "forever" has become attached to Leah.

While not rejecting higher interpretations, may we be forgiven for reading the sonnet somewhat biographically as most critics have done. Leah is Juana, the butcher's daughter and legal wife of Lope; Rachel is the "Lucinda" who serves an ideal. As we have repeated, Lope is at his best when he can transform his experience into poetry.

For its fittingness in relation to the figure of Lope his sonnet on the Iberian theme of Doña Inés de Castro (CLXXXI) merits a word of recognition. This tragic Portuguese lady is embroiled in *pundonor*, the fierce system of honor. As Don Pedro's beloved, for reasons of state she cannot be his wife, and she is executed. How, then, can Don Pedro act in the presence of her body? Extravagantly, of course; as Vélez de Guevara's play explores it, Don Pedro has her reign after being dead. Lope of course exalted this extravagent system of honor in the poetry of his plays; in the prose of his life both he and Cervantes had female family members seduced, and the seducer was not struck down. Of course Doña Inés is also Portuguese, with that *saudade*, the languid love of this race. Thus this pair is a couple tritely but truly after Lope's own heart. In Lope's dramatic sonnet, then, Don Pedro is in the presence of the dead Doña Inés, his emotions wildly alternating. "Of palest hue, in raging anger's fires . . . He tender then draws near, irate retires." His whole being is "to her alabaster image wed." Weeping, he then speaks to her, naturally in heaven, so that she can appreciate how he is reacting:

> You'll see I am, in honoring your remains,
> A Pedro hard, a Portuguese in love,
> Monarch in might, and in revenge a lover."

Although Lope's loves always dribbled away into the stern realities of life, in his febrile imagination he was a Don Pedro.

As Montesinos indicated years ago, Lope in his development of classical and Biblical themes anticipated the manner later called Parnassian, with emphasis upon the image frozen as in a snapshot. Properly cited as the example of Biblical themes is "To Judith's Triumph (XCV). The first part of the sonnet focusses upon the tyrant Holofernes, first his shoulders, then his left hand, finally his "trunk consumed in gore." Then the scene widens to the city wall where "now crowned / By hosts of Israel, the Hebrew chaste / Armed with the head shines forth resplendently." A second example translated, also Biblical, is the sonnet "Of Absalom" (CIV). From the opening line to the last the poet creates a Parnassian image of Absalom, suspended from the branches of a tree (following 2 Samuel 18:9). Absalom's beautiful locks entwine with the leaves, his eyes are eclipsing; thus pride and ambition have destroyed the prince. But the specific conceit of the poem concerns earth and air. "What is it you tried to usurp from earth?" the poet asks. Now Absalom by a quirk of fate does not even touch the earth: he hangs grotesquely suspended in the air in a Parnassian image imprinted on the mind of the reader.

As a confident Renaissance poet Lope does not limit himself to the amorous theme; he must also show himself as a defender of noble heroism, in general the virtue of that day. In Sonnet XXXVIII, "To Pedro Liñán," a long-time friend, the poet declares "the noble breast / can only esteem / Wealth that the soul holds as nobility"; and later in the poem, "The virtuous man for riches has no need." The common-place but powerful lines build toward the final one: "For Virtue truly is its own reward." Now sober critics have either chortled, guffawed or mourned that Lope would have the gall to write such a poem, for his letters show him sickeningly abasing himself before the Duke of Sessa. But this is unjust to Lope, who *believed in* the ideal of virtue, even if his own life betrayed the opposite. Among Lope's poems dedicated to nobles in life and death has come down as an anthology piece his "On the Death of the Duke of Pastrana" (C). This is a dramatic sonnet in classical fashion: As personifications Death, Mars, and Love himself in the presence of the body in state extol the fallen Duke's uniqueness. In hyperbole Mars declares that he has lost "light, Spain sun, Flanders thunderstroke." Lope of course could take these poems seriously, and it is not to our glory that we usually cannot.

Toward the end of the *Rhymes*, Lope sneaks in what have come to be called the *Manso* (or "bellwether") sonnets (CLXXXVIII and CLXXXIX). There are also two more sonnets, from other sources, which fit the bellwether pattern. Now these are *pastoral* poems, from an ancient tradition even in Spain, but Lope manages to infuse a "salty" tactile note in them which has made them memorable. "Let my bellwether go, head shepherd strange" begins the first sonnet; thus Lope evokes again that first turbulent love in which he was struggling against a stronger competitor, a noble. The bellwether (or *Manso*) as the lady offers a problem since the word is masculine in Spanish (and neuter in English). In the poem the battle is between false "gold" and honest "tin." The shepherd poet declares the sheep to be his, and dares the head shepherd to let it go so that it can return to his cabin, "For these its master's hands some salt still hold." In this single line Lope revitalizes an old tradition with an earthy, even a sexual note. In the second sonnet, although the "salt" is still present, the erotic note forceful, the language is at a more elevated level as the poet demonstrates his cultural knowledge, even of "anacardium." But it is in the final tercet where the poet flaunts his beloved conceits: he offers himself to the bellwether-beloved: "Here is your woods, your vega, and your hill." As if this were not enough he flashes the old *ganado-perdido* conceit (ganado as "flock" and "won"; *perdido* as "lost"). In English this line can become "You flock of one, and I your poor soul lost." (The translator can play this game, if not always perfectly.) This little body of sonnets (when put together) remains one of Lope's solid achievements.

Toward the end of *Rhymes* Lope at one extreme is a Neoplatonist, reaching upward, at the other a poet reaching out to ordinary life, and in both cases with a certain balance. In a sonnet of Neoplatonic vision (CLXXIX), his Lucinda is an "angel blest" blessed with "Pulchritude of artificer supernal," and that beauty is to make him eternal. The poet's expression in the first tercet is clearly Neoplatonic: "Fair center of my soul . . . In whom the structure and accord declare / The world superior I contemplate and see." It does not severely undercut this Neoplatonism that in the final tercet Lucinda is "morning, sky, daylight, sunshine," and that the poet ends emphasizing his *desire*, surely a key word in Lope. In human contrast stands Sonnet CXCI, one of the last ones, which begins with that simplicity for which Lope is often praised: "The woman is the best thing that man knows / And it is foolishness to say the worst." We must admit that Lope goes on to abuse the clever alternating contrasts still dear in his time, so that woman is life and death, heaven and hell, angel and harpy. Surely Lope was proud of his concluding line, where she "At times gives health, and other times she slays."

For Lope de Vega, despite its lack of thematic progression, probably the *Rhymes* remained the flagship of his lyric fleet. His faith in the elegance of the imported Italian hendecasyllable and the Petrarchan sonnet never wavered and he remained bedazzled by the power of the conceit in poems of idealistic touch. In this book he was able to humanize Neoplatonism a bit by turning his own realistic and even tawdry love into the Lady Camila Lucinda. By Sonnet III, from custom the poet has begun a palinode, but his limitless *deseo*, his vitalism imposes itself and he can declare that "Love's remedy" is "to want to conquer love."

In chronological order after the early Moorish and pastoral ballads of the 1590's and the essential *Rhymes* of 1602, the *Sacred*

Rhymes of 1614 mark another essential achievement in Lope de Vega's lyric poetry. The *Sacred Rhymes* are the outgrowth of a severe religious crisis in Lope's life, a crisis of conscience following the death of his young son and the turbulence of his domestic relations, specifically the death of his legal wife Juana. The turning away from Neoplatonic love to the religious theme is of course not just a Spanish phenomenon. Sir Philip Sidney also wrote his *Psalms of David*, and later a significant part of John Donne's poetry is religious. In Spain, it is striking that in 1613 Quevedo, somewhat younger than Lope, published his *Christian Heraclitus*, a book of Christian repentance also, complete with palinodes.

In this *Sacred Rhymes*, as the title suggests a grab bag of forms, themes, and manners, Lope creates poems of at least three recognizable types, the first of which has been accepted by modern critics, albeit somewhat grudgingly. (The other two will be touched upon later.) As model poets in the religious vein, Lope could look back to Fray Luis de León and St. John of the Cross. Fray Luis was, despite being a religious figure, more a Renaissance Platonist than a religious poet; St. John in his great poems began in an elevated state of mysticism and then soared still higher. Lope, who chose not to follow either of these, presents himself as an abject sinner, floundering in the flesh, seeking forgiveness from a personal Jesus, and vowing to improve. From Montesinos onward the modern reader can approve this "sincerity," but there is difficulty in accepting the groveling of the poet's repentance. Nevertheless, this core of religious sonnets forms an enduring part of Lope's essential poetry.

Probably Lope began the *Sacred Rhymes* with the idea of a controlled book in which he would struggle through his religious crisis to a perfect Christian state, but Lope was still young enough that his life kept spilling over into other areas of life and literature. The matter of Lope's religious sonnets is of course the accumulation of centuries in Spain: the stubborn sinner pursuing the false pleasures of this world living in *engaño* or self-deception, ignores God and Jesus; finally, through *desengaño* or disillusionment, a term negative in form but positive in meaning, the repentant Christian realizes that this life has little importance and he prepares himself for death and the promise of eternal life. In his First Sonnet, generally following Petrarch, Lope comes as close to a palinode as he ever gets, so that if we took him seriously the rest of the sonnets would be unnecessary. To begin, the poet goes back to a famous line by Garcilaso de la Vega, although in the Toledan poet the line introduces his poetry of courtly love: "Cuando me paro a contemplar mi estado." As Lope stops to contemplate the state of his life, he marvels that a man "so wholly lost" now knows "the error of his ways." In a "labyrinth," he has entrusted the thread of his life to "Late-apprehended disillusionment"; indeed Lope keeps "approaching" this disillusionment. Finally, in the sonnet at least, with his "blind deception" destroyed "Lost reason to its home returns content." In this sonnet, as in many others, the structure is impressive: the two quatrains begin with *when* clauses and the sestet offers a firm resolution of the problem of the sonnet.

In a few sonnets Lope dares to re-invent the pastoral. From the time of the Psalms the Lord has been a shepherd. In Sonnet XIV, however, Lope begins in the tradition of the pastoral novel, with the shepherds given over to the amorous. Surely Lope was also aware of one of St. John's lesser known poems, "El pastorcico," in which a shepherd turns out to be suffering not from amorous pains, but from being nailed on a cross. In Lope's poem the shepherd has called out to the poet as sleeping flock: "Shepherd who with amorous whistles sweet / From my profound dream-sleep awakened me." The shepherd sleeping (because he is content) is of course a pastoral theme; here the poet is asleep in regard to Christ's sacrifice. This Jesus has fashioned a staff from that "tree" from which he now entreats. The Sheep that is the poet thus gives his solemn word to follow his "sweet-voiced whistles" and his "precious feet." Then in urgency he addresses this Shepherd who dies "for love affairs"; Lope uses the word *amores* with this normal sense. In this urgency he commands the Shepherd: "Await, therefore, and listen to my cares." Then he realizes the wrong of telling Jesus to wait when he suffers the terrible immobility on the Cross: "Yet how can I tell you to wait for me / If you await your feet nailed to the Cross?" The very next sonnet (XV) also ends with this fierce concentration upon the Cross: "Now that today I turn in tears to you, / Then you nail me to you upon your tree, / And you'll have me secure with those three nails."

Without doubt Lope's most famous religious sonnet is Sonnet XVIII with its extremely simple first line: "What do I have, that you my friendship seek?" Last century Longfellow, one of the early Hispanists, left us an adequate version of this sonnet, with his usual looseness in regard to fidelity. Apparently through this translation Emily Dickinson, struggling Puritan that she was, was captured by the image of Jesus, wet with evening dews, spending the nights before the sinner's door. In this sonnet Lope blames his procrastination in responding to Jesus upon the attraction of the Beauty of the Greeks.

"How many, Sovereign Beauty, did I cry / We'll let him in tomorrow certainly, / Then tomorrow always gave the same reply!" Years ago Allison Peers identified the phrase "Sovereign Beauty" as coming down from St. Augustine.

Another recognizable type of sonnet in the *Sacred Rhymes* is one in which the language of courtly love of the Lady is simply applied to Jesus himself. The model of this type is Sonnet XXIX, which begins: "Light of my eyes, I made a promise strong / A mortal beauty of this earth to sing." Up to this day the poet has sung this "mortal beauty," but he vows from this day forth to sing to and for Jesus: "I'll sing out loud your name of King divine, / And to your beauty fair eternally / I consecrate my pen, voice, wit, and hand." In Sonnet XLVI the "celestial beauty" of the subject is initially addressed, but then the poet exalts the "golden" head, the free-streaming hair like "budding tendrils," the "neck of ivory," the hand like "hyacinth" of the Lord. This language is exactly that usually used to exalt the Lady. In Sonnet XXXI the initial phrase is *yo me muero de amor*—"of love I'm dying." This is a great (though stock) phrase of courtly love; in Spain it became a great (though stock) phrase of the mystics such as Saint Teresa. These sonnets provide a potent argument against the contemporary critical practice of divorcing the "text" from author and book. The overall "conceit" of these sonnets is that the language gains power from Neoplatonic love; Lope's authorship and the title *Sacred Rhymes* keep us oriented toward the religious theme.

To appreciate the simple power of this (for Lope) brief series of sonnets in the first part of the book we encourage the reader to read thoughtfully through the poems, letting the effect gradually accumulate. A few sonnets stand out, for a particular conceit, a surprise of emphasis, an arresting line, but in general the sonnets develop the religious theme of the seeking, repentant sinner without sharp exaggeration. The reader must accept with patience the flow of Christian themes which lack novelty and shock; in our time the pressure to achieve novelty often obscures meaning. Lope's first and last lines are often clean, firm, powerful: "I go inside myself my self to know," (III); "What blindness brought me all these hurts intense?" (V); "For it's not counsel that comes late, in vain," (X); "How many times, O Lord, you've called to me" (XV); "For I to love myself stopped loving you" (XXXI). Indeed, a model for this effortless expression is Sonnet XVI, which begins, "Life dying is, and without life I live / Offending life with my death now begun," and ends, "To die for him will be divine accord; / But you are all my life, O Christ my Lord, / And since I have it not, it cannot lose."

This series of personal religious poems has received a fair hearing in our times. As for the other two types of poems, from Montesinos onward Lope has been judged to be either puerile or silly in creating one type, unbelievably ingenuous in creating the other. In the first type here the poet takes a consecrated religious figure (usually a saint) and presents him or her in an exaggerated manner, since the stories are already well-known. With humility we have dared to translate a few of these sonnets (LX, LXI, LXII, XLII). Montesinos focuses upon the "puerilities" of LX and LXI, which treat of St. Lawrence and St. Sebastian. Now these two saints, given the striking nature of their martyrdom, unhinged the Baroque poets. Quevedo, for example, a sober scholar usually, left us a sonnet on St. Lawrence in which the main conceit is that the tyrant who burned the saint is more burned than the saint that the saint is burning—but happily! Lope too runs a bit wild in his sonnet on St. Lawrence. In the first place, his title reads, "To a Bone of St. Lawrence," a puzzling title if we remember that the burning body is usually the focus. In Lope's sonnet, while Christ waits at the table, the focus throughout the poem is upon Lawrence as a "lamb" cooking upon the grill: sweet smoke is rising, the meat is turning pinkish, meat to which "Love" has given flavor. The "candid dove" (his soul) should fly off to "better Hemisphere and Araby." When this meat has a fine crust, Christ should eat quickly, "For this most Christian King awaits a bone." Is this "bone" to be a valued relic, or the bone where the most succulent meat remains? Certainly Lope has taken the situation of Jesus-communion-martyr and stretched it to the breaking point. Lope's sonnet for St. Sebastian (LXII) plays extensively with the conceit of target shooting indulged in by both God and man. Of course God wins, with perfect aim, "For on God's arrows (man) his arrows broke." Now this cannot be childish, but are we so sure it is "silly"? In our age, even the humorous grotesque is "serious"—say a young nymph fornicating against the hump of a back. In Lope this is serious poetic effort, a bit extravagant to be sure.

The third type of poems now generally ignored or deplored by the contemporary critic are the series of ballads upon the time-honored biblical themes, especially those relating to Christ. Among his few minor poems St. John of the Cross preceded Lope in working with this material in ballad form. Now Lope's ballads are simple, ingenuous, with emphasis upon realistic details: indeed they remain with an innocence unconvincing in our time. As we have stressed, however, although Lope was a "monster of nature" in literary production, he was in fact a fairly simple human being. As examples of the religious ballad, we have chosen two: "On the Farewell to Christ Our Blessing by His Most Holy Mother; Ballad," and "On Putting Him on the Cross (Ballad)." Of the first, the initial stanza, which technically could be considered blasphemous, emphasizes the ingenuousness of the poet:

> The sweetest spouses are these two
> The sweethearts tenderest,
> Because they Christ, his mother are,
> As mother and son the best.

In the ballad, first Mary speaks at some length to the Son; then the Son speaks directly to her. Mary laments her coming solitude when Jesus departs; Jesus finally like a little boy says farewell: "The Cross calls me, may God bless you / My Lady, cuddle me." This "Lady" is also the Lady of courtly love. Finally the poet asks his own soul to contemplate these two in their utter solitude, "For she remains without a son, / He without mother parts," and the poet hopes to accompany the Virgin in her tribulations. The second ballad is filled with fiercely realistic detail, the initial focus being the hole where the Cross is to be placed. Then a number of stanzas focus upon the stripping away of his "seamless garments" made by "Mary beautiful": "As they his clothing strip away, / His wounds re-bloom afresh, / and there among the folds appeared / Chunks of his bloody flesh." Even in simplicity, however, the poet cannot entirely escape his conceits; for example, although Jesus is upon his back on the hard cross, he so many sorrows suffers that this seems like rest. Lope concludes by attacking the "soul of Porphry and marble" (like himself) who is asleep to Christ's sufferings.

In the latter pages of the *Sacred Rhymes* Lope slips in a rather long poem dear to his heart, a "Song" in the Italian sense, "On the Death of Carlos Félix." "This of my very bowels tender fruit," he says with humility he offers to the shrine of God. Critics have always used this poem to illustrate Lope's excessive sentimentality, his sincerity to excess, quoting some of the few lines spoken directly to the child: "And you child blest, who in the seven years / You had of life, in that time never had / A disobedient act mean-spirited. . . ." And later, "I gave to you the best home that I could / For your birth here. . . ." In general, however, the long poem (we have translated nine of its fifteen stanzas) is a philosophical meditation upon God and his universe, with complicated syntax and rhyme. Certainly the poem is Lopesque in transforming one of the most poignant experiences of his turbulent life.

In his later years, Lope de Vega keeps developing (in theme and manner, not in form) the ballad of his youth, the years of the pastoral and Moorish ballads, and of his middle years, the religious ballads of the *Sacred Rhymes*. Even at his most popular and traditional, there is always something of the cultivated, the classical, or the Renaissance in Lope's poetry; thus in the later ballads from *La Dorotea* (of 1632) these effects are emphasized. The typical examples have now become culture pieces, where the prudent poet in his hard-earned wisdom (this is the Senecan tradition in Spain) speaks of his own life and problems in a general way, as a lesson for his reader. By now he has polished the ballad stanza to perfection, each self-contained quatrain in octosyllables and assonance flaunting condensed syntax and expressive metaphor. The two best-known of these ballads have become anthology pieces.

In the first of them, the poet in the initial line speaks to his soul as a "Poor little sailing bark," a metaphor which extends throughout the ballad. Lope continues one of his favorite metaphors; for example, Sonnet CL of the earlier *Rhymes*, begins with this identical phrase. Lope's ballad begins in a strongly moral vein, a type of theme still popular in his age. Quevedo, for instance, left a series of sonnets which he called moral. In Lope's ballad he displays a seasoned prudence (comparable to disillusionment in the religious area) which we associate with the Roman writers. Essentially the poet keeps warning the bark of his soul concerning the dangers in the sea which is life. "It's true in one's own land / That Virtue fares not well," says the poet; naturally the soul as virtuous can expect trouble. Lope manages to bring in the sea traffic between Spain and the world, a traffic earlier heroic, but now only dangerous, and by Lope's last years under attack:

> Don't those examples choose
> That have the water crossed,
> For those who had success
> Have many others lost.

It would not be Lope, however, not to slip in a romantic note. Indeed, the poet escaping a shipwreck finds himself in a bower where "Her husband she called me / And I called her my bride." In the final stanza, the poet shows the sharp disappointment of not being listened to by that now departed love (and the world), but he manages to end in prudent resignation:

> But you're not hearing me!
> However, brief is life:
> While living, all is scarce,
> In dying, things are rife.

The other anthology piece from the late ballads is "Back from my solitudes I come." In this single word *soledades* Lope the poet has seized upon a term of widest resonance. For Lope, Gongora's towering failure the *Soledades* was still around as a vague challenge. Later the great German Hispanist Karl Vossler wrote a book on *soledad* in Spanish poetry. (In the 20th century, from Machado to García Gómez, the term has persisted, as existential anguish.) It is interesting that humankind eternally dissatisfied ever flees the boring and barbarous countryside for the teeming city, then soon begins to scorn the city for the pastoral. Although we look back at Lope's time as Spain's Golden Age, Lope in his ballad is lamenting a Golden Age already gone and carping at a miserable present. From his first stanza the ultimate refuge is that of his own mind and thoughts:

> Back from my solitudes I come,
>   To solitudes I go,
> Because when I walk by myself
>   Sufficient my thoughts grow.

(At about this same time the English poet said, "My mind to me a kingdom is.") In Lope's poem, in "this village," where he "lives and dies each day," he is an outsider living inside himself. Again the basic theme is prudence, which comes from a wisdom which is humble; naturally the enemy becomes the fools and the falsely proud of the world. In his ideal the poet is sure of one thing: "That captive to the body is / A man who is soul pure." In his modesty the poet quotes Socrates: "I only know I nothing know"; in actual fact we assume that Lope was no more modest than Socrates.

The heart of the ballad is a firm but not strident attack against the age in which he lives. While we have concluded that Lope lived in a Golden Age, he insists that even a "Silver Age" has gone and this his age is now one of "copper," or brass. Above all the Spaniard of valor is no more; now the famous "sense of honor" has been cast aside. Now Virtue and Philosophy are "blind pilgrims" who go about weeping and begging. The poet ends the ballad with a confession of envy (the Spaniard's outstanding trait, said Unamuno), envy of these who "without books, paper, and accounts, / Relations, tales to tell, / Whenever they desire to write / They even beg inkwell." His final stanza returns to the solitudes:

> With this the envy thus confessed,
>   And more that I forego,
> Back from my solitudes I come,
>   To solitudes I go.

Here is the Lope of deep contradictions. Throughout his heavily-engaged life (in contrast, say, with Herrera's or Gongora's), he sought company, especially that of women, and gave them of his time and energy; yet he also treasured his solitude, when he escaped into his study to write those two million lines.

Another important collection of lyrics in the form of songs, dances, and sonnets is scattered throughout his hundreds of *comedias* or plays. In fact, Sainz de Robles begins his well-known anthology of *Obras escogidas* with an extensive selection from the dramatic works. The collection is quite varied in form, theme, and length; there are tiny seguidillas, May songs, Wedding songs, poems for dance, poems in dialogue, and many others. Since many of the lyrics are brief and cast in short lines, they are a terror to translate; luckily the translator can pick and choose. Since our selection is very brief, we have tried to pick outstanding, varied, and well-known examples. These being generally popular lyrics (and by Lope the amorous), naturally the predominant theme is love.

For many the jewel among the many tiny seguidillas is one Lope dedicated to Seville and the river Guadalquivir:

> River of Seville,
>   O sparkling scene,
> With snow-white caravels
>   And garlands green.

Although Lope was a *madrileño* born and bred, he (for various reasons) knew and lived in Toledo, Valencia, Seville. In Lope's time, Seville still suggested the bustle and romance of traffic with the New World. Many of the seguidillas are light and playful, in part because Lope was this way:

> Sweet lass, on Thursdays green
>   Your eyes are seen;
> If only they were blue
>   They'd not be green.

Later, Lorca took these same popular types and cast them as grimly tragic. As popular poems, the base of these lyrics is usually pastoral.

> Sweet meadows mild
> Let grow your grass;
> My golden flock
> Through them must pass.

A longer lyric which has come down as an anthology piece is the one of the *Trébole*, sweet clover, which has the values of our four-leaf clover. Found in the play *Peribáñez*, the song in its complicated form seems to be a variation of the Arabic *zéjel*. Lope is in his element with the fortune of all the basic classes of women: there is the sweet clover of the woman wed, the maiden lass, the girl still single, and even the widow, who "Outside, a head-dress white wears she; / Inside, bright colors lend accent." Poetically, these bright colors indicated her everblooming vitality, comparable to the poet's own. The movement, the repetition, the vitality is surely what has sustained this lyric.

Without any doubt Lope's most famous poem from a play is the one which is used as theme for *El Caballero de Olmedo*, one of his rare tragic efforts. (In Spain Lope of course served to establish *comedia* as the word for "play" in general.) In four tiny lines is encapsulated the story of the three-act tragedy:

> So they struck down this Knight
>   At darkest hour,
> Medina's pride and joy,
>   Olmedo's flower.

Was Lope following an anonymous lyric coming down in the tradition or inventing a poem of popular type to serve as leitmotif? We do not know, but in a conflict between love and duty (along with some weak plotting) the protagonist, after proving both the amorous and the heroic in his nature, meets his death at night upon a lonely road.

Lope de Vega's final book of poetry and one of his solidest efforts is of complicated title: *Rhymes Human and Divine of the Licentiate Tomé de Burguillos*. In this book Lope reaches the realistic, and thus he authenticates himself for our age. This title and the introductory pages offer a complicated thicket of materials. The poems are still *Rhymes*, that is, poems of the usual forms—sonnet, ballad, song; indeed, the poet as a quirk of technical mastery casts all 164 of the sonnets in the most difficult Petrarchan form, with the double-triple (cdc, dcd) rhyme in the sestets. But these are not the *Rhymes* of his earlier book where the poet retains the idealistic stance of the Renaissance; these are Human—and thereby hangs a tale of importance. Whereas before Lope transformed the women of his life into symbols of Neoplatonic love (admittedly with a few realistic touches), in this book his Juana surprisingly does not spring from a life model, and toward her the poet assumes a mocking, gently burlesque stance in regard to the Neoplatonic, while at the same time exalting her human value. (This theme bears developing later.) As for the *Divine* in this book, the title is almost a trick. Lost at the end of the book are a few varied religious poems which add little to the *Sacred Rhymes*. (With the poet now old, we might expect important religious poems of final confidence; it is perhaps surprising that Lope poetically exhausted his religious vein of guilty failure and desperate yearning during his middle years.) Indeed, instead of the divine, Lope sneaks in a mock-epic poem called *La Gatomachia*, in which with humor and fancy the poet develops the loves of a triangle of cats. Under the pressure of the age, Lope kept trying to achieve an epic poem. As for Tomé de Burguillos, in his "Notice" to the reader Lope explains that he met this *alter ego* in Salamanca, when he was working on his important poem for the canonization of St. Isidore. Tomé is the common man's Stoic, a figure in Spain who begins with Sem Tob and comes down to Machado's Juan de Mairena.

Beyond the lengthy title itself, the introductory material of this book is rich and striking. First, the book is dedicated to the Duke of Sessa, Lope's patron and intimate for years. By chance there remains a massive collection of letters from Lope to this Duke, "Great Admiral of Naples," Count of this and that, and Knight of the Order of Santiago. Yet for Lope the Duke is neither heroic or idealistic; in fact, he is a figure pathetically (but safely) aberrant. As for the censors of this book, no less a figure than Quevedo resoundingly praises it. Here Quevedo, holding in abeyance his vicious streak toward competitors, emphasizes Lope's style; it is not only respectable but outstanding, "in which the Castilian tongue presumes a victory over the Latin." It is a style with a grace that never sinks to malice or to the scabrous, even in vocabulary. In short, Quevedo compares Tomé's style to that of Lope, "whose name has been universally proverbial for everything good." In his own "Notice" Lope with gentle mockery defends his "faithful style" as more Castilian than cultish, that is, natural, and he correctly predicts that the natural will prevail in later ages. His final mocking emphasis comes in an introductory sonnet, where Tomé (or Lope) "likes olives more than laurel" and always crowns himself with thyme, which grows wild. Thus these brief but rich materials prepare us for a series of sonnets toward the realistic, so essential to our age. Again we shall find that "realistic" does not mean vicious, scabrous, or grotesque; Lope is always a poet of moderation and balance.

As in the case of the earlier *Rhymes*, the *Human Rhymes* begins as a book of poems for a Lady, a special lady in fact, but soon the poet drifts into quite diverse themes—his problems as he ages, his place in the literary world, even the praise of the noble in both heroism and death. Again as in the *Rhymes* the initial sonnet "Distrust in His Verses" establishes both his poetry and the Lady. Surprisingly, Blecua ignores this keystone sonnet in his extensive collection from this book. The poet, to the feigning poets of his day, urges them to hear "from Chaos deep the matter prime," presumably a poetic substance closer to the realistic. This matter is to be expressed in a language "pure, clean, simple, free." However, the poet wonders if this poetry that he invents, Love writes, and Time polishes will sell—surely a realistic note. In the final tercet he introduces the lady: if the poems do not sell or bring him fame, "May she a copy wear who brands my name: / Enough of laurel is her lovely breast." Here is still the courtly exaggeration, but in a later sonnet we learn that this is indeed a lovely breast—not the bosom of Platonic ideas.

The special Lady is gradually identified in earlier sonnets of the *Human Rhymes*, beginning with the second. After a burst of reference to earlier poets and their ladies (Vergil, Amaryllis, etc.), the poet declares that Love has commanded him to celebrate his Jane, since her "soapbubbles" are worth more to him than all the classic figures together. The epigraph to the seventh sonnet subtly identifies her further: "He doesn't dare to paint his Lady very beautiful so as not to lie, which is much for a poet." This lady must be real, since the Neoplatonic Lady knows no degree of beauty. After the poet insists that he can write Neoplatonic poetry, if the reader is disturbed by this "hyperbolic love" he points to a portrait of Jane, to whom he declares: "Enough it is you pretty be for me." This simple line consecrates the particularity of the real and personal. The special lady is not clearly identified until the nineteenth sonnet, "He tells how Love is engendered, speaking like a Philosopher." For eleven lines the poet traces the communication of "Spirits" necessary for Neoplatonic love, then hits us with the final tercet: "Look, Jane, what love, look what deceitful pose: / I'm speaking Natural Philosophy / To one who's hearing me while soaping clothes!" Thus the lady is named *Juana*, in our phrase plain Jane. Since life imitates art (as Wilde preached), Lope's earlier plain and ugly wife, the butcher's daughter, was named Juana, but that was a score of years ago. Surely here Lope intends mainly that his Jane be real, since he touts her as being real. So real is she in fact that she is a washer lass (in other sonnets she is fresh and young).

The poet in fact does little to particularize this real lady, and at times his expression begins to approach the hyperbole of Neoplatonic love, although gentle and self-effacing humor replace the grim seriousness of the Neoplatonic lover. What remains constant in this group of sonnets (and thus runs counter to contemporary notions) is Jane's disdain, as fierce as that of the courtly lady. Apparently his Jane sings (and naturally folksongs), for in Sonnet 146, his Jane is singing seguidillas at the river while washing clothes. But in almost everything the poem is little popular and much the expanded conceit so important to the poet. The whole sonnet develops Jane singing as a siren, the poet a Ulysses being tested by the music. Finally the poet begs the "crystals sweet" to avenge his love and desire, for her "two ivories" are showing there. This is about the limit of Lope's daring in this book. Gradually the poet tends to return to the hyperbole of Neoplatonic love. In Sonnet 75, for example, "The poet reasons how Jane's mouth might be a rose," he develops a courtly conceit of the Love gods throwing roses in a stream; Jane drinks; the roses stick to her lips. Then what a transformation for her lips, "To crystals drink / and turn to roses thus."

The outstanding feature of the *Human Rhymes* is the diversity of specific themes. The bane of both courtly and religious poetry tends to be monotony: perfection in both beauty and goodness becomes cloying for most humans, especially in our time where novelty is highly prized. Here Lope looks out upon the imperfection surrounding his later life and seizes upon some varied and surprising moments. For example, in Sonnet 39, "The nag speaks," his subject the "ripping of a belly one bullfight day." In the sonnet Goldipants, "Arabian" in origin, is the poor nag offered up by his master the *picador* to the bull's horns. "Ill-starred," he tells us, "one Tuesday I perfumed the place." it seems he was doing rather well, but his master attacked a "Fierce One" and his "poor belly paid." He is furious not to get respect: "Because

they all while I was raising dust / Called nothing what a goring was
to me, / Cursed by the man who puts in horns his trust!" Here are both
humor and pathos with a light touch except, as the nag notes, for him!
In Sonnet 107, the poet tells his friend Claudio about an outing, not "to
see a Mystery Play," but one in which the King has collected various
ladies who work for pay for the amusement of his official party. The
poet remains "chaste" (apparently age has made him cautious) while
the others go for the ladies. Later the King retired, the lovers left, "And
in the place faint scent of Court remained / Like inner chamber where
some gloves had been." Years ago Montesinos seized upon the
delicacy of these lines, conveniently forgetting the basic matter of the
sonnet. Although these are Tomé de Burguillos's poems, not Lope's,
surprisingly Sonnet 149 is a return to Belisa, as we have seen a wife of
Lope's youth. In the sonnet, the poet as Evander has had his friend
Felipe de Liaño paint Belisa's portrait as she lies dead. Liaño's portrait,
however, captures her at "That moment when to him she looked her
best." Lope surely approves, for in his vitalism he lived for the present
moment whatever his religious outlook might be.

Since Tomé de Burguillos is an aging commoner (not a noble
Renaissance figure like Lope with nineteen towers on his family
crest!), he can ruefully record his amatory failures and disappoint-
ments. In the early Sonnet 10, for example, the poet describes the
Renaissance bower, with privacy, overarching trees, flowing water,
etc., following the model of Garcilaso. After extended description of
this perfect scene, however, the poet concludes that in it, "To me there
never happened anything." In Sonnet 14, the poet begins with a
situation that is common, since the lady, usually amorous, closed the
door on him (in courtly love, of course, the door was never expected
to be open). But the poet chastises her at the end with a classical sally:
"I'm not so proud that I as Tarquin pass / Nor you so Roman as to be
Lucrece." In Sonnet 40, the poet begins in high fashion: his love has
him "so overwrought"; day and night he finds himself "Inside the shell
of Venus tied up taut." Then he tells her: "From Garcilaso is this verse,
my Jane: / So people filch. . . ." Finally he tells her that he regrets more
"being without soutane" than the "rabid ill" of the love he has for her.
In Sonnet 85, with humor but a dose of pique, the poet describes how
a gallant one night brought a crossbow with him to court his lady, and
when a neighbor lady came to spy upon them with a pot on her head,
the gallant fired a noisy arrow upon the pot. But the poet's point is
anger at nosy neighbors and if the lover wants to protect himself,
"Then moving is the only remedy." Finally Lope is at his domestic best

in Sonnet 113, "Loving, there is no problem." His lady (here Inez) has asked him for coal, their supply having been given to the maid's boyfriend, the groom of a noble. If she had asked for light, the "by-fire-dazed" Troy of his soul could find her some, but for coal he has to plod off to the store, his "cassock raised." Then he remembers that mighty Hercules adopted a distaff, Jupiter Diana's petticoats. In these sonnets Lope is forgetting that, not his *alter ego*, supposed author of these poems, but he was wearing a cassock, and in fact proud of his friar's commission from Rome itself. In the sonnets of the *Human Rhymes* the poet with humorous irony descends to the domestic, but almost all of them also flaunt ironic classical references.

Through his *alter ego* Burguillos Lope de Vega treats his literary reputation and his style in a significant number of fine sonnets. Surely the best of these in a sardonic, general way is Sonnet 77, "What the truly talented should do on hearing gossip." Presented is a beautiful Irish wolfhound, walking pridefully along the street. Yapping at him comes a pack of curs, the kind the moon leads totally astray. Reaching the pack at the corner, "This wolfhound noble, indifference on display / Wet down the corner quite, his leg raised high, / And through them with firm step went on his way." Transparently, the wolfhound is the great dramatist and poet, two million lines of verse behind him; the curs are the little authors, short on talent but long on false pride and envy. In "He trimming his pen, the two speak" (Sonnet 28), Burguillos is having an argument with his pen over style. The pen (since such is now in fashion) wants to write like Góngora; the poet wants to write "simple verse and easy rhyme." The pen ends up wanting to go back to the goose, since it is sad "To be born flying and to end up feigning." The Gongorists indeed fly in style, but for Lope it is a false flight. In Sonnet 73, the poet is arguing with his scholarly friend, Francisco López, who insists that not a man in Spain knows Greek; the poet insists that they all "write in Greek." He goes on to take a slap at Góngora whom he accuses of filching from the Italians; indeed "he writes in Greek, in euphuistic cult." The strongest attack against the euphuists (that is, the Gongorists) is found in Sonnet 120, where the poet is exorcizing a euphuist demanding that he speak true Castilian. The Gongorist replies in his best language: "Why are you torquing me barbaric-so-ly?", and finally confessing that he is "Polack."

In three of these sonnets Lope de Vega shows perhaps a more personal touch. In Sonnet 109 the great but always poor poet finds a way to exalt his distinction, though perhaps a bit ruefully. For thirteen lines the order of Nature and the universe is turned inside out—lovers understand each other, gold has no power, elephants fly, virtue triumphs; then the concluding line: "For here's a rich man calmly writing verse." In facing Góngora, Lope, a gentle (or perhaps a timid) enemy, in Sonnet 147 addresses his Baroque rival under a classical pseudonym: "Livio, I've remained your advocate / And worth of friendship never would abjure." The poet continues, however, to mourn that Góngora has of late "broken the bonds of consonance." Góngora is remote, too subtle, his tropes are impossible; Lope is "gentle, facile, elegant, and pure." The fine concluding stanza refers to both invective and poetry: "To solid core of meaning I attend, / So that both pen and punishment may leave / My blotter dark, and clear my poetry." In an even more generous mood, Lope in one of the final sonnets of the book (156) heaps great praise upon Don Francisco de Quevedo, perhaps in return for Quevedo's words of praise we mentioned earlier. As we have emphasized, Lope adored the "ideal conceit," and he declares that Quevedo's conceits are the subtlest in the world. Warming up, the poet gushes to Quevedo that he is "stirred to be, write, sing sublime / By your clear Sun, O Phaeton new-crowned." Even Apollo's chorus tells Burguillos that if he wants to tinge his pen in gold, "Bathe it in great Quevedo's stunning wit." Lope is of course correct in his praise: particularly in venomous and grotesque wit Quevedo is without peer in the Golden Age.

In three late sonnets of the book (including the final one) Lope continues to show preoccupation with his style. In Sonnet 136, Burguillos (the later Lope) speaks directly with Lope (the earlier courtly-heroic Lope) concerning the "pickpocket muses" Burguillos is following. He promises to invoke "those tried and true," the classical ones, and even bursts into a high-flown passage worthy of Góngora. But he cannot go on because his "Dishevelled muse of simple home-spun wool" keeps calling out to him. In Sonnet 137, as the title reads "The same apology continues." Where "all this world is one mad theme," the muses of Burguillos, "in hemp sandals," not in buskins, make their way. In the final lines he declares that "Jane has never studied Philosophy," and that he can well trust in his own taste. In the final sonnet of the book (161) one last time "The poet apologizes for his humble style." He is addressing "the sacred lights of heaven," and, like Chaucer, not quite believing that his *Canterbury Tales* were better than his saints' lives, Burguillos-Lope almost dares to believe in his plain and more realistic style. For one last time the poet focusses upon himself in his study: "But I in such reproofs one good possess, / That it's not possible that envy see: / Two books, three oil paintings, and four flowers."

Of all the 161 sonnets (plus two special ones) of the *Rhymes Human and Divine* is there one we can dare to call the best? From Montesinos (who thought little of the book) onward to Blecua, no critic has declared a clear choice. We boldly select Sonnet 76, "The poet grows weary of the delay of his hope." In courtly love, the poet lived (and perfected himself) in the *delay* of his hope, though knowing it was futile. Lope's first and eleventh lines are magnificent: "¡Tanto mañana y nunca ser mañana! . . . Siempre mañana y nunca mañanamos." In the latter line "tomorrowing" becomes a first person plural of the verb. Here there is a double meaning: life is nothing now, it's toward tomorrow; yet that tomorrow is never, there is nothing to come. Although this poem is beyond love into life in total, Lope the incurable lover will not leave love. But "Love now is cawing crow," the crow involving an unexpressed conceit. (In Latin, *cras* is both "tomorrow" and the caw of the crow.) Perhaps under the pressure of "tomorrow" the poet lapses into two Baroque lines: "In what place will the sun's car lodging see / For this impossible hope tramontane?" This vain hope evokes two powerful but inelegant metaphors; it is "Like old lame mule" or "ship that lugs at sea." Even as real, his lady Jane is abusing the poet as old and powerless. But the old poet will not give up; he and Love will commence a "search for this tomorrow." This poet, however, who has enjoyed a string of conquests in the past, ends without hope: "If I your fierce disdain cannot subdue / Let crows pluck from the boughs of greenery / Your eyes. But no, that they are mine is true!" It is strange that Lope rather lost this sonnet in the middle of the book, for it expresses the infinite sadness of a poet who in his "desire" set out to conquer love and almost succeeded. Then, as he a good Christian would say, he ran out of love and life.

As a kind of footnote to the *Human Rhymes*, after the sonnets, after the mock-epic on cats, among a group of poems tossed into the book, Lope slips in a tiny *redondilla* (a quatrain rhyming abba in octosyllables used in his plays) which reads thus:

> Today Antonia's thirteen and she
> Deserves two thousand birthdays more;
> There would be nothing else to implore
> If she thirteen could always be.

Then in impeccable *quintillas* (five line stanzas) the poet in forty more lines develops a poem which glosses his quatrain. This Antonia is Antonia Clara, child of his old age and daughter of his last great love,

Amaryllis. Here the poet has captured her in the age of perfection for the father: she has that combination of budding beauty, pride, confidence, and innocence of a girl near womanhood and yet unbattered by the demands and dangers of life. In fact a few years later, she was enticed away from home by a Don Juan of some rank, and the poor Lope mourned her the rest of his life. He dutifully recorded this experience without much transformation in his eclogue *Phyllis*.

Only a year after the publication of the *Human Rhymes*, Lope de Vega rather suddenly became seriously ill, but forgetting idle things such as literature, he had time to prepare himself for a "good dying," as the Spanish say. His death and burial were resoundingly Spanish both personally and nationally. In his final agony Lope declared himself "the biggest sinner of all times," for which he can now become the greatest repentant. His burial evoked national mourning and the promise to eternalize his memory, but in a few years material promises failed and his bones were tossed into the common boneyard. To merit the designation of "biggest sinner" honestly meant that Lope did a lot of living, and it is this deep but ordinary experience that pervades his poetry. Years ago Montesinos called him the greatest Spanish poet of circumstance, a phrase intended to be positive.

In final summary, then, what is the worthy and honest thing to say about Lope de Vega Carpio (1562-1635)? First, we remain in awe at his creation of two million lines of poetry, perhaps a thousand plays in verse, six epics in verse form, a novel or two, and 1600 sonnets among his lyric poetry. Yet no recluse he, he wrote all of this by hand while living more than a full domestic, professional, and public life, giving of himself throughout that life. His legacy of lyric poetry is solid, varied, and generally complete for the Golden Age: his significant contribution to the artistic ballad with his Moorish and pastoral ballads, the *Rhymes*, the *Sacred Rhymes*, a group of later artistic ballads, an imposing group of songs and poems from the plays, and the *Rhymes Human and Divine*. It is proper that we respect the fact that he inherited a respect for the classical, the ideals of Neoplatonism, and a solid Catholic faith, and in his poetic stance he could chip away at these ideals, push them toward the human, without destroying them. That the contemporary poet adopts a stance in which the world is a personal dunghill from which with agony a pearl or two may be saved is proper for our time, but it is not necessarily eternal or universal. From his generally Renaissance stance Lope transformed his great *desire*, his persistent amorousness into lyric poetry. He became a master of the forms of his time, especially the ballad and the sonnet.

Of the three great poets of the Golden Age, Quevedo pushed toward the grotesque and the anguish of the existential; Gongora practically exhausted the limits of poetic language. Both of these have enjoyed revivals in our time, Góngora after the 1920's, and Quevedo since 1950. Lope's particular contribution to Spanish poetry is that he personalized both the courtly and the religious themes, making them more human, more of this earth. In his final position (in the *Human Rhymes*) he exalts the ordinary, the common, with the courtly and the heroic subjected to gentle irony; thus for us he becomes a prophet toward our times. Yet there remains a certain sense of balance in Lope's poetry; and balance not being the mark of our age, Lope's revival has been a modest one. Significantly, there is still no full-fledged study of his poetry. It is impossible not to be disappointed in him that, given his genius, he did not concentrate more, organize better, dig deeper into things—but that was not his genius. As the emphases of our time moderate—the stress upon text, ignoring the poet, the seduction of the rebellious and the grotesque—perhaps Lope de Vega will gain new respect as a poet who lived fully and then transformed that experience into poetry that represents him, his age, and in a balanced measure, all ages.

Footnotes

[1] José F. Montesinos, *Estudios sobre Lope* (Mexico: Colegio de Mexico, 1951), p. 237.

[2] Lope de Vega, *Lírica*, Selección, introducción y notas por José María Blecua (Madrid: Clásicos Castalia, 1981), p. 7.

[3] From *La Dorotea*, quoted in his *Lírica*, edited by *Blecua*, p. 50.

[4] Quoted in Amado Alonso, *Materia y forma en poesía* (Madrid: *Editorial Gredos*, 1965), p. 127.

[5] The Facsimile Edition (without explanatory materials) reads *Rimas humanas y divinas del Licenciado Tomé de Burguillos*, por Fray Lope Félix de Vega Carpio (Madrid: Inprenta del Regno, 1634).

Romances Moriscos y Pastorales

Moorish and Pastoral Ballads

El mayor Almoralife . . .

El mayor Almoralife
de los buenos de Granada,
el de más seguro alfanje
y el de más temida lanza,
el sobrino de Zulema,   5
visorrey de la Alpujarra,
gran consejero en la paz,
fuerte y bravo en la batalla,
en socorro de su rey
se va a la mar desde Baza,   10
más animoso y galán
que el hijo del moro Audalla;
tanto que al mundo su nombre
seguras fianzas daba
que verdaderas saldrían   15
sus dichosas esperanzas.
Albornoz de seda verde
y de pajizo de gualda,
marlota de raso al uso,
de [verdes] lirios sembrada,   20
por mostrar que allá en la guerra
encubre con esperanzas
los lirios, que ya son verdes
y fueron flores moradas;
con cuatro moros detrás   25
solo en una yegua baya,
que quien quiere adelantarse
bien es que delante vaya,
recogiendo, pues la rienda
cesando el trote paraba   30
por no sentir por la posta
la ausencia de Felisalva.
Saca un retrato del pecho,
que aun a sacalle no basta,
porque salen tras la vista   35
las imágenes del alma.

The Almoralife most renowned . . .

The Almoralife most renowned
    Of Granada's most endeared,
He of the cutlass ever sure,
    He of the lance most feared,

The Alpujarra land's vice-king,   5
    The nephew of Zuleme,
Great counsellor in times of peace,
    In bravery extreme,

From Baza he goes down to sea,
    To see the king's wars won,   10
More gallant and more spirited
    Than Moor Audalla's son;

So much so that his name did give
    The world firm guarantee
That all his happy hopes and plans   15
    Would know true victory.

Burnoose of finest silk in green,
    In yellow and pale tan,
Tight-fitting gown with lilies strewn,
    In style Mohammedan;   20

So as to show that off in war
    He dwells upon hopes keen,
The lilies, which in green now are,
    Before had purple been;

Four Moors behind, he rides in front,   25
    Alone upon bay mare,
For one who wants to get ahead,
    To stay in front must dare;

Now gathering up the slackened reins
    He curbs the horse's trot,   30
That Filisalva's absence keen
    In posting he feel not.

He takes a portrait from his breast,
    But it cannot console,
For after just one look comes forth   35
    The image of her soul.

—Amada mora—le dice—,
—que parece que me hablas
con ceño porque te dejo
y dejándote me agravias,   40
¿cómo me miras alegre,
pues yo te vi esta mañana
tan enojada conmigo
que contigo te enojabas?
Si no lloras como peña   45
que está dura y echa un agua,
¡mucho me quieren tus ojos,
mucho debo a tus entrañas!
Si el arrancar tus cabellos
no es sentimiento que engaña,   50
¡muchos cabellos, amiga,
por mi respeto te faltan!
Habla ya que a tu pintura
le darán vida mis ansias
dejando mi cuerpo triste   55
vacío y con fuerzas flacas.
Felisalva, no te entiendo,
las suertes están trocadas,
hoy callas tú y hablo yo,
ayer hablaste y callaba.   60
¡Malhaya aquel amador
que al retrato de su dama
le dice sus sentimientos,
pues que no sienten las tablas!
¡Malhaya aquel que la mira   65
en retrato mesurada,
él llorando, flaco y triste,
y ella compuesta y ufana!
¡Ay pundonor que me llevas
a meterme en una barca   70
y entre las ondas y el cielo
cargado de acero y malla!
¡Ay mis baños y jardines
que el mejor tiempo os dejara!
Mas si dejo mi contento   75
¿qué hago en dejar mi casa?

"Dear Moorish lass," he says to her,
      "It seems you speak to me
With frown because I'm leaving you,
      And thus you then wound me;   40

"How can you view me happily
      Since I saw you myself
At dawn as furious with me
      As you were with yourself?

"If you don't weep like cliff that's hard   45
      And makes the waters flow,
So much your eyes are fond of me,
      Much I your heart's core owe!

"If tearing out your hair is not
      To throw me off the track,   50
So many locks of hair, dear friend,
      In my respect you lack.

"Speak then, for to your picture now
      My worries will give life,
My empty body leaving sad,   55
      My forces weak from strife.

"Filisalva, I don't understand,
      Our fates are turned around:
Now you are mute, I talk; before
      You talked, I made no sound.   60

"A curse upon that lover who
      To his lady's picture appeals
By telling it his sentiments—
      It's board that nothing feels!

A curse upon one who sees her   65
      In portrait dignified,
He weeping, skin-and-bones and sad,
      And she calm, full of pride.

"Ay, point of honor that sticks me
      Inside a ship to sail,   70
Between the heavens and the waves,
      Weighed down by steel and mail!

"Ay, all my gardens and my baths,
      To leave you this time best!
What does it serve to leave my home   75
      If I leave peace and rest?

Amiga, por nuestro amor
que si vives en mi alma
suspirando me la envíes,
que no venceré sin alma—.   80
Con esto los cuatro moros
a media rienda le alcanzan;
esconde el retrato y pica
hablando de guerra y armas.

Ensíllenme el potro rucio ...

«Ensíllenme el potro rucio
del alcaide de los Vélez;
denme el adarga de Fez
y la jacerina fuerte,
    una lanza con dos hierros,   5
entrambos de agudos temples,
y aquel acerado casco
con el morado bonete,
    que tiene plumas pajizas
entre blancos martinetes   10
y garzotas medio pardas,
antes que me vista, denme.
    Pondréme la toca azul
que me dio para ponerme
Adalifa la de Baza,   15
hija de Zelín Hamete,
    y aquella medalla en cuadro
que dos ramos la guarnecen
con las hojas de esmeraldas,
por ser los ramos laureles,   20
    y un Adonis que va a caza
de los jabalíes monteses,
dejando su diosa amada,
y dice la letra «Muere».»

"Dear friend of mine, for all our love
    If you live in my soul,
Then, sighing, send me it for I
    Can't conquer without soul."   80

At this, the four Moors at half rein,
    His company now seeking,
He hides the portrait, spurs his mare,
    Of arms and battles speaking.

Go saddle the colt of silver gray . . .

"Go saddle the colt of silver gray
    The Vélez' warden has;
Give me the coat of mail so strong,
    The oval shield from Fez,

"A lance with its two iron shafts,   5
    Both sharp and tempered true,
And that good helmet made of steel,
    With cap of purple hue,

"That has those rich straw-colored plumes,
    Between some herons white   10
And herons tinged toward brown—give me,
    Before I dress to fight.

"I'll put on my head-dress in blue
    That gave to me to wear
Adalifa she of Baza town,   15
    Hamete's daughter fair,

"And that medallion in its frame,
    Adorned with branches two,
And since the branches laurel are,
    With leaves of emerald hue,   20

"And an Adonis with wild boars
    His skill at hunting tries,
His precious goddess leaving alone,
    With words below, 'He dies.'"

Esto dijo el moro Azarque,   25
antes que a la guerra fuese,
aquel discreto, animoso,
aquel galán y valiente,
    Almoralife el de Baza,
de Zulema descendiente,   30
caballeros que en Granada
paseaban con los reyes.
    Trajéronle la medalla,
y suspirando mil veces,
del bello Adonis miraba   35
la gentileza y la suerte,
    «Adalifa de mi alma,
no te aflijas ni lo pienses;
viviré para gozarte,
gozosa vendrás a verte;   40
    breve será mi jornada,
tu firmeza no sea breve.
Procura, aunque eres mujer,
ser de todas diferente;
    no te parezcas a Venus,   45
aunque en beldad le pareces,
en olvidar a su amante
y no respetalle ausente.
    Cuando sola te imagines,
mi retrato te consuele,   50
sin admitir compañía
que me ultraje y te desvele;
    que entre tristeza y dolor
suele amor entremeterse,
haciendo de alegres tristes,   55
como de tristes alegres.
    Mira, amiga, mi retrato
que abierto[s] los ojos tiene,
y que es pintura encantada,
que habla, que vive y siente.   60
    Acuérdate de mis ojos,
que muchas lágrimas vierten,
y a fe que lágrimas suyas
pocas moras las merecen.»

This said the Moor Azarque named,   25
    Before to war he went,
The one discreet, brave, spirited,
    In love self-confident;

Almoralife in Baza he,
    Descendant of Zuleme,   30
Those knights who in Granada lived
    And knew the kings' esteem.

They brought him this medallion then,
    And with a thousand sighs,
On fair Adonis' grace and fate   35
    He firmly cast his eyes:

"Dear Adalifa of my soul,
    With grief don't even toy:
You'll joyful see yourself, I'll live
    Your favors to enjoy.   40

"My journey will be brief, let not
    Brief be your constancy,
And strive, although you woman are,
    That you may different be.

"Like Venus I'll not have you be   45
    (Though you in beauty are),
Forgetting her own lover true,
    Not honoring him afar.

"May, when you fancy you're alone,
    My portrait bring relief,   50
Without admitting company
    For my ill and your grief.

"Between despondency and pain
    Love often will intrude,
The sad ones making happy ones,   55
    The happy changing mood.

"Look, friend, upon my portrait then,
    Wide open are the eyes,
For it an enchanted painting is
    That speaks, and lives, and sighs.   60

"May you remember well my eyes,
    Which many tears have shed;
Few Moorish lasses with their own
    Such tears have merited."

En esto llegó Gualquemo   65
a decille que se apreste,
que daban priesa en la mar
que se embarcase la gente.
   A vencer se parte el moro,
aunque gustos no le vencen,   70
honra y esfuerzo lo animan
a cumplir lo que promete.

Gallardo pasea Zaide . . .

   Gallardo pasea Zaide
puerta y calle de su dama,
que desea en gran manera
ver su imagen y adorarla,
porque se vido sin ella   5
en una ausencia muy larga,
que desdichas le sacaron
desterrado de Granada,
no por muerte de hombre alguno
ni por traidor a su dama,   10
mas por dar gusto a enemigos,
si es que en el moro se hallan,
porque es hidalgo en sus cosas
y tanto que al mundo espantan
sus larguezas, pues por ellas   15
el moro dejó su patria;
pero a Granada volvió
a pesar de vil canalla,
porque siendo un moro noble
enemigos nunca faltan.   20
Alzó la cabeza y vido
a su Zaida a la ventana,
tan bizarra y tan hermosa
que al sol quita su luz clara.

At this Gualquemo came to him   65
    And said he should make haste,
The troops were ready to embark,
    There was no time to waste.

Though willingness him conquers not,
    To conquer parts the Moor: 70
His honor and his effort make
    His promises secure.

Now Zaide boldly walks the street . . .

Now Zaide boldly walks the street
    Before his lady's door,
For he desires in great degree
    Her image to adore,

For without it, he saw himself   5
    In absence for long while,
Because misfortunes took him from
    Granada in exile,

Not for the death of any man,
    Or treason to his dame,   10
But more to please his enemies
    If such this Moor can claim;

Since he is noble in his ways,
    His gifts much awe command,
The Moor because of his largesse   15
    Then left his fatherland;

But to Granada he returned
    In spite of riffraff vile,
For enemies will never lack
    A Moor with noble style.   20

He raised his head, at window gazed,
    And Zaida met his sight,
So gallant and so beautiful,
    She robs the sun of light.

Zaida se huelga de ver   25
a quien ha entregado el alma,
tan turbada y tan alegre
y cuanto alegre turbada,
porque su grande desdicha
le dió nombre de casada,   30
aunque no por eso piensa
olvidar a quien bien ama.
El moro se regocija
y con dolor de su alma,
por no tener más lugar,   35
que el puesto no se la daba,
por ser el moro celoso
de quien es esposa Zaida,
en gozo, contento y penas
le envió aquestas palabras: 40
—¡Oh más hermosa y más bella
que la aurora aljofarada,
mora de los ojos míos,
que otra en beldad no te iguala!
Dime, ¿fáltate salud   45
después que el verme te falta?
Mas según la muestra has dado
amor es el que te falta.
Pues mira, diosa cruel,
lo que me cuestas del alma   50
y cuántas noches dormí
debajo de tus ventanas;
y mira que dos mil veces,
recreándome en tus faldas,
decías: —El firme amor   55
sólo entre los dos se halla.
Pues que por mí no ha quedado,
que cumplo, por mi desgracia,
lo que prometo una vez,
cúmplelo también, ingrata.   60
No pido más que te acuerdes,
mira mi humilde demanda,
pues en pensar sólo en ti
me ocupo tarde y mañana—.

Thus Zaida is thrilled to see   25
    Him who her soul did get,
So happy and upset is she,
    As happy as upset,

Because her great misfortune was
    In name to be a wife,   30
Though she no thought has to forget
    The love that is her life.

The Moor rejoices in his love
    And in his soul's fierce pain,
Since he in fact has not much place,   35
    Not much could he obtain,

For jealous is the Moor of him
    Who Zaida has as wife;
In joy, in grief, in pleasure he
    Sent her these words of strife: 40

"More beauteous, more beautiful
    Than dawn with pearls of dew,
O Moorish lass, joy of my eyes,
    No other equals you!

"Tell me, is it good health you lack   45
    Since you're not seeing me?
Love is the thing that you don't have
    By all the signs I see.

"Consider then, cruel goddess mine,
    How much my soul you cost;   50
How many nights I sleeping there
    Beneath your windows lost;

"And look you that two thousand times
    You said, my courting you,
'Between us only can be found   55
    A love that's firm and true.'

"That love has not remained for me;
    I keep, to my own woe,
My promises, ungrateful one,
    May you keep yours also.   60

"I only ask that you recall,
    Look to my humble demand;
Through morning into afternoon
    You all my thoughts command."

Su prolijo razonar   65
creo el moro no acabara
si no faltara la lengua
que estaba medio turbada.
La mora tiene la suya
de tal suerte, que no acaba   70
de acabar de abrir la gloria
al moro con la palabra.
Vertiendo de entrambos ojos
perlas con que le aplacaba
al moro sus quejas tristes,   75
dijo la discreta Zaida:
—Zaide mío, a Alá prometo
de cumplirte la palabra
que es jamás no te olvidar,
pues no olvida quien bien ama;   80
pero yo no me aseguro
ni estoy de mí confiada,
que suele, el cuerpo presente,
ser la vigilia doblada,
y más que tú lisonjeas,   85
que ya lo tienes por gala,
de ser como aquí lo has dicho,
no habiendo en mí bueno nada.
Sé muy bien lo que te debo
y pluguiese a Alá quedara   90
hecho mi cuerpo pedazos
antes que yo me casara,
que no hay rato de contento
en mí, ni un punto se aparta
este mi moro enemigo   95
de mi lado y de mi cama,
y no me deja salir
ni asomarme a la ventana
ni hablar con mis amigas
ni hallarme en fiestas o zambras—.   100
No pudo escuchalla más
el moro, y así se aparta
hechos los ojos dos fuentes
de lágrimas que derrama.

I think this Moor long-reasoning   65
    Might thus be talking yet,
If his poor tongue had not failed him,
    It being half-upset.

The Moorish lass finds hers in such
    A way she has not stirred   70
To open glory for this Moor
    With her refreshing word.

Thus pouring out from both her eyes
    The pearls sent to appease
The sad complainings of the Moor,   75
    Said Zaida to please:

"My Zaide, I will keep my word
    (I ever Allah praise),
That word you never to forget:
    True lover loves always;   80

"But I cannot be confident,
    Or have security,
That I may not, since he is here,
    The vigil doubled see;

"And though you hold it as your charm   85
    With flattery to speak,
Here in this case, as you have said,
    You've nothing good to seek.

"I well know what I owe to you;
    Then I with Allah pled   90
That my poor body pieces were
    Before I came to wed;

"There is no moment of content
    In me; this other Moor,
My foe, not for a minute leaves   95
    My side, my bed, be sure.

"He never lets me leave the house,
    Or at the window sit,
Or go to fiesta or Moorish dance,
    Or talk with girls a bit."   100

The Moor could hear her words no more
    And thus away he heads,
His eyes a pair of fountains made
    Of tears that he now sheds.

Zaida, no menos que él,　　　　　　　　　　　105
se quita de la ventana,
y aunque apartaron los cuerpos,
juntas quedaron las almas.

Mira, Zaide, que te aviso . . .

«Mira, Zaide, que te aviso
que no pases por mi calle
ni hables con mis mujeres,
ni con mis cautivos trates,
　　ni preguntes en qué entiendo　　　　　　5
ni quién viene a visitarme,
qué fiestas me dan contento
o qué colores me aplacen;
　　basta que son por tu causa
las que en el rostro me salen,　　　　　　　10
corrida de haber mirado
moro que tan poco sabe.
　　Confieso que eres valiente,
que hiendes, rajas y partes
y que has muerto más cristianos　　　　　　15
que tienes gotas de sangre;
　　que eres gallardo jinete,
que danzas, cantas y tañes,
gentil hombre, bien criado
cuanto puede imaginarse;　　　　　　　　20
　　blanco, rubio por extremo,
señalado por linaje,
el gallo de las bravatas,
la nata de los donaires,
　　y pierdo mucho en perderte　　　　　　25
y gano mucho en amarte,
y que si nacieras mudo,
fuera posible adorarte;

And Zaida, no less than he,   105
    From the window now does fade,
And though their bodies were apart,
    Their souls together stayed.

Look, Zaide, I say to you . . .

"Look, Zaide, I say to you
    Along my street don't walk;
Don't say things to my women folk,
    Or with my captives talk;

"Don't ask me what I'm going to do,   5
    Or who's to visit me,
What parties I enjoy the most,
    What colors I like to see;

"Enough it is that because of you
    This one in my face shows;   10
Upset I am at having seen
    Moor that so little knows.

"That you are valiant I confess,
    That you rip, slash, give pain,
That, count the drops of blood you have,   15
    More Christians you have slain;

"That you a gallant horseman are,
    You dance and play and sing,
A man of class, and well brought up,
    Beyond all reckoning;   20

"Outstanding as to lineage,
    Both fair and blond to excess,
The cock of challenge arrogant,
    Elite in gracefulness.

"I lose a lot in losing you,   25
    In loving you much win;
To adore you would be possible,
    Had you at birth mute been;

y por este inconviniente
determino de dejarte,   30
que eres pródigo de lengua
y amargan tus libertades,
    y habrá menester ponerte
quien quisiere sustentarte
un alcázar en el pecho   35
y en los labios un alcaide.
    Mucho pueden con las damas
los galanes de tus partes,
porque los quieren briosos,
que rompan y que desgarren;   40
    mas tras esto, Zaide amigo,
si algún convite te hacen
al plato de sus favores
quieren que comas y calles.
    Costoso fue el que te hice;   45
venturoso fuera[s], Zaide,
si conservarme supieras
como supiste obligarme.
    Apenas fuiste salido
de los jardines de Tarfe   50
cuando heciste de la tuya
y de mi desdicha alarde.
    A un morito mal nacido
me dicen que le enseñaste
la trenza de los cabellos   55
que te puse en el turbante.
    No quiero que me la vuelvas
ni quiero que me la guardes,
mas quiero que entiendas, moro,
que en mi desgracia la traes.   60
    También me certificaron
cómo le desafiaste
por las verdades que dijo,
que nunca fueran verdades.
    De mala gana me río;   65
¡qué donoso disparate!
No guardas tú tu secreto
¡y quieres que otri le guarde?

"And for this inconvenience
   I vow to let you go;   30
Tongue prodigal, your liberties
   With me now bitter grow;

"Whoever wants to live with you,
   Be sure that she equips
Your breast with Moorish fortress strong,   35
   With warden your loose lips.

"The gallants with your qualities
   With the ladies much can do;
They want men who are spirited,
   Who slash and break things too;   40

"But after this, friend Zaide,
   If they hold out some treat
Upon their plate of favors they
   Want you to hush and eat.

"The one I offered you much cost;   45
   You fortunate would be
If, Zaide, you would me support
   The way you entangle me.

"You barely had departure made
   From Tarfe's gardens fine,   50
When you began to spread around
   Your woes along with mine.

"To some mean Moor not born to class
   They tell me that you showed
The special lock of hair that I   55
   Inside your turban stowed.

"I ask that you not give it back,
   And not keep it also;
I want you, Moor, to understand
   You bear it for my woe.   60

"They too affirmed to me that you
   Him challenged to a fight,
Because of certain truths he said—
   Oh that they were not right!

"I have to laugh unwillingly,   65
   What a blunder made by you!
You your own secret fail to keep,
   What, then, will others do?

No quiero admitir disculpa;
otra vez vuelvo a avisarte   70
que esta será la postrera
que me hables y te hable.»
    Dijo la discreta Zaida
a un altivo bencerraje
y al despedirle repite: 75
«Quien tal hace, que tal pague».

Di, Zaida, ¿de qué me avisas?

«Di, Zaida, ¿de qué me avisas?
¿Quieres que muera y que calle?
No te fíes de mujeres
fundadas en disbarates.
    Y si pregunté en qué entiendes   5
y quién viene a visitarte,
son fiestas de mis tormentos
ver qué colores te aplacen.
    Dices que son por mi causa
las que en el rostro te salen;   10
por la tuya, con mis ojos,
tengo regada la calle.
    Dícesme que estás corrida
de Zaide que poco sabe;
no sé poco, pues que supe   15
conocerte y adorarte.
    Confiesas que soy valiente,
que tengo otras muchas partes;
pocas tengo pues no puedo
de una mentira vengarme;   20
    mas ha querido mi suerte
que ya en quererme te canses;
no busques inconvinientes,
si no que quieres dejarme.

"I will not make apology;
    I echo warning plain: 70
You speak to me, I speak to you
    The last time ever again."

Thus spoke this Zaida discreet
    To a Moor long on self-praise,
And she dismissing him repeats:
    "One who such does, such pays."

Say, Zaida, what advice is this?

"Say, Zaida, what advice is this?
    You'd have me hush and die?
Don't put your trust in women who
    Use foolishness and lie.

"And if I asked you what you like,   5
    Who comes to visit you,
They're fiestas of my own torments,
    To see your colors true.

"You say that it's because of me
    Such colors your face greet;   10
Because of yours, I with my eyes
    Have watered down the street.

"You tell me too that you're upset
    That Zaide little knows:
That I could meet and worship you   15
    No little talent shows.

"That I have valor you confess,
    And many other sides;
I must have few, I can't avenge
    The lie that still abides;   20

"But now you tire of loving me
    My fortune has decreed;
Unless you want to leave me now
    Excuses you don't need.

No entendí que eras mujer   25
a quien mentiras le placen,
mas tales son mis desdichas
que en mí lo imposible hacen;
    hanme puesto en tal extremo
que el bien tengo por ultraje: 30
lóasme para hacerme
la nata de los galanes;
    yo soy quien pierdo en perderte
y yo quien gano en amarte
y aunque hables en mi ofensa,   35
no dejaré de adorarte.
    Dices que, si fuera mudo,
fuera posible adorarme;
si en tu daño no lo he sido,
enmudesca en disculparme.   40
    Si te ha ofendido mi vida
y si gustas de matarme,
basta decir que hablo mucho
para que el pesar me acabe.
    Es mi pecho un fuerte muro   45
de tormentos inmortales
y mis labios son silencio,
que no han menester alcaide.
    El hacer plato o banquete
es de hombres principales,   50
mas da[r] les de sus favores
sólo pertenece a infantes.
    Zaida cruel, que dijistes
que no supe conservarte:
mejor te supe obligar   55
que tú supiste pagarme.
    Mienten las moras y moros
y miente el traidor de Zarque
que si yo le amenazara,
bastara para matarle.   60
    A ese perro mal nacido
a quien [yo] mostré el turbante
no fié yo del secreto:
en pecho bajo no cabe.

"I never imagined that with you 25
    Lies would be acceptable,
But such as my misfortunes are,
    They work the impossible;

"In such extremes I'm placed that I
    The good as outrage hold: 30
You sing my praises to make me
    The cream of gallants bold;

"I'm he who loses losing you,
    I win adoring you,
And though you speak in my offense 35
    I won't stop loving you.

"You say that if I silent were
    Your love such would produce;
If to your hurt I talked, let me
    Be mute as my excuse. 40

"If my life has offended you,
    You'd like to kill your friend,
Let me just say I talk a lot
    So that my woes may end.

"My breast is still enduring wall 45
    Of hurts immutable,
And silence are my very lips,
    That need no constable.

"To offer plate or banquet is
    Of men predominant, 50
But for them favors of all kinds
    Are what infantes grant.

"In short, I couldn't hold on to you,
    Cruel Zaida, you did say;
I better was at obliging you, 55
    Than you knew how to pay.

"Since Moors both men and women lie,
    Then Zarque's traitor must lie;
Yet if I chanced to threaten him
    He would fall down and die. 60

"I showed the turban to that dog,
    Low-born and dispossessed;
I kept the secret though, for it
    Can't fit in vulgar breast.

Yo le quitaré la vida   65
y escribiré con su sangre
lo que tú, Zaida, replicas:
«Quien tal hace, que tal pague».

En la prisión está Adulce . . .

En la prisión está Adulce
alegre porque se sabe
que está preso sin razón
y le quieren mal de balde.
Esto es causa que en el moro   5
es la pena menos grave,
pues no quiere libertad
si con ella han de culpalle.
Piensan que ha de hacer por fuerza
lo que de agrado no hace,   10
enmudeciendo las leyes
para que los mudos hablen.
Arrimado está a una reja
que hace más fuerte la cárcel,
pena un tiempo de traidores   15
castigo ya de leales.
Alzó los ojos al cielo
temiendo que se le cae
y dijo: —Siempre padezco
por leal y por amante.   20
¡Ay Aja ingrata! ¿Qué es esto,
que en medio de mis pesares
hallo viva la memoria
de mis bienes y mis males?
Y todo porque no pueda,   25
ingrata, desengañarme,
pues con quererte en naciendo
pienso que te quise tarde.

"I'll take his life away from him,   65
  And with the blood that sprays
Write what you, Zaida, retort:
  'One who such does, such pays.'"

In prison cell Adulce lies . . .

In prison cell Adulce lies,
  Content because it's known
That he's in jail without real cause,
  For nothing he's alone.

It's for this reason that the Moor   5
  His troubles less grave feels,
For he does not want liberty
  That any guilt conceals.

They think that can be done by force
  What one's not pleased to do,   10
The normal laws thus silencing,
  So that the mute speak true.

He's pressing now against a grille
  That stronger makes the jail,
For traitors once a punishment,   15
  For the faithful now travail.

He raised his eyes up to the skies
  In fear they tumble down,
And said: "As faithful lover I
  In suffering have my crown.   20

"Ungrateful Aja, ay! What's this,
  Here where my troubles spill,
I find alive the memory
  Of both my good and ill?

"And everything so that I can't,   25
  Cruel one, myself set straight,
For with my loving you from birth,
  I think I loved you late.

A otra reja me vi asido,
más baja, porque alcanzase   30
las promesas de tu boca,
puesto que ya no se guarden.
¿Cómo quieres, di, que crea
que el aire se las llevase,
estando los dos tan cerca   35
que apenas pasaba el aire?
¿Cómo no te desengañas
de que así quise engañarte
si en medio de los favores
siempre me viste cobarde?   40
¡Agora, ingrata, te pesa
de que te sirva y te ame
y no quieres ser querida
quizá por desobligarte!
¿Quién derribó por el suelo   45
el edificio admirable
que alzó amor a las estrellas,
de que apenas hay señales?
Déjanse sus ruïnas
una piedra que declare   50
la mudanza que hizo el tiempo
sin poder jamás mudarme.
Mucho debo a sus amigos,
todos dicen que me guarde,
mas ¿de qué sirve, cruel,   55
si viene el consejo tarde?
¿De qué aprovecha el socorro
y que todo el pueblo llame
si está la casa abrasada
cuando la campana tañen?   60
¿Quieres, ingrata, que pierda
el premio de ser constante
y que si es la causa firme
que la pena sea mudable?
No, para tanta belleza   65
no hay tormento que sea grave,
pues la ofensa de quererte
se defiende con amarte.

"I saw myself at another grille,
    One lower, so that I   30
Might reach the promise of your lips,
    For they unguarded lie.

"Say, how can you want me to think
    That the air took them away,
Since we so close together were,   35
    No air could pass that way?

"Why can't you undeceive yourself
    That I would you deceive;
Since you saw me as cowardly,
    Could I those favors thieve?   40

"Ungrateful, it now weighs on you
    That I you serve and love,
And you don't want my love perhaps
    Obligations to remove.

"Who dashed completely to the ground   45
    The edifice much-praised,
Of which there are not many signs,
    That to the stars Love raised?

"The ruins of the building leave
    A stone that makes one see   50
The change that time has slowly made,
    Though never changing me.

"I owe a great deal to her friends,
    They all tell me to wait,
And yet, cruel one, what good can be   55
    Advice that comes too late?

"Of what advantage is such help,
    What good that people yell,
The house already lost in flames,
    When they go ring the bell?   60

"Ungrateful, shall I lose the prize
    For being unchangeable,
And whether this might be firm cause
    That hurts be changeable?

"No, for such beauty no torment   65
    Is grave; for my offense
Of loving you, just loving you
    Becomes its own defense.

Los ojos vuelve, enemiga,
y podrá ser que eso baste,   70
pues para corta ventura
cualquier favor será grande.
Verás lo mucho que quiero
y lo poco que me vale
y que no es bien que me pierda   75
donde es justo que me gane—.
Llamaron en esto al moro,
que le esperaba su paje,
que venía muy contento
con una carta que trae,   80
donde Adalifa le escribe
el pésame de sus males,
Y Adulce dijo: —¿Qué importa
si Aja gusta que me acaben?

Sale la estrella de Venus . . .

        Sale la estrella de Venus
al tiempo que el sol se pone
y la enemiga del día
su negro manto descoge,
        y con ella un fuerte moro   5
semejante a Rodamonte
sale de Sidonia airado,
de Xerez la vega corre,
        por donde entra Guadalete
al mar de España, y por donde   10
Santa María del Puerto
recibe famoso nombre.
        Desesperado camina,
que siendo en linaje noble,
le deja su dama ingrata   15
porque se suena que es pobre,

"Your eyes show me, my enemy,
    Perhaps that will suffice,   70
Since for a scanty enterprise,
    Any favor will be nice.

"You'll see the much that I love you,
    And the little it brings in,
And it's not good that I should lose,   75
    It's right that I should win."

At this, they called out to the Moor,
    That his page was waiting there,
That he was coming quite content,
    A letter he does bear,   80

Where Adalifa writes to him
    Condolence for his ills.
Then Adulce said: "What matters it
    If Aja my end wills?"

The star of Venus now comes out . . .

The star of Venus now comes out
    Just as the sun goes down,
And that old enemy of day
    Outspreads her thick, black gown,

And with the night a mighty Moor,   5
    Like Rodamont in deeds,
In anger leaves Sidonia,
    Across Jerez' plain speeds,

There where the Guadalete flows
    Into the sea of Spain,   10
And where Saint Mary of the Port
    Its famous name does gain.

Though he's of noble lineage,
    He's riding insecure,
For his cruel lady is leaving him,   15
    Because they hint he's poor;

y aquella noche se casa
con un moro feo y torpe
porque es alcaide en Sevilla
del Alcázar y la Torre.   20
    Quejándose tiernamente
de un agravio tan inorme,
y a sus palabras la vega
con dulces ecos responde:
    «Zayda, dice, más airada   25
que el mar que las naves sorbe,
más dura e inexorable
que las entrañas de un monte,
    ¿cómo permites, cruel,
después de tantos favores,   30
que de prendas de mi alma
ajena mano se adorne?
    ¿Es posible que te abraces
a las cortezas de un roble,
y dejes el árbol tuyo   35
desnudo de fruta y flores?
    ¿Dejas tu amado Gazul,
dejas tres años de amores
y das la mano a Albenzaide,
que aun apenas le conoces?   40
    Dejas un pobre muy rico
y un rico muy probre escoges,
pues las riquezas del cuerpo
a las del alma antepones.
    Alá permita, enemiga,   45
que te aborrezca y le adores
y que por celos suspires
y por ausencia le llores
    y que de noche no duermas
y de día no reposes   50
y en la cama le fastidies
y que en la mesa le enojes
    y en las fiestas, en las zambras,
no se vista tus colores,
ni aun para verlas permita   55
que a la ventana te asomes;

That very night she is to wed
   A dull Moor who looks ill,
For of the Alcázar, the Tower both,
   He's warden in Seville;   20

Lamenting he so tenderly,
   So terrible a wrong,
And at his words the plain responds
   With echoes sweet and long:

"Dear Zaida, angrier than sea   25
   That drinks of ships its fill,
More flinty and inexorable
   Than bowels of craggy hill,

"How, after favors without count,
   Can you permit, cruel one,   30
That alien hand adorn itself
   With gifts my soul thought won?

"Is it even possible that you
   Should clasp an oak's rough bark,
And leave without both bloom and fruit   35
   Your own tree standing stark?

"You give up your much-loved Gazul,
   Three years of love let go,
And Albenzaide give your hand,
   Though him you barely know.   40

"You leave a poor man very rich
   And rich one poor you choose,
For riches of the body you
   With those of soul confuse.

"That he hate you, and you love him,   45
   May Allah grant you, foe,
And may you sigh with jealousy,
   His absence wailing go,

"And that you never sleep at night,
   And never rest by day,   50
That you may bother him in bed,
   At table him dismay;

"May he in fiesta and in dance
   Your colors never wear,
Nor let you at the window sit   55
   To glimpse them anywhere;

y menosprecie en las cañas,
para que más te alborotes,
el almaizar que le labres
y la manga que le bordes   60
　　y se ponga el de su amiga
con la cifra de su nombre,
a quien le dé los cautivos
cuando de la guerra torne;
　　y en batalla de cristianos   65
de velle muerto te asombres
y plegue a Alá que suceda,
cuando la mano le tomes,
　　que si le has de aborrecer,
que largos años le goces;   70
que es la mayor maldición
que pueden darte los hombres.»
　　Con esto llegó a Xerez
a la mitad de la noche;
halló el palacio cubierto   75
de luminarias y voces,
　　y los moros fronterizos
que por todas parten corren,
con sus hachas encendidas
y con libreas conformes.   80
　　Delante del desposado
en los estribos alzóse;
arrojóle una lanzada,
de parte a parte pasóle;
　　alborotóse la plaza,   85
desnudó el moro un estoque
y por mitad de la gente
hacia Sidonia volvióse.

"And may he scorn in reed-spear games,
    To see you furious grow,
The sleeve that you embroidered for him,
    The veil for him you sew;   60

"And may he wear his lady friend's
    Which her initials bears;
Let him give her the captive slaves
    When he from war repairs;

"His fighting Christians, may you be   65
    Overcome to see him dead;
Grant Allah as you take his hand,
    His life will then be fled;

"And if you're going to bear him hate,
    Enjoy it long years through;   70
This is the greatest curse for sure
    That men can lay on you."

On this, he at Jerez arrived
    In the middle of the night;
He found the palace overspread   75
    With voices and torch-light;

The Moors who on the frontier lived
    Were moving rapidly
With lighted torches held aloft
    And proper livery.   80

Before the bridegroom he stood up
    In stirrups him to view,
And hurled his trusty lance at him,
    And pierced him through and through.

The plaza fell into uproar;   85
    The Moor then bared a blade,
And toward Sidonia through the throng
    His way he slowly made.

El tronco de ovas vestido . . .

El tronco de ovas vestido
de un álamo verde y blanco
entre espadañas y juncos
bañaba el agua del Tajo,
y las puntas de su altura,   5
del ardiente sol los rayos,
y todo el árbol, dos vides
entre racimos y lazos.
Al son del agua y las ramas
hería el céfiro manso   10
en las plateadas hojas,
tronco, punta, vides, árbol.
Este con llorosos ojos
mirando estaba Belardo,
porque fue un tiempo su gloria   15
como ahora es su cuidado.
Vio de dos tórtolas bellas
tejido un nido en lo alto
y que con arrullos roncos
los picos se están besando.   20
Tomó una piedra el pastor
y esparció en el aire claro
ramas, tórtolas y nido,
diciendo alegre y ufano:

Redondillas

«Dejad la dulce acogida,   25
que la que el amor me dio
envidia me la quitó
y envidia os quita la vida.
Piérdase vuestra amistad,
pues que se perdió la mía,   30
que no ha de haber compañia
donde está mi soledad.
Tan solo pena me da,
tórtola, el esposo tuyo,
que tú presto hallarás cuyo,   35
pues Filis le tiene ya.»

The trunk with river weeds adorned . . .

The trunk with river weeds adorned
    Of a poplar green and white
Among the rushes and reeds was bathed
    By Tagus' waters bright,

And highest measure of its crown   5
    In ardent sunlight glowed,
And over all the tree two vines
    A thousand tendrils showed.

With sound of waters and of boughs,
    A zephyr meek aggrieves—   10
Of trunk, of crown, of vines, of tree—
    The silver-tinted leaves.

Upon this tree so tearfully
    Belardo fixed his stare,
For what was once his glory bright   15
    Has now become his care.

He saw that two fair turtledoves,
    On high entwined their nest,
Were cooing in a husky voice
    And billing without rest.   20

The shepherd then picked up a stone
    And scattered in clear air
The branches, nest, and turtledoves
    And said with prideful flair:

Quatrains

"From this sweet shelter leave, I say;   25
That love that she once gave to me
Now envy has taken away from me
And envy takes your life away.

"And may your friendship know distress
As mine was truly lost to me,   30
For there can be no company
Where reigns my utter loneliness.

"The only thing that brings me pain
Is you good husband, turtledove,
For you'll soon find another love,   35
As Phyllis has another swain."

Sigue el romance

Esto diciendo el pastor,
desde el tronco está mirando
adónde irán a parar
los amantes desdichados.   40
Y vio que en un verde pino
otra vez se están besando;
admiróse y prosiguió,
olvidado de su llanto:

Redondillas del fin

«Voluntades que avasallas,   45
Amor, con tu fuerza y arte,
¿quién habrá que las aparte,
que apartarlas es juntallas?
Pues que del nido es eché
y ya tenéis compañía,   50
quiero esperar que algún día
con Filis me juntaré.»

Por las riberas famosas . . .

Por las riberas famosas
de las aguas del Jarama,
junto del mesmo lugar
que Tajo las acompaña,
alegre sale Belardo   5
a recibir justa paga
de tantos años de amor,
celos, temor y mudanza.
¡Dichoso el pastor que alcanza
tan regalado fin de su esperanza!   10

The Ballad continues

This saying, the shepherd sets his gaze
    Upon a trunk in sight
Where both the lovers unfortunate
    Are ready to alight.   40

He saw that in a verdant pine
    They're billing and cooing again.
He, lost in wonder, then went on,
    Now out of mind his pain:

Concluding Quatrains

"O love, you who enslave wills quite,   45
With all your power and your art;
Whoever could tear them apart
When separate becomes unite?

"Since you from your nest I did sever
And yet you now have company,   50
I'd like to hope some day to see
Myself with Phyllis joined forever."

Along the famous river banks . . .

Along the famous river banks
    Where Jarama's waters go,
Close by the same locality
    Where they join Tagus' flow,
Belardo happily comes forth   5
    His just reward to prove
For many years of jealousy,
    Of fear, of change, of love.

    How blest that shepherd who redeems
Such pleasant end for all his hopes and dreams!   10

Vase a casar a su aldea
con Filis su enamorada,
que se la entrega su padre
después de tantas desgracias.
Contento lleva el villano,   15
por los ojos muestra el alma,
que al fin de tanta fortuna
promete el cielo bonanza.
¡Dichoso el pastor que alcanza
tan regalado fin de su esperanza!   20

Va mostrando en el vestido
las esperanzas del alma,
tan cerca ya de cumplirlas
como tardías y largas.
Guardadas lleva en el seno   25
de Filis todas las cartas,
que si son obligaciones
quiere pagar y borrallas.
¡Dichoso el pastor que alcanza
tan regalado fin de su esperanza!   30

Llegó Belardo a la villa
y de su suegro a la casa,
sale a tener el estribo,
mientras de la yegua baja,
Filis, abiertos los brazos;   35
marido y señor le llama,
él señora y dulce esposa;
besóla y ella le abraza.
¡Dichoso el pastor que alcanza
tan regalado fin de su esperanza!   40

Contemplando estaba Filis . . .

Contemplando estaba Filis
a la medianoche sola
una vela a cuya lumbre
labrando estaba una cofia,

In her own village he's to wed
    With Phyllis, his sweetheart,
Whose father will give her to him,
    Past troubles now apart.
The country swain contentment bears,   15
    His soul shines through his eyes,
For many tempests come and gone,
    Now heaven grants sweet prize.

    How blest that shepherd who redeems
Such pleasant end to all his hopes and dreams!   20

He in his dress displays the hopes
    That to his soul belong,
So near now to fulfilling them,
    As they are late and long;
He, guarded, Phyllis' letters bears   25
    In bosom's hiding-place,
For if there obligations are,
    He'll pay and them erase.

    How blest that shepherd who redeems
Such pleasant end to all his hopes and dreams!   30

Belardo reached the little town,
    And father-in-law's house there,
Who comes to hold his stirrup for him,
    Dismounting from his mare,
And Phyllis calls him husband, lord,   35
    With open arms him faces;
He calls her lady and sweet wife,
    Kissed her, she him embraces.

    How blest that shepherd who redeems
Such pleasant end to all his hopes and dreams!   40

Dear Phyllis contemplating was . . .

Dear Phyllis contemplating was,
    At midnight hour alone,
While on a coif embroidering,
    A candle whose light shone,

porque andaba en torno della   5
una blanca mariposa,
quemándose los extremos
y cerca de arderse toda.
Suspendióse, imaginando
el avecilla animosa,   10
tomóla en sus blancas manos
y así le dice, envidiosa:
«¿Adónde tienes los ojos,
que de esta luz te enamoras,
la boca con la que besas   15
y el gusto con que la gozas?
¿Adónde tienes tu ingenio
y dónde está la memoria?
¿Con qué lengua la requiebras?
¿Con qué despojos la adornas?   20
¿Qué le dices cuando llegas,
cuando en su fe presurosa
le dejas alguna prenda
de la afición que la adoras?
Y sin haberte ido vienes   25
y después de volar tornas
hasta el punto que tu vida
entre las llamas despojas,
viendo que no será justo
dilatar su muerte y gloria.»   30
En diciendo estas razones,
llegóse al fuego y quemóla.
«Dichosa fuiste, avecilla
—Filis prosigue—, pues gozas
en los brazos de tu amigo   35
vida y muerte glorïosa;
que la vida sin contento
mucha falta y poca sobra
y solo el sosiego es bueno
adonde el alma reposa.   40
Mas ¿cómo yo con tu ejemplo
no me doy la muerte agora?
Morir quiero, pues me anima,
y acabar con tantas cosas.

Because near it was fluttering 5
    A fragile moth all white,
Now singeing its extremities,
    Near burning up outright.

She sat astonished, thinking on
    This birdie spirited; 10
In her white hands she fondled it
    And envious thus said:

"Where do you, creature, have your eyes,
    That this light charms you so,
And where the mouth you kiss it with, 15
    The pleasure that you know?

"Where do you have your memory,
    Where your good sense inborn?
In what tongue do you flatter it,
    With what spoils it adorn? 20

"What do you tell it when you come,
    When in your faith's elation
You leave it for some precious gift
    To prove your adoration?

Not having left you then arrive, 25
    And flying around return
To such a point that your own life
    Among the flames you burn,
Now seeing it would not be right
    Your death and glory to spurn." 30

It reached the fire, which burned it quite,
    While she was reasoning.
"You, tiny bird, were fortunate,"
    Says Phyllis, continuing,
"In your friend's arms you can enjoy 35
    A life and death like king;

"For life devoid of happiness
    Much lacks and little shows;
Serenity is only good
    Where soul lies in repose. 40

"But why should I not kill myself
    And your example extend?
I want to die, for it drives me
    So many things to end.

He sabido que Belardo   45
su vida pasa con otra,
porque le enojan mis celos
y mis desdichas le enojan.»
Del paño de su labor
un corto cuchillo toma   50
y dijo, toda turbada:
«¡Oh Belardo, aquí fue Troya!»
Pero primero que fuese
puesto el intento por obra,
quiso probar el dolor,   55
que es mujer y temerosa.
Con la aguja que labraba
picóse el dedo, y turbóla
de su muy querida sangre
el ver salir una gota.   60
Pide un paño a la criada,
intento y cuchillo arroja;
lloró su sangre perdida,
que su amante no la llora.

Amada pastora mia . . .

Amada pastora mía,
tus descuidos me maltratan,
tus desdenes me fatigan,
tus sinrazones me matan.
A la noche me aborreces   5
y quiéresme a la mañana;
yo te ofendo a mediodía,
ya por la tarde me llamas:
ahora dices que me quieres,
y luego que te burlabas;   10
ya ríes mis tibias obras,
ya lloras por mis palabras.

"I've found out that Belardo now   45
    His time with another spends,
Because my jealousy chafes him,
    My misery him offends."

From sewing kit she quickly takes
    A knife small like a toy,   50
And firmly said, all overwrought,
    "Belardo, here was Troy!"

Before, however, her intent
    Could as a deed remain,
She as a woman, timorous,   55
    Set out to prove the pain.

She with the needle of her work
    Her finger gently pricked,
And seeing of her precious blood
    One drop she was transfixed.   60

She asks the maid to bring a cloth,
    Intent and knife forgot;
She wept her lost blood bitterly,
    He lover weeps it not.

Beloved shepherd girl of mine . . .

Beloved shepherd girl of mine,
    Your scorn has my strength bled,
Your negligence leaves me abused,
    Your follies strike me dead.

At night you hold me in contempt,   5
    And mornings you love me;
I hurt your feelings at mid-day,
    You afternoons call me.

You say you love me; afterward
    You say 'twas tongue-in-cheek;   10
Now you laugh at my lukewarm works,
    Now weep to hear me speak.

Cuando te dan pena celos
estás más contenta y cantas,
y cuando estoy más seguro   15
parece que te desgracias.
A mi amigo me maldices
y a mi enemigo me alabas;
si no te veo, me buscas,
y si te busco, te enfadas.   20
Partíme una vez de ti,
lloraste mi ausencia larga,
y ahora que estoy contigo,
con la tuya me amenazas.
Sin mar ni montes en medio,   25
sin peligro ni sin guardas;
mar, montes y guardas tienes
con una palabra airada.
Las paredes de tu choza
me parecen de montaña,   30
un mar en llegar a vellas
y mil guardas tus desgracias.
Como tienes en un punto
el amor y la mudanza,
pero bien le pintan niño,   35
poca vista y muchas alas.
Si Filis te ha dado celos,
el tiempo te desengaña,
que como ella quiere a uno
pudo por otra dejalla.   40
Si el aldea lo murmura,
siempre la gente se engaña,
y es mejor que tú me quieras,
aunque ella tenga la fama.
Con esto me pones miedo   45
y me celas y amenazas.
Si lloras, ¿cómo aborreces?
Y si burlas, ¿cómo amabas?
Esto Belardo decía
hablando con una carta,   50
sentado al pie de un olivo
que el dorado Tajo baña.

When jealousy does cause you grief,
    You sing with happy heart;
And when I have most confidence   15
    It seems you fall apart.

You curse me to my dearest friend,
    And praise me to my foe;
If I don't see you, you seek me,
    Seek I, you anger show.   20

From you I parted once and you
    Did my long absence moan,
And now that I am here with you
    You threaten with your own.

With neither sea nor hills between,   25
    With neither risk nor guard,
Sea, wooded hills, and guards you have
    With just an angry word.

The very walls your cabin has
    To me as mountain loom;   30
A sea it is just reaching them,
    A thousand guards your gloom.

How you both love and fickleness
    At single point unite,
But well they picture him a boy,   35
    With many wings, faint sight.

If Phyllis you has jealous made,
    Time will you undeceive,
For she now loves someone who could
    One for another leave.   40

And if the village gossip spreads,
    The people are to blame;
It's better you be fond of me,
    Though she may have the fame.

With this, then, you arouse my fears   45
    And threaten and reprove.
If you can weep, how can you hate?
    And scoff, how can you love?

All this Belardo put in words,
    And in a letter saves,   50
There seated 'neath an olive tree
    The golden Tagus laves.

De una recia calentura . . .

De una recia calentura,
de un amoroso accidente,
con el frío de unos celos,
Belardo estaba a la muerte.
    Pensando estaba en la causa,   5
que quiso hallarse presente
para mostrar que ha podido
hallarse a su fin alegre.
    De verle morir la ingrata
ni llora ni se arrepiente,   10
que quien tanto en vida quiso
hoy en la muerte aborrece.
    Empezó el pastor sus mandas
y dice: «Quiero que herede
el cuerpo la dura tierra,   15
que es deuda que se le debe;
    sólo quiero que le saquen
los ojos y los entreguen,
porque los llamó su dueño
la ingrata Filis mil veces.   20
    Y mando que el corazón
en otro fuego se queme
y que las cenizas mismas
dentro de la mar las echen,
    que por ser palabras suyas,   25
en la tierra do cayeren,
podrán estar bien seguras
de que el viento se las lleve.
    Y pues que muero tan pobre
que cuanto dejo me deben,   30
podrán hacer mi mortaja
de cartas y de papeles;
    y de lo demás que queda
quiero que a Filis se entregue
un espejo porque tenga   35
en que se mire y contemple.

Within the grip of fever harsh . . .

Within the grip of fever harsh
    Of amorous accident,
In icy jealousy, near death,
    Belardo's life lay spent.

He fell to thinking on the cause,   5
    Who wanted to stay near
To show that she as his end comes
    Can tarry in good cheer.

She selfish neither repents nor weeps
    On seeing his life abate,   10
For she who loved so much in life
    Today in death shows hate.

The shepherd started his bequests:
    "I give and bequeath," he said,
"My body to unyielding earth,   15
    A debt that must be paid.

"I only ask they remove the eyes
    And bury them apart,
For selfish Phyllis oft called them
    The master of her heart.   20

"And I ask further that my heart
    Be burned in another flame,
And also that the ashes themselves
    The deepest ocean claim,

"For if like all those words of hers   25
    They down toward earth should stray,
They could be very sure the wind
    Would carry them away.

"And since I die so very poor
    Life owes me all I leave,   30
My letters and my papers serve
    My winding sheet to weave.

And of the things now left, I ask
    That someone designate
A glass for Phyllis that she look   35
    In it, and contemplate.

Contemple que su hermosura
es rosa cuando amanece
y que es la vejez la noche
a cuya sombra se prende,   40
    y que sus cabellos de oro
se verán presto de nieve,
y con más contento y gusto
goce las horas que duerme.

Romance de Lope de Vega
cuando se iba a Inglaterra

De pechos sobre una torre
que la mar combate y cerca
mirando las fuertes naves
que se van a Ingalaterra,
    las aguas crece Belisa   5
llorando lágrimas tiernas,
diciendo con voces tristes
al que se parte y la deja:
    «*Vete, cruel, que bien me queda*
en quien vengarme de tu agravio pueda.»   10
    «No quedo con solo el hierro
de tu espada y de mi afrenta,
que me queda en las entrañas
retrato del mismo Eneas,
    y aunque inocente, culpado,   15
si los pecados se heredan;
mataréme por matarle
y moriré porque muera.
    «*Vete, cruel, que bien me queda*
en quien vengarme de tu agravio pueda.»   20
    «Mas quiero mudar de intento
y aguardar que salga fuera
por si en algo te parece,
matar a quien te parezca.

"Yes, contemplate her beauty fair,
    Which is a rose at dawn,
And then old age which is the night
    Whose shadows always yawn,   40

"And that her hair now touched with gold
    The snow too soon will steep,
And may she with more bliss and ease
    Enjoy her hours of sleep."

Ballad of Lope de Vega When He
Was Going to England

Now leaning out from tower high
    That the sea holds in command,
And seeing the mighty galleons
    Soon off to Engeland,
Belisa makes the waters rise   5
    In weeping tender tears;
To him who parts and leaves her here
    Now voicing her sad fears:

"Go off, cruel one, there is someone
In whom I can avenge the wrong you've done."   10

"I don't just have your steely sword
    And the wrong I did myself;
For there remains beneath my heart
    Portrait of Aeneas himself,
And guilty, although innocent,   15
    If sins can be passed on;
I'll kill myself thus to kill him,
    And die to see him gone.

"Go off, cruel one, there is someone
In whom I can avenge the wrong you've done."   20

"But I will change my mind and wait
    Until I can him view,
Then if he looks like you at all,
    Kill him who looks like you.

Mas no le quiero aguardar,   25
que será víbora fiera,
que rompiendo mis entrañas,
saldrá dejándome muerta.
        «Vete, cruel, que bien me queda
en quien vengarme de tu agravio pueda.»   30
        Así se queja Belisa
cuando la priesa se llega;
hacen señal a las naves
y todas alzan las velas.
        «Aguarda, aguarda, le dice,   35
fugitivo esposa, espera . . .
May ¡ay! que en balde te llamo;
¡plega Dios que nunca vuelvas!»
        «Vete, cruel, que bien me queda
en quien vengarme de tu agravio pueda.»   40

Hortelano era Belardo . . .

        Hortelano era Belardo
de las güertas de Valencia,
que los trabajos obligan
a lo que el hombre no piensa.
        Pasado el hebrero loco,   5
flores para mayo siembra,
que quiere que su esperanza
dé fruto a la primavera.
        El trébol para las niñas
pone a un lado de la huerta,   10
porque la fruta de amor
de las tres hojas aprenda.
        Albahacas amarillas,
a partes verdes y secas,
transplanta para casadas   15
que pasan ya de los treinta,

"But I don't want to wait for him,   25
    Fierce viper he will be,
For he'll destroy my very womb,
    Be born and dead leave me."

"Go off, cruel one, there is someone
In whom I can avenge the wrong you've done."   30

Belisa thus complaining is
    When urgency prevails;
They signal to the fighting ships
    And all of them hoist sails.
"Wait, wait, my husband fugitive."   35
    She "Wait!" says with concern.
"But ay! I call to you in vain;
    Pray God you never return!"

"Go off, cruel one, there is someone
In whom I can avenge the wrong you've done."   40

Belardo was a gardener . . .

Belardo was a gardener
    In Valencia's garden spot,
For hardships change a man's prospects,
    Although he may think not.

With mad February now behind   5
    He flowers sows for May,
For he would have it that his hope
    In Spring some fruit display.

Beside the garden for the girls
    He does the clover plant,   10
So that from its three leaves they learn
    How fruits of love enchant.

Sweet basil of a yellow cast,
    With parts of dry and green,
He transplants for the women wed   15
    Who've more than thirty seen;

y para las viudas pone
muchos lirios y verbena,
porque lo verde del alma
encubre la saya negra.   20
    Toronjil para muchachas
de aquellas que ya comienzan
a deletrear mentiras,
que hay poca verdad en ellas.
    El apio a las opiladas   25
y a las preñadas almendras,
para melindrosas cardos
y ortigas para las viejas.
    Lechugas para briosas
que cuando llueve se queman,   30
mastuerzo para las frías
y asenjos para las feas.
    De los vestidos que un tiempo
trujo en la Corte, de seda,
ha hecho para las aves   35
un espantajo de higuera.
    Las lechuguillazas grandes,
almidonadas y tiesas,
y el sombrero boleado
que adorna cuello y cabeza,   40
    y sobre un jubón de raso
la más guarnecida cuera,
sin olvidarse las calzas
españolas y tudescas.
    Andando regando un día,   45
vióle en medio de la higuera
y riéndose de velle,
le dice desta manera:
    «¡Oh ricos despojos
de mi edad primera   50
y trofeos vivos
de esperanzas muertas!
    ¡Qué bien parecéis
de dentro y de fuera,
sobre que habéis dado   55
fin a mi tragedia!

Much iris and verbena too
 For the widows he provides,
Because the bloom stored in the soul
 A black skirt often hides.   20

Balm-gentle for the older girls,
 Those ready to begin
To spell out lies, because with them
 The truth can little win.

For those obstructed, celery,   25
 For the prudish, thistles bold,
Some almonds for the pregnant ones,
 And nettles for the old.

Leaf-lettuce for the spirited
 Who burn when rains oppress;   30
Some wormwood for the ugly ones,
 For the cold ones, watercress.

Of those silk garments that one time
 He sported at the Court,
He in a figtree scarecrow made,   35
 For birds of thieving sort.

A massive ruff of Holland cloth
 All starched and stiff outspread,
And dashing hat with rounded crown
 That graces neck and head,   40

And over velvet doublet neat
 A leather jacket goes,
Without forgetting with their lines
 His Spanish, Teuton hose.

Upon the tree he this did see   45
 Out watering one day,
And laughing as he looked at it
 He speaks of it this way:

 Oh, spoils extravagant
  Of first age fled,   50
 And trophies still alive
  Of hopes now dead!

 How fine inside and out
  You seem to be,
 For you've brought to an end   55
  My tragedy.

¡Galas y penachos
de mi soldadesca,
un tiempo colores
y agora tristeza!   60
    Un día de Pascua
os llevé a mi aldea
por galas costosas,
invenciones nuevas.
    Desde su balcón   65
me vio una doncella
con el pecho blanco
y la ceja negra.
    Dejosé burlar,
caséme con ella,   70
que es bien que se paguen
tan honrosas deudas.
    Supo mi delito
aquella morena
que reinaba en Troya   75
cuando fue mi reina.
    Hizo de mis cosas
una grande hoguera,
tomando venganzas
en plumas y letras.»   80

Mil años ha que no canto . . .

    Mil años ha que no canto
porque ha mil años que lloro
trabajos de mi destierro,
que fueran de muerte en otros.
    Sin cuerdas el instrumento,   5
desacordado de loco,
con cuatro clavijas menos,
cubierto y lleno de polvo;

My days of soldiering,
    Of plumes and show,
At one time colors bright,
    And now just woe.   60

One Easter in my town
    I dressed in you
To see the costly pomp,
    Inventions new.

A lass from balcony   65
    Then did me sight,
Her lovely breast white snow,
    Her brow black night.

She let herself be tricked,
    I married her: 70
That honorable debts be paid,
    All will concur.

That dark-complexioned lass
    Heard of my crime,
She who in my Troy reigned   75
    As queen one time.

She made of all my things
    A great bonfire,
On pen and papers wreaked
    Her vengeance dire.   80

A thousand years I have not sung . . .

A thousand years I have not sung
    Since I've a thousand cried
The troubles of exile from which
    Some others would have died.

My instrument bereft of strings   5
    And madly out of tune,
Without four of its tuning pegs,
    With dust both filled and strewn;

ratones han hecho nido
en medio del lazo de oro,   10
por donde el aire salía,
blando, agudo, grave y ronco.
   Muchos piensan, y se engañan,
que, pues callo, piedras cojo,
y mala landre me dé   15
si no es de pereza todo;
   fuera de que ha pocos días
que ciertos poetas mozos
dan en llamarse Belardos,
hurtándome el nombre solo.   20
   Substitutos de mis bienes
y libres de mis enojos,
revocan mis testamentos,
de mi desdicha envidiosos.
   Un codicilo se canta,   25
en que dicen que revoco
todas las mandas pasadas:
Dios sabe lo que me corro.
   Los estrelleros de Venus
le dan más priesa que al moro   30
que a Sidonia se partía
a impedir el desposorio.
   En fe de mi nombre antiguo
cantan pensamientos de otros,
quizá porque, siendo males,   35
yo triste los pague todos.
   Por algún pequeño hurto
echan de la casa a un mozo
y si algo falta después,
aquel se lo llevó todo.   40
   ¡Oh Filis, cuán engañada
te han tenido maliciosos,
pues ha tres años y más
que aun a solas no te nombro!
   Si escribo de ajenos gustos   45
algunos versos quejosos,
gentilhombres de tu boca,
te los pintan como propios;

The mice have made a nest among
    Its golden tracery,   10
From where soft, sharp, or raucous, grave,
    The air escape did see.

Now many wrongly think, since I
    Am mute I just rocks throw;
If it's not laziness alone,   15
    May I a tumor grow;

Except that for some little time
    Young poets athirst for fame,
"Belardo" dare to call themselves,
    Thus filching just my name.   20

They of my riches substitutes,
    And from my rages free,
My oaths revoke, and for my woes
    They harbor jealousy.

A codicil is sung in which   25
    They say that I revoke
All legacies of former times:
    Lord knows this makes me choke!

Stargazers of dear Venus fair
    Pursue her with more speed   30
Than Moor who to Sidonia went
    The nuptials to impede.

With faith they have in my old name,
    They thoughts of others sing,
Perhaps because, mine being ills,   35
    I pay for everything.

They banish from the house a lad
    For any theft though small;
If something's missing afterward,
    They say he took it all.   40

Oh, Phyllis, how malicious folk
    With lies have filled your ears,
For I, alone, have ignored your name
    For more than three long years!

If I of alien pleasures write   45
    Some verses of complaint,
Those noble poets of your mouth
    As theirs to you them paint;

y con estar por tu causa
que aun apenas me conozco,   50
y con tres años de ausencia,
quieren decir que te adoro;
   y plega a Dios que si hoy día
a su brazo poderoso
para ti no pido un rayo,   55
que a mí me mate con otro.
   ¿Soy por dicha Durandarte?
¿Soy Leandro? ¿Soy Andronio,
o soy discípulo suyo
o tú del viento furioso?   60
   ¡Mal hayan las tortolillas,
mal haya el tronco y el olmo
de do salieron las varas
que el vulgo ha tirado al toro!
   Lisardo, aquel ahogado,   65
como Narciso, en el pozo,
antes que a la guerra fuese
dijo bien esto del olmo.
   Oh, guarde Dios a Riselo,
guarda mayor de mi soto,   70
que mi vega maldecía
por barbechar sus rastrojos.
   Todo el mundo dice y hace;
yo lo pago y no lo como,
y hecho Atlante de malicias   75
sustento un infierno en hombros.

Mirando está las cenizas . . .

   Mirando está las cenizas
de aquel saguntino fuego,
los vanos anfiteatros,
vivos ejemplos del tiempo,

They say I still don't know myself
    Since you I can't forget,   50
And absent for three years they say
    That I adore you yet;

And if of God I now ask not
    That with arms heralded
He send a bolt for you, may he   55
    With another strike me dead.

Am I Leander? Durandart?
    Or am I Androcles
Or as disciple of him then;
    Or you of furious breeze?   60

A curse upon the turtledoves,
    Cursed be the trunk, the elm
From which came poles with which the folk
    The bull did overwhelm!

Lisardo, that one drowned much like   65
    Narcissus, in the well,
Before he sallied off to war
    This of the elm said well.

May God my friend Riselo guard,
    My thicket's major guard,   70
Because my vega cursed to plow
    And see its stubbly sward.

The whole world often says and does;
    I pay and yet don't eat;
I bear a hell upon my back,   75
    Made Atlas by deceit.

Now looking at the ashes cold . . .

Now looking at the ashes cold
    Of that fire Saguntine,
The pompous amphitheaters,
    Of time live models fine,

Belardo, que allí llegó   5
con sus cabras y becerros,
antes morador del Tajo
y ya del río Monviedro;
y viendo entre sus ruïnas
del tiempo tantos ejemplos   10
así le dice, llorando
sobre un peñasco de pechos:
—¿Quién se ha de poner contigo
a fuerza, tiempo ligero,
teniendo tantos testigos   15
de tus poderosos hechos?
¡Qué acabaste de ciudades,
qué deshiciste de imperios,
qué de triunfos has traído
a sepultura de muertos!   20
Los mármoles que cubrían,
de púrpura y oro llenos,
yacen por el suelo ahora
de inútil yerba cubiertos.
Aquí, donde recitadas   25
alegres comedias fueron,
unos alegres sombríos
está recitando el tiempo,
y el lugar que tan apriesa
ocuparon sus asientos   30
a mis cabras lo agradezca
que su yerba están paciendo,
y sólo de sus balidos
por derribados cimientos
estas bóvedas escuchan   35
tristes y espantables ecos.
No pienses que soy, Sagunto,
Belisardo ni Pompeyo,
pero soy un desterrado
por uno de tus sucesos,   40
que como la piedra cae
y sube a su esfera el fuego,
he venido a esta lugar
como a verdadero centro.

Belardo, who with goats and calves   5
    Arrived there recently
(Before, he near the Tagus dwelled,
    Monviedro now knows he);

And seeing in its crumbling ruins
    So many examples of time,   10
He weeping speaks, now perched upon
    A crag he's had to climb:

"Who, fleeting time, is going to dare
    Your force invincible,
There being so many witnesses   15
    Of your deeds powerful?

"How many cities you've laid low,
    Through empires chaos spread;
How many triumphs you have brought
    To graveyards of the dead!   20

"The marbles that were everywhere
    With purple and gold replete,
Now covered with some useless grass,
    Lie here before my feet.

"Here where at one time were declaimed   25
    Those happy comedies,
The time declaims insistently
    Some happy elegies,

"And in the place where rapidly
    They occupied their seat,   30
My flock of goats are grateful now
    That they the grass can eat;

"Among foundations overthrown,
    These vaults that with age creak,
Can in their bleating sounds alone   35
    Hear echoes sad and bleak.

"Saguntum: Pompey, Belisard
    I'm not, nor make pretense,
But I'm a man in exile cast,
    By one of your events;   40

"For as the stone forever falls,
    And fire its sphere seeks too,
I've come to this locality
    As to my center true.

Ya fuiste ciudad insigne   45
y fuí yo dichoso un tiempo,
tus mármoles levantabas
y yo mi ventura al cielo;
tú por ser buena ciudad,
yo por ciudadano bueno   50
ambos en el suelo estamos,
tú difunta, yo muriendo.
Sobra de malos amigos
en este lugar me han puesto;
tu muerte fué honrada vida,   55
pues fué de enemigos buenos.
Por haber sido agradable
a tan inclemente cielo
me pagan desta manera
que ves que penando muero.   60
Consuélate, ciudad mía,
pues en tus manos me han puesto
en agradable prisión
yerros de mi propio dueño.

Llenos de lágrimas tristes . . .

Llenos de lágrimas tristes
tiene Belardo los ojos
porque le muestra Belisa
graves los suyos hermosos.
Celos mortales han sido   5
la causa injusta de todo,
y porque lo aprenda, dice
con lágrimas y sollozos:
«*El cielo me condene a eterno lloro*
si no aborrezco a Filis y te adoro.»   10

"You once a city were renowned,   45
    I once was fortunate;
Your marble you raised up, and I
    My luck did elevate;

"You since you were a city good,
    I as good townsman fled,   50
Now both are fallen to the ground,
    I dying and you dead.

"Too many lying, evil friends
    Have put me in this place;
Your death a life with honor was,   55
    Good foes did you erase.

"For having been agreeable
    In clime so inclement,
They pay me thus, for you can see
    I'm grieving, my life spent.   60

"Console yourself, my city fair,
    For in this prison bower
Mistakes of my own master guide
    Have placed me in your power."

Now welling with the saddest tears . . .

Now welling with the saddest tears
    Belardo's eyes are full,
Because Belisa shows him grave
    Her own so beautiful.

A mortal jealousy has been   5
    The unjust cause of all,
And so that she such learn, he says
    With sighs and tears that fall:

"The Lord doom me to weeping evermore
If I don't Phyllis hate and you adore."   10

Mal haya el fingido amigo,
lisonjero y mentiroso,
que juzgó mi voluntad
por la voz del vulgo loco;
    y a mí, necio, que dejé   15
por el viejo lodo el oro
y por lo que es propio mío
lo que siempre fue de todos.
      «El cielo me condene a eterno lloro
si no aborrezco a Filis y te adoro.»   20
    Mis enemigos me venzan
en pleitos más peligrosos
y mi amigo más querido
me levante testimonio,
    jure falso contra mí,   25
y el jüez más riguroso
de mis enemigos sea
del lado parcial devoto.
      «El cielo me condene a eterno lloro
si no aborrezco a Filis y te adoro.»   30
    Y jamás del claro Tajo
vuelva a ver la orilla y soto
ni a ver enramar sus vides
por los brazos de los olmos;
    enviuden las tortolillas   35
viendo que gozas a otro;
jamás tenga paz contigo
y siempre guerra con todos.
      «El cielo me condene a eterno lloro
si no aborrezco a Filis y te adoro.»   40
    Cubra el cielo castellano
los más encumbrados sotos
porque el ganado no pazca
y muerto lo coma el lobo.
    Llévese el viento mi choza,   45
el agua falte a mis pozos,
el fuego abrase mi parva,
la tierra me trag[u]e solo.
      «El cielo me condene a eterno lloro
si no aborrezco a filis y te adoro.»   50

A curse upon the feigning friend
   With lying, flattering word,
Who judged my will by gossiping
   Of the mad and vulgar herd;

A curse on me, a fool, who let   15
   My gold into mud fall,
And left that which is really mine
   For what belonged to all.

"The Lord doom me to weeping evermore
If I don't Phyllis hate and you adore."   20

Let conquer me my enemy
   In trials that horrify,
And let my very dearest friend
   Against me testify;

May I false swear against myself,   25
   And the judge most rigorous
Go over to my enemies
   And be solicitous.

"The Lord doom me to weeping evermore
If I don't Phyllis hate and you adore."   30

May I not ever see again
   Clear Tagus' grove and shore,
The arms entwining of the elms
   The vines see nevermore;

May turtledoves all lose their mates   35
   You seeing love another;
May you no peace find with yourself
   And war find with your brother.

"The Lord doom me to weeping evermore
If I don't Phyllis hate and you adore."   40

May all the highest grazing lands
   Castilian sky deplete,
So that the flock not graze, and dead
   Then let the wolf it eat.

Let water fail in all my wells,   45
   My hut away be blown,
Burn my supply of unthreshed grain,
   The earth gulp me alone.

"The Lord doom me to weeping evermore
If I don't Phyllis hate and you adore."   50

Cuando las secas encinas . . .

Cuando las secas encinas,
álamos y robles altos,
los secos ramillos visten
de verdes hojas y ramos
y las fructíferas plantas   5
con mil pimpollos preñados
brotando fragantes flores
hacen mil colores varios
para pagar el tributo
al bajo suelo, ordinario   10
natural de la influencia
qu'el cielo les da cada año,
y secas las hierbezuelas
de los secretos contrarios
por naturales efectos   15
al ser primero tornando,
de cuyos verdes renuevos
hacen mil colores varios
de miles distintas flores
que esmaltan les verdes prados,   20
de lechales cabritillos
y los corderos balando
corren a los alcaceles
ya comiendo, ya jugando,
cuando el pastor Albano suspirando,   25
con lágrimas, así dice llorando:
«Todo se alegra, mi Belisa, ahora;
solo tu Albano se entristece y llora.»
    Los romeros y tomillos
de cuyos floridos ramos   30
las fecundas abejuelas
sacan licor dulce y claro,
y con la mucha abundancia,
su labor melificando
hinchen el penal nativo   35
de poleo tierno y blanco,

When all the scrub-oaks, lofty oaks . . .

When all the scrub-oaks, lofty oaks,
    And poplars now bare seen
On barren twigs put on new dress
    Of boughs and leaves all green,

And when the plants fructiferous   5
    With pregnant shoot and sprout,
The fragrant flowers bursting forth,
    A thousand colors shout,

In order tribute to bestow
    Upon the earth austere,   10
A natural delivery
    That heaven sends each year,

And all the little grasses dry
    From secrets contrary,
Returning by innate effects   15
    To being primary,

With their renewal green there are
    A thousand colors seen,
Of thousands of distinctive blooms
    That tint the meadows green;   20

The little kids that need their milk,
    And everywhere lambs bleating,
Go running to the barley fields,
    Now playing and now eating,

When that good shepherd Albano falls to sighing,   25
With flowing tears, and thus he says while crying:
"Belisa mine, now everything joy shows;
Your Albano weeps alone, his sadness grows."

The wild rosemary and the thyme,
    From whose bloom now complete   30
The fecund little honeybees
    Take liquor clear and sweet,

And with so much luxuriance,
    Their native penal site
They swell, for honey laboring,   35
    With pollen soft and white,

de cuyos preñados huevos
los hijuelos palpitando
salen, por gracia divina,
a poblar ajenos vasos;   40
las laboriosas hormigas
de sus provistos palacios
seguras salen a ver
el tiempo sereno y claro
y los demás animales,   45
aves, peces, hierba o campo,
desechando la tristeza,
todos se alegran ufanos
previniste tiempo alegre;
mas triste, el pastor Albano,   50
a su querida Belisa
dice, el sepulcro mirando:
«Todo se alegra, mi Belisa, ahora;
solo tu Albano se entristece y llora.»
       Belisa, señora mía,   55
hoy se cumple justo un año
que de tu temprana muerte
gusté aquel potaje amargo.
Un año te serví enferma,
¡ojalá fueran mil años,   60
que así enferma te quisiera,
contino aguardando el pago!
Solo yo te acompañé
cuando todos te dejaron,
porque te quise en la vida,   65
y muerta te adoro y amo;
y sabe el cielo piadoso,
a quien fiel testigo hago,
si te querrá también muerta
quien viva te quiso tanto.   70
Dejásteme en tu cabaña
por guarda de tu rebaño,
con aquella dulce prenda
que me dejaste del parto,

And from whose eggs so copious
   A pulsing progeny
Comes surging forth, by grace divine,
   To alien vessel see;   40

The string of ants laborious
   From their well-stocked demesne
Now confident come out to see
   The time clear and serene,

And all the other animals,   45
   Birds, fishes, grass or field,
Their sadness firmly casting off,
   To happiness all yield,

Anticipated happy time;
   But to his Belisa dear   50
The shepherd Albano, very sad,
   Says, seeing her tomb near:

"Belisa mine, now everything joy shows;
Your Albano weeps alone, his sadness grows."

Belisa, one long year ago,   55
   My lady and my bride,
Because of your untimely death
   That bitter brew I tried.

I served you sick for one whole year,
   Would it a thousand were!   60
Thus ill I loved you waiting for
   That last reward to occur.

Thus I alone stayed at your side,
   When others all withdrew,
For I loved you in life, and dead   65
   I love and worship you.

And well knows heaven merciful,
   Who will my heart foreknow,
If he who so loved you alive
   Will love you dead also.   70

You left me in your cabin there,
   Guard of your flock to be,
With that sweet treasure wonderful
   You from the birth left me,

que por ser hechura tuya   75
me consolaba algún tanto
cuando en su divino rostro
contemplaba tu retrato;
pero duróme tan poco
qu'el cielo, por mis pecados,   80
quiso que también siguiese
muerta tus divinos pasos.
«Todo se alegra, mi Belisa, ahora;
solo tu Albano se entristece y llora.»

And being a handiwork of yours   75
    I was somewhat consoled
When I in her dear countenance
    Your portrait could behold;

But she so little time did stay
    Since heaven for sins of mine   80
Desired that she should follow dead
    In your footsteps divine.

"Belisa mine, now everything joy shows;
Your Albano weeps alone, his sadness grows."

Rimas

Rhymes

Soneto Primero

Versos de amor, conceptos esparcidos,
engendrados del alma en mis cuidados;
partos de mis sentidos abrasados,
con más dolor que libertad nacidos;

expósitos al mundo, en que, perdidos,   5
tan rotos anduvistes y trocados,
que sólo donde fuistes engendrados
fuérades por la sangre conocidos;

pues que le hurtáis el laberinto a Creta,
a Dédalo los altos pensamientos,   10
la furia al mar, las llamas al abismo,

si aquel áspid hermoso no os aceta,
dejad la tierra, entretened los vientos:
descansaréis en vuestro centro mismo.

II

Cleopatra a Antonio en oloroso vino
dos perlas quiso dar de igual grandeza,
que por muestra formó naturaleza
del instrumento del poder divino.

Por honrar su amoroso desatino,   5
que fue monstruo en amor, como en belleza,
la primera bebió, cuya riqueza
honrar pudiera la ciudad de Nino.

Mas no queriendo la segunda Antonio,
que ya Cleopatra deshacer quería,   10
de dos milagros reservó el segundo.

Quedó la perla sola en testimonio
de que no tuvo igual, hasta aquel día,
bella Lucinda, que naciste al mundo.

First Sonnet

Verses of my love, conceits set free,
Engendered in the soul my cares to frame,
The offspring of my senses set aflame,
Born more in suffering than in liberty;

As foundlings in the world you raggedly   5
Went wandering and lost, without a name;
Where you were engendered only can you claim
By blood alone to have identity.

For since you rob the labyrinth from Crete,
From Daedalus his thoughts of highest worth,   10
Flames from the abyss, rage from the sea's unrest,

If that enchanting asp would you ill treat,
Then entertain the winds, fly from the earth,
In your own center you will come to rest.

II

For Anthony Cleopatra in rich wine
Would cast two pearls of equal majesty,
Which Nature formed to serve symbolically
As instrument of sovereignty divine.

To honor her wild caprice in love's sign   5
(A monster was in love and beauty she),
The first he drank, whose value well could be
Esteemed in Ninus' city libertine.

The second not desiring Anthony,
Which Cleopatra hoped to melt away,   10
Of these two marvels, he the second saved.

The pearl unique remained as surety
That it no equal had, until that day,
Lucinda fair, when you the world first braved.

III

Cuando imagino de mis breves días
los muchos que el tirano amor me debe
y en mi cabello anticipar la nieve
más que en los años las tristezas mías,

veo que son sus falsas alegrías   5
veneno que en cristal la razón bebe
por quien el apetito se le atreve
vestido de mis dulces fantasías.

¿Qué hierbas del olvido ha dado el gusto
a la razón, que sin hacer su oficio   10
quiere contra razón satisfacelle?

Mas consolarse quiere mi disgusto,
que es el deseo del remedio indicio,
y el remedio de amor, querer vencelle.

IV

Era la alegre víspera del día
que la que sin igual nació en la tierra
de la cárcel mortal y humana guerra
para la patria celestial salía;

era la edad en que más viva ardía   5
la nueva sangre que mi pecho encierra
cuando el consejo y la razón destierra
la vanidad que el apetito guía,

cuando amor me enseñó la vez primera
de Lucinda en su sol los ojos bellos   10
y me abrasó como si rayo fuera.

Dulce prisión y dulce arder por ellos;
sin duda que su fuego fue mi esfera
que con verme morir descanso en ellos.

III

When of my fleeting days the mind's eye sees
The many that the tyrant love me owes,
And in my hair to anticipate the snows
More than in years in my despondencies,

I see that these deceptive gaieties   5
Are venom reason drinks from glass that glows,
Through which the appetite its daring shows,
Decked out in my seductive fantasies.

What herbs of forgetfulness has pleasure doled
To reason, that, ignoring its design,   10
It wants against the reason that it approve?

But my displeasure well may be consoled:
Desire is for the remedy the sign,
Love's remedy to want to conquer love.

IV

It was upon the eve of that day grand
That she, unequalled, born to earth's domains
In mortal jail and human strife and pains,
Departed for celestial fatherland;

It was also the time when like firebrand   5
New blood was burning that my breast contains
(When reason and advice are put in chains
By vanity which appetites command),

When Love for that first time to me showed clear
Lucinda's lovely eyes in her sun's diadem,   10
And it like lightning bolt my heart did sear.

Sweet prison and sweet longing fire for them;
Without a doubt their fire became my sphere,
For seeing myself die I rest in them.

V

Sirvió Jacob los siete largos años,
breves, si el fin cual la esperanza fuera;
a Lía goza y a Raquel espera
otros siete después, llorando engaños.

Así guardan palabra los extraños,   5
pero en efecto vive y considera
que la podrá gozar antes que muera,
y que tuvieron término sus daños.

Triste de mí, sin límite que mida
la que un engaño al sufrimiento cuesta,   10
y sin remedio que el agravio pida.

¡Ay de aquel alma a padecer dispuesta,
que espera su Raquel en la otra vida,
y tiene a Lía para siempre en ésta!

VII

Éstos los sauces son y ésta la fuente,
los montes éstos y ésta la ribera
donde vi de mi sol la vez primera
los bellos ojos, la serena frente.

Éste es el río humilde y la corriente,   5
y ésta la cuarta y verde primavera
que esmalta el campo alegre y reverbera
en el dorado Toro el sol ardiente.

Árboles, ya mudó su fe constante.
Mas, ¡oh gran desvarío!, que este llano,   10
entonces monte le dejé sin duda.

Luego no será justo que me espante
que mude parecer el pecho humano,
pasando el tiempo que los montes muda.

V

Jacob served those seven lengthy years,
Brief though, if issue with the hope complies;
He Leah enjoys, and Rachel fills his sighs
For seven more, deceits him bringing tears.

Thus strangers keep their promise it appears, 5
But in effect he lives and verifies
That her he can enjoy before he dies,
And for his troubles fair solution nears.

How sad am I, no limit thus imposed
To mark what costs a fraud turned into strife, 10
And without remedy the wrong amiss.

Woe to that soul to suffering disposed,
Who waits for Rachel in the other life,
And Leah has forever here in this!

VII

These are the willows, this as fountain shows,
The wooded hillocks these, and this the shore
Where of my sun I saw that day before
The lovely eyes, the brow in sweet repose.

This is the humble river, where it flows, 5
And this the greening Spring now number four
That sun in Taurus does vibrations pour
And on the joyous fields enamel sows.

You trees, already she has changed her constancy.
But now this very plain—oh madness strange!— 10
I left it then a hill, of that I'm sure.

Thus it's not right that I surprised should be
The human heart would seem to suffer change:
With passing time even hills cannot endure.

VIII

De hoy más las crespas sienes de olorosa
verbena y mirto coronarte puedes,
juncoso Manzanares, pues excedes
del Tajo la corriente caudalosa.

Lucinda en ti bañó su planta hermosa;   5
bien es que su dorado nombre heredes,
y que con perlas por arenas quedes,
mereciendo besar su nieve y rosa.

Y yo envidiar pudiera tu fortuna,
mas he llorado en ti lágrimas tantas   10
(tú, buen testigo de mi amargo lloro),

que, mezclada en tus aguas, pudo alguna
de Lucinda tocar las tiernas plantas
y convertirse en tus arenas de oro.

X

Cuando pensé que mi tormento esquivo
hiciera fin, comienza mi tormento,
y allí donde pensé tener contento,
allí sin él desesperado vivo.

Donde enviaba por el verde olivo,   5
me trajo sangre el triste pensamiento;
los bienes que pensé gozar de asiento
huyeron más que el aire fugitivo.

Cuitado yo, que la enemiga mía
ya de tibieza en hielo se deshace,   10
ya de mi fuego se consume y arde.

Yo he de morir y ya se acerca el día,
que el mal en mi salud su curso hace,
y cuando llega el bien, es poco y tarde.

VIII

You hence your temples' curls with odorous
Verbena, myrtle can a crown concede,
Reed-heavy Manzanares, who exceed
The Tagus with your currents bounteous.

Lucinda bathed in you foot beauteous;   5
Well may her golden name to you succeed,
And you with pearls for grains of sand proceed,
Full worthy both her snow and rose to buss.

And I your fortune could well envy you,
But I in tears have wept in you so much   10
(You of my bitter weeping witness stand),

That mixed among your waters one tear true
Lucinda's feet so delicate could touch,
And change itself into your golden sand.

X

When I thought that my torment negative
Would reach an end, commences my torment,
And there where I thought I would be content,
There discontent I desperate must live.

Where I sought olive branch that peace can give,   5
I was brought blood by thought's sad argument;
The wealth I would enjoy as affluent
Fled from me more than breezes fugitive.

Distressed I am, for my dear enemy
Now from lukewarmness changes into ice;   10
Now with my fire she burns in flames that flare.

I am to die and now the day I see;
Now evil works my health to sacrifice,
And when the good arrives, it's late and spare.

XIII
A una tempestad

Con imperfectos círculos enlazan
rayos el aire, que en discurso breve
sepulta Guadarrama en densa nieve,
cuyo blanco parece que amenazan.

Los vientos campo y naves despedazan;   5
el arco el mar con los extremos bebe;
súbele al polo, y otra vez le llueve;
con que la tierra, el mar y el cielo abrazan.

Mezcló en un punto la disforme cara
la variedad con que se adorna el suelo,   10
perdiendo Febo de su curso el modo.

Y cuando ya parece que se para
el armonía del eterno cielo,
salió Lucinda y serenóse todo.

XIV

Vierte racimos la gloriosa palma
y sin amor se pone estéril luto;
Dafnes se queja en su laurel sin fruto,
Narciso en blancas hojas se desalma.

Está la tierra sin la lluvia en calma,   5
viles hierbas produce el campo enjuto;
porque nunca al Amor pagó tributo,
gime en su piedra de Anaxarte el alma.

Oro engendra el amor de agua y de arenas;
porque las conchas aman el rocío,   10
quedan de perlas orientales llenas.

No desprecies, Lucinda hermosa, el mío,
que al trasponer del sol, las azucenas
pierden el lustre, y nuestra edad el brío.

XIII
To a Tempest

Imperfect circles making now enlace
The lightning bolts the air, which in brief flow
The Guadarrama buries in dense snow,
Whose white it seems they threaten to erase.

The winds lay waste the fields and ships apace;   5
The rainbow drinks the sea with points below,
To Pole takes it, as rain makes it reflow,
So that the earth and sea and sky embrace.

The monstrous visage in one place did blend
All that the earth flaunts as variety,   10
With Phoebus off his course no longer seen.

And when it seems that now will reach an end
The sempiternal heavens' harmony,
Lucinda appeared, and all became serene.

XIV

Date-clusters streams the arching, glorious palm,
Which without love mourns sterile disrepute;
Fair Daphne frets in laurel without fruit,
Narcissus in white leaves endures a qualm.

The earth without the rain shows mortal calm;   5
Vile herbs and weeds the parching fields pollute;
Because to Love she never paid tribute,
Anaxarete in stone wails without balm.

Love can from sand and water gold create;
Because the oyster shells so love the dew,   10
They filled with Oriental pearls will be.

My love, Lucinda fair, don't deprecate,
For lilies when the sunset fades from view
Their luster lose, our years their energy.

XXXV

Árdese Troya, y sube el humo escuro
al enemigo cielo, y entretanto,
alegre, Juno mira el fuego y llanto:
¡venganza de mujer, castigo duro!

El vulgo, aun en los templos mal seguro,   5
huye, cubierto de amarillo espanto;
corre cuajada sangre el turbio Janto,
y viene a tierra el levantado muro.

Crece el incendio propio el fuego extraño,
las empinadas máquinas cayendo,   10
de que se ven rüinas y pedazos.

Y la dura ocasión de tanto daño,
mientras vencido Paris muere ardiendo,
del griego vencedor duerme en los brazos.

XXXVIII
A Pedro Liñán

Liñán, el pecho noble solo estima
bienes que el alma tiene por nobleza;
que, como vos decís, torpe riqueza
está muy lejos de comprar su estima.

¿A cuál cobarde ingenio desanima   5
segura, honesta y liberal pobreza,
ni cuál, por ver pintada la corteza,
quiere que otro señor su cuello oprima?

No ha menester fortuna el virtuoso;
la virtud no se da ni se recibe,   10
ni en naufragio se pierde, ni es impropia.

¡Mal haya quien adula al poderoso,
aunque fortuna humilde le derribe,
pues la virtud es premio de sí propia!

XXXV

Troy lies in flames, and rises smoke obscure
Up to the heavens enemy; meanwhile
Gay Juno views the fire and woe with smile:
A woman's vengeance, castigation sure!

The folk, even in the temples insecure,   5
Go fleeing covered with fright's yellow bile;
The turbid Xanthus runs with blood the while,
And down to earth comes wall once high, secure.

The conflagration feeds extraneous fire,
The towering machines of war capsizing,   10
Where ruins and rubble still remain astir.

And the fierce occasion of such damage dire,
While vanquished Paris burns, is agonizing,
Sleeps in the arms of her Greek conqueror.

XXXVIII
To Pedro Liñán

Liñán, the noble breast can only esteem
Wealth that the soul keeps as nobility,
For as you say, crude wealth held torpidly
Is very far from buying its esteem.

The fearful genius will disesteem   5
Safe, generous, and honest poverty;
Nor does one seeing mottled crudity
Want someone else to oppress it in extreme.

The virtuous man for riches has no need,
For virtue is not given or received,   10
Nor improper is, nor does shipwreck record.

Curse him who to the powerful pays heed,
Although by humble fortune he be grieved,
For virtue truly is its own reward!

XLIII

Al sol que os mira, por miraros miro,
que pienso que la luz de vos tomando
en sus rayos la vuestra estoy mirando,
y luego de dos soles me retiro.

Aguila soy, a Salamandra aspiro;   5
este Dédalo amor me está animando,
pero anochece, y como estoy llorando,
en el mar de mis lágrimas expiro.

Y como donde estoy sin vos no es día,
pienso cuando anochece vos fuistes   10
por quien perdió los rayos que tenía.

Porque si amaneció cuando le vistes,
dejándole de ver, noche sería
en el ocaso de mis ojos tristes.

XLIV

Que otras veces amé, negar no puedo,
pero entonces Amor tomó conmigo
la espada negra, como diestro amigo,
señalando los golpes en el miedo.

Mas esta vez que batallando quedo,   5
blanca la espada y cierto el enemigo,
no os espantéis que llore su castigo,
pues al pasado amor amando excedo.

Cuando con armas falsas esgremía,
de las heridas truje en el vestido   10
(sin tocarme en el pecho) las señales;

mas en el alma ya, Lucinda mía,
donde mortales en dolor han sido
y en el remedio heridas inmortales.

XLIII

Sun that sees you I scan to see your fire,
For I think that the light he's from you prying
In his bright rays is yours that I am spying,
And later I from these two suns retire.

I eagle am, to salamander aspire;   5
This Daedalus my love is vivifying,
But dusk is coming on, and since I'm crying,
In deep sea of my weeping I expire.

Since where I am without you is not day,
I think when it grows dark that it was you   10
For whom he lost the beams that he did prize.

For if it dawned when you saw him at play,
Then seeing him no more, night would be due
Here in the sunset of my wistful eyes.

XLIV

That other times I loved, I can't deny,
But then the god of Love took up with me
The black-tipped sword, like friend who skillfully
Could mark the hits with fear to identify.

But now this time as I in battling vie,   5
White steel the sword and clear the enemy,
That I its chastening weep, don't frightened be,
Since loving I exceed all love gone by.

When with false arms I used to fence as role,
I for my wounds upon my garment bore   10
The marks (without a touch upon my breast);

But now, Lucinda, in my very soul,
My wounds have mortal been as heartache sore,
And wounds immortal remedy attest.

XLVIII

El pastor que en el monte anduvo al hielo,
al pie del mismo derribando un pino,
en saliendo el lucero vespertino,
enciende lumbre y duerme sin recelo.

Dejan las aves con la noche el vuelo,   5
el campo el buey, la senda el peregrino,
la hoz el trigo, la guadaña el lino:
que al fin descansa cuanto cubre el cielo.

Yo solo, aunque la noche con su manto
esparza sueño y cuanto vive aduerma,   10
tengo mis ojos de descanso faltos.

Argos los vuelve la ocasión y el llanto,
sin vara de Mercurio que los duerma:
que los ojos del alma están muy altos.

LVII

Silvio en el monte vio con lazo estrecho
un nudo de dos áspides asidas,
que, así enlazadas, a furor movidas,
se mordían las bocas, cuello y pecho.

«Así—dijo el pastor—, que están, sospecho,   5
en el casado yugo aborrecidas
dos enlazadas diferentes vidas,
rotas las paces, el amor deshecho.»

Por dividir los intrincados lazos,
hasta la muerte de descanso ajenos,   10
alzó el cayado, y prosiguió diciendo:

«Siendo enemigos, ¿para qué en los brazos?
¿Para qué os regaláis y os dais venenos?
Dulce morir, por no vivir muriendo.»

XLVIII

The shepherd walked the hills in icy white,
At foot of them then breaking down a pine,
And as the evening star begins to shine,
He lights a fire and sleep finds without fright.

At coming darkness birds give up their flight,   5
The ox the fields, the road soul peregrine,
The scythe the flax, the sickle wheatstalk fine:
All under heaven then rests for the night.

I only, though the night with mantle slow
Spreads drowsiness and leaves all things asleep,   10
I with my eyes so wanting rest stand by.

And Argos them occasion brings and woe,
Without a Mercury's wand to give them sleep:
For these eyes of the soul remain on high.

LVII

Silvio in the hills saw in close tie
Two knotted asps each by the other seized,
Who thus enlaced, to raging fury teased,
In biting mouths and neck and breast did vie.

"Thus" (said the shepherd) "I suspect they lie   5
In yoke of marriage hatefully displeased,
Two lives completely different tightly squeezed,
Their union shattered, and their love gone dry."

To tear apart ties intricate as these,
For down to death no peace can they declare,   10
He raised his staff, and words continued sighing:

"Why in each other's arms, being enemies?
Why one another clasp, and venom share?
Sweet death is yours, so that you not live dying."

LX

Quien dice que en mujeres no hay firmeza,
no os puede haber, señora, conocido;
ni menos el que dice que han nacido
de un parto la crueldad y la belleza.

Un alma noble, una real pureza   5
de un cuerpo de cristal hicieron nido;
el mismo ser está con vos corrido,
y admirada de sí naturaleza.

Firme sois, y mujer, si son contrarios;
hoy vuestro pecho con vitoria quede,   10
de que es sujeto que los ha deshecho.

Bronce, jaspe, metal, mármoles parios,
consume el tiempo; vuestro amor no puede:
que es alma de diamante en vuestro pecho.

LXI

Ir y quedarse, y con quedar partirse,
partir sin alma, y ir con alma ajena,
oír la dulce voz de una sirena
y no poder del árbol desasirse;

arder como la vela y consumirse   5
haciendo torres sobre tierna arena;
caer de un cielo, y ser demonio en pena,
y de serlo jamás arrepentirse;

hablar entre las mudas soledades,
pedir prestada, sobre fe, paciencia,   10
y lo que es temporal llamar eterno;

creer sospechas y negar verdades,
es lo que llaman en el mundo ausencia,
fuego en el alma y en la vida infierno.

LX

He who says woman has no constancy
Cannot, my lady, ever have known you;
Much less he who says from one labor due
Were born both beauty fair and cruelty.

A noble soul, a royal purity   5
Found in a crystal body dwelling true;
Even very life embarrassed is with you,
And Nature with herself surprised must be.

You constant are, and woman, if foils these are;
Today your heart a victory should prove,   10
As subject who has put them to the test.

Bronze, jasper, Parian marble, metal bar
Time quite consumes, but never can your love:
Diamantine soul it is inside your breast.

LXI

To go, to stay, with staying, to be sent,
Leave spiritless, with alien spirit go;
To hear the voice of siren sweetly flow
And from the tree to let go impotent;

To burn like candle as life blood is spent   5
In building castles in soft sand to show;
To fall from heaven, demon's pain to know,
And being demon, never to repent;

To speak among the speechless solitudes,
To borrow patience, using faith as bond,   10
And what is temporal, as eternal sell;

To trust suspicions, gainsay certitudes
To absence in the world must correspond,
Fire in the soul and in one's life a hell.

LXIII
A la jornada de Inglaterra

Famosa Armada de estandartes llena,
partidos todos de la Roja Estola,
árboles de la Fe, donde tremola
tanta flámula blanca en cada entena.

Selva del mar a nuestra vista amena,   5
que del cristiano Ulises la Fe sola
te saca de la margen española,
contra la falsedad de una Sirena.

Id y abrasad el mundo, que bien llevan
las velas viento y alquitrán los tiros,   10
que a mis suspiros y a mi pecho deban.

Seguras de los dos podéis partiros;
fiad que os guarden, y fiad que os muevan:
tal es mi fuego, y tales mis suspiros.

LXVI
A Lupercio Leonardo

Pasé la mar cuando creyó mi engaño
que en él mi antiguo fuego se templara;
mudé mi natural, porque mudara
naturaleza el uso, y curso el daño.

En otro cielo, en otro reino extraño,   5
mis trabajos se vieron en mi cara,
hallando, aunque otra tanta edad pasara,
incierto el bien y cierto el desengaño.

El mismo amor me abrasa y atormenta,
y de razón y libertad me priva.   10
¿Por qué os quejáis del alma que le cuenta?

¿Que no escriba decís, o que no viva?
Haced vos con mi amor que yo no sienta,
que yo haré con mi pluma que no escriba.

LXIII
On the Journey to England

Armada famous, decked with pennants bright,
Derived from that Red Banner in some way,
Trees of the Faith, where flutter in display
At every mast so many streamers white.

A forest in the sea, sweet to our sight,   5
That Christian Ulysses One Faith to obey
From these dear Spanish shores takes you away,
Against a Siren's falsehood thus to fight.

Go out and scourge the world, for well now bear
The sails the wind, the shot pitch-residue,   10
Which to my sighs and to my heart much owe.

You can set sail, secure in both this pair;
Trust in their guarding and their moving you:
Such is my fire, and such my sighs also.

LXVI
To Lupercio Leonardo

Deception reigning, overboard I went
In hope my ancient fire might tempered be;
I custom changed, that Nature might decree
Her custom changed, and course the detriment.

In kingdom strange, in other firmament,   5
My labors in my visage one might see,
And finding, though another age might flee,
The good unsure, sure disillusionment.

For very love inflames and torments me,
And does my reason and my freedom steal.   10
Why frown you when a soul must love recite?

That I not write, you say, not live (for me)?
Then you see to it I my love don't feel,
And I'll see to it that my pen not write.

LXX

Quiero escribir, y el llanto no me deja;
pruebo a llorar, y no descanso tanto;
vuelvo a tomar la pluma, y vuelve el llanto:
todo me impide el bien, todo me aqueja.

Si el llanto dura, el alma se me queja;   5
si el escribir, mis ojos; y si en tanto
por muerte, o por consuelo, me levanto,
de entrambos la esperanza se me aleja.

Ve blanco, al fin, papel, y a quien penetra
el centro deste pecho que me enciende   10
le di (si en tanto bien pudieres verte)

que haga de mis lágrimas la letra,
pues ya que no lo siente, bien entiende:
que cuanto escribo y lloro todo es muerte.

LXXXI

Lucinda, yo me siento arder, y sigo
el sol que deste incendio causa el daño;
que porque no me encuentre el desengaño,
tengo al engaño por eterno amigo.

Siento el error, no siento lo que digo;   5
a mí yo propio me parezco extraño;
pasan mis años, sin que llegue un año
que esté seguro yo de mí conmigo.

¡Oh dura ley de amor, que todos huyen
la causa de su mal, y yo la espero   10
siempre en mi margen, como humilde río!

Pero si las estrellas daño influyen,
y con las de tus ojos nací y muero,
¿cómo las venceré sin albedrío?

LXX

I want to write, and weeping won't let me;
I seek to cry, and not much rest I gain;
I take my pen, and weeping comes again:
It all impedes the good, all wearies me.

If weeping lasts, my soul complains to me;   5
If writing, then my eyes; and if my pain
Concerning death and comfort I sustain,
From both of them my hope escapes from me.

Stay blank, then, paper, and to her who nears
The center of this breast that fire now brands,   10
Tell her (if you would such a blessing reap)

That she her letters fashion from my tears,
Since she who feels it not, well understands:
That everything is death I write and weep.

LXXXI

Lucinda, I now feel a glowing and pursue
The sun that brings the damage of this fire;
So that plain truth my heart cannot acquire,
I keep deception as friend ever true.

The error, not the words I say, I rue;   5
I strangeness even in myself inspire;
My years pass by, and not one year entire
Can I sure friendship with myself renew.

Oh rigid law of love, that all must flee
The cause of their own ill, and always I   10
Await it by my shores, like humble rill!

But if the stars through harm influence me,
And with those of your eyes I live and die,
How can I conquer them without free-will?

LXXXIII

Yo no espero la flota, ni importuno
al cielo, al mar, al viento por su ayuda,
ni que segura pase la Bermuda,
sobre el azul tridente de Neptuno.

Ni tengo yerba en campo, o rompo alguno   5
con el arado en que el villano suda,
ni del vasallo que con renta acuda
provecho espero en mi favor ninguno.

Mira estas hiedras, que con tiernos lazos,
para formar sin alma su himeneo,   10
dan a estos verdes álamos abrazos.

Y si tienes, Lucinda, mi deseo,
hálleme la vejez entre tus brazos,
y pasaremos juntos el Leteo.

LXXXVII
De Europa y Júpiter

Pasando el mar el engañoso toro,
volviendo la cerviz, el pie besaba
de la llorosa ninfa, que miraba
perdido de las ropas el decoro.

Entre las aguas y las hebras de oro   5
ondas el fresco viento levantaba,
a quien con los suspiros ayudaba
del mal guardado virginal tesoro.

Cayéronsele a Europa de las faldas
las rosas al decirle el toro amores,   10
y ella con el dolor de sus guirnaldas,

dicen que, lleno el rostro de colores,
en perlas convirtió sus esmeraldas,
y dijo: «¡Ay triste, yo perdí las flores!»

LXXXIII

I don't await the fleet, or importune
The sky, the sea, the winds to ask their aid;
Nor have I crossing of Bermuda made,
Upon the azure trident of Neptune.

I grow no plants, nor have I any strewn   5
With plow, at which the peasant sweats unpaid;
Nor from the vassal, who brings rents all paid,
Do I hope for whatever sort of boon.

Behold this ivy, which with tender ties,
To form a wedding song without soul-charms,   10
Embraces these green poplars with firm tether.

And if, Lucinda, my desire you prize,
Let old age find me nestled in your arms,
And we will cross the Lethe joined together.

LXXXVII
Of Europa and Jupiter

The sea outdaring, that deceitful bull,
His neck bowed down, the foot kissed avidly
Of that nymph whimpering, who then did see
Decorum lost in her dress dutiful.

Between the waters and gold bountiful,   5
Soft ripples raised fresh wind continually
And aided with its sighs that one to be
Of mal-watched virgin treasure possible.

The roses, while the bull love words was sharing,
Fell from Europa's skirts now disarranged,   10
With her the sharp pain of her garlands bearing.

They say that color touched her face in showers,
Her emeralds she for clear pearls exchanged,
And said, "Ay, poor, poor me, I lost my flowers!"

LXLIX

Perderá de los cielos la belleza
el ordinario curso, eterno y fuerte;
la confusión, que todo lo pervierte,
dará a las cosas la primer rudeza.

Juntaránse el descanso y la pobreza;   5
será el alma inmortal sujeta a muerte;
hará los rostros todos de una suerte,
la hermosa, en varïar, Naturaleza.

Los humores del hombre, reducidos
a un mismo fin, se abrazarán concordes;   10
dará la noche luz y el oro enojos.

Y quedarán en paz eterna unidos
los elementos, hasta aquí discordes,
antes que deje de adorar tus ojos.

XCII
A Pedro Liñán de Riaza

Señor Liñán, quien sirve sin estrella
en átomos del sol quimeras hace,
pues cuanto más el duro yugo abrace,
tanto más su fortuna le atropella.

De mí estoy cierto que nací sin ella;   5
pues ¿qué porfía el que sin ella nace?
La forma sin materia se deshace;
cantar no puedo en Babilonia bella.

Sin premio, cosa injusta me parece
perder el tiempo, encanecer temprano,   10
ídolos de dosel, confuso abismo.

Dichoso vos a quien el cielo ofrece
tabla en el mar, y en el profundo mano,
sirviendo a dueño que se da a sí mismo.

LXLIX

The beauty of the heavens changed will see
Its ordinary course, eternal and strong;
Confusion, which perverts the whole to wrong,
Will give to things form rudimentary.

Together poverty and rest will be;   5
The soul immortal will to death belong;
And Nature fair, in varying her song,
Will make all faces of one quality.

The humors of mankind, to single end
Reduced, will then embrace in sweet accord;   10
Night will give light, and all will gold despise.

And in eternal peace secure will blend
The elements, before now in discord,
Before I stop adoring your bright eyes.

XCII
To Pedro Liñán de Riaza

Liñán, to serve without a star each one
Of sunbeams makes chimeras in his art;
However much he take hard yoke to heart,
Much more his fortune does him overrun.

Myself, I'm certain I was born with none,   5
And without such, how can one even start?
The form without the content falls apart;
Sing I cannot in beautiful Babylon.

Without reward it seems unjust to me
To waste my time, grow gray before my due,   10
Confused abyss and idols' canopy.

O happy you, since heaven offers you
Hand for all things profound, plank in the sea,
A master serving to his own self true!

XCV
Al triunfo de Judit

Cuelga sangriento de la cama al suelo
el hombro diestro del feroz tirano,
que opuesto al muro de Betulia en vano,
despidió contra sí rayos al cielo.

Revuelto con el ansia el rojo velo   5
del pabellón a la siniestra mano,
descubre el espectáculo inhumano
del tronco horrible, convertido en hielo.

Vertido Baco, el fuerte arnés afea
los vasos y la mesa derribada,   10
duermen las guardas, que tan mal emplea;

y sobre la muralla coronada
del pueblo de Israel, la casta hebrea
con la cabeza resplandece armada.

XCVII

Tristezas, si el hacerme compañía
es fuerza de mi estrella y su aspereza,
vendréis a ser en mí naturaleza,
y perderá su fin vuestra porfía.

Si gozar no merecen de alegría   5
aquellos que no saben qué es tristeza,
¿cuándo se mudará vuestra firmeza?
¿Cuándo veré de mi descanso el día?

Sola una gloria os hallo conocida:
que si es el fin el triste sentimiento   10
de las alegres horas desta vida,

vosotras le tendréis en el contento;
mas, ¡ay!, que llegaréis a la partida,
y llevaráse mi esperanza el viento.

XCV
To Judith's Triumph

In dripping blood hangs from the bed to floor
The dexterous shoulder of fierce tyrant slain,
Who, enemy of Bethulia's wall in vain,
Against himself those bolts from heaven bore.

Disturbed, the scarlet veil, fear at the fore,   5
Of rich pavilion by left hand in strain,
Inhuman spectacle makes clearly plain,
Now turned to ice, the trunk consumed in gore.

The armor strong deform, with Bacchus drowned,
The glasses and the table turned to waste;   10
Ill-chosen sentinels sleep drowsily;

And there upon the city wall, now crowned
By hosts of Israel, the Hebrew chaste
Armed with the head shines forth resplendently.

XCVII

Despondencies, if keeping me as company
Does power of my star's ill humor show,
Your perseverance will its aim let go;
My very nature you will come to be.

It they don't merit basking in their glee   5
Those who what sadness is don't even know,
When will some changes in your firmness flow?
When will I my own day of rest thus see?

One glory alone I find that you display:
For if life's purpose is sad sentiment   10
Of all the happy hours one is alive,

You will possess it being well-content,
But ay! you at a parting will arrive,
And all my hope the wind will take away.

C
A la muerte del Duque de Pastrana

—¿Quién llora aquí? —Tres somos, quita el manto.
—La Muerte soy. —¿La muerte? Pues ¿tú lloras?
—Sí, que conté de sus fatales horas
a un César español término tanto.

    —¿Y tú, robusto? —Marte soy. —¿Con llanto   5
el resplandor del claro arnés desdoras?
—Perdí por otras manos vencedoras
yo luz, España sol, Flandes espanto.

    —Y tú, niño, ¿quién eres? —Antes era
Amor, pero murió mi nombre y llama,   10
muerto el más bello que la fama escribe.

    —Muerte, Amor, Marte, no lloréis que muera
don Rodrigo de Silva: que la fama
de su valor eternamente vive.

CI

Cayó la torre que en el viento hacían
mis altos pensamientos castigados,
que yacen por el suelo derribados,
cuando con sus extremos competían.

    Atrevidos, al sol llegar querían   5
y morir en sus rayos abrasados,
de cuya luz, contentos y engañados,
como la ciega mariposa, ardían.

    ¡Oh siempre aborrecido desengaño,
amado al procurarte, odioso al verte,   10
que en lugar de sanar, abres la herida!

    Pluguiera a Dios duraras, dulce engaño:
que si ha de dar un desengaño muerte,
mejor es un engaño que da vida.

C
On the Death of the Duke of Pastrana

"Who's weeping here?" "We're three; remove the cloak."
"I'm Death." "You Death, and even you can cry?"
"Yes, for a Spanish Caesar it was I
Who counted of his hours the fatal stroke."

"And you, robust one?" "Mars I am." "You soak   5
His armor's splendor bright with weeping eye?"
"Through other conquering hands we lost thereby
I light, Spain sun, and Flanders thunderstroke."

"And you, lad, who are you? "I was before
Called Love itself, but died my fire and name   10
Once dead the fairest fame inscribed will see."

"Death, Love, and Mars, weep not that past death's door
Be Don Rodrigo de Silva, since the fame
Of his great valor lives eternally."

CI

The tower fell that my thoughts ever high
Upon the wind kept making, thoughts distressed
That upon the ground lie prostrate, dispossessed
When with their opposites they used to vie.

Courageous, they to reach the sun did try   5
And thus to perish by its rays possessed,
In whose light they, deceived as well as blessed,
Kept burning like unseeing butterfly.

Oh, disillusionment always despised,
Loved being sought, reached hated unto death,   10
You, healing not, wound open as with knife.

God have you linger, sweet deception prized,
For if a disillusionment gives death,
Much better is deception that gives life.

CIV
De Absalon

Suspenso está Absalon entre las ramas,
que entretejen sus hojas y cabellos,
que los que tienen la soberbia en ellos
jamás expiran en bordadas camas.

Cubre de nieve las hermosas llamas,   5
al eclipsar de aquellos ojos bellos,
que así quebrantan los altivos cuellos
las ambiciones de mayores famas.

¿Qué es de la tierra que usurpar quisiste,
pues apenas la tocas de liviano,   10
bello Absalon, famoso ejemplo al suelo?

Esperanza, ambición, cabellos diste
al viento, al cielo, a la ocasión tan vano,
que te quedaste entre la tierra y cielo.

CXXIII

Cayó la Troya de mi alma en tierra,
abrasada de aquella griega hermosa:
que por prenda de Venus amorosa
Juno me abrasa, Palas me destierra.

Mas como las reliquias dentro encierra   5
de la soberbia máquina famosa,
la llama en las cenizas vitoriosa
renueva el fuego y la pasada guerra.

Tuvieron y tendrán inmortal vida
prendas que el alma en su firmeza apoya,   10
aunque muera el troyano y venza el griego.

Mas, ¡ay de mí!, que, con estar perdida,
aun no puedo decir: «Aquí fue Troya»,
siendo el alma inmortal y eterno el fuego.

CIV
Of Absalom

Hangs Absalom among the branches there,
Which now their leaves and locks of hair entwine;
For those who in their locks their pride define
Will never expire in beds that ruffles wear.

    The slow eclipsing of those eyes so fair   5
With snow now hides those precious flames ashine;
For thus ambition that would fame enshrine
Will bring down low the necks caught in pride's snare.

    What is it you tried to usurp from earth?
You barely touch it as you light remain,   10
Fair Absalom, far-famed example fallen quite.

    Ambition, hope, abundant hair from birth
You gave to wind, to sky, to occasion vain,
While you mid earth and heaven did alight.

CXXIII

    The Troy that is my soul fell in earth's mire,
Burned by that Grecian lady beauteous;
Thus as a pawn of Venus amorous,
Me Pallas exiles, Juno sets afire.

    But since the great machine that all admire   5
Within confines the relics presumptuous,
May in the ashes flame victorious
Renew the previous conflict and the fire.

    Immortal life thus did and will possess
Charms that the constant soul's support enjoy,   10
Though Greek may win and Trojan may expire.

    But, woe is me, with soul lost in distress,
I still cannot quite utter, "Here was Troy,"
Immortal being the soul, eternal the fire.

CXXVI

Desmayarse, atreverse, estar furioso,
áspero, tierno, liberal, esquivo,
alentado, mortal, difunto, vivo,
leal, traidor, cobarde y animoso;

    no hallar fuera del bien centro y reposo,   5
mostrarse alegre, triste, humilde, altivo,
enojado, valiente, fugitivo,
satisfecho, ofendido, receloso;

    huir el rostro al claro desengaño,
beber veneno por licor süave,   10
olvidar el provecho, amar el daño;

    creer que un cielo en un infierno cabe,
dar la vida y el alma a un desengaño:
esto es amor: quien lo probó lo sabe.

CXXVII

Con una risa entre los ojos bellos
bastante a serenar los accidentes
de los cuatro elementos diferentes
cuando muestra el amor del alma en ellos;

    con dulce lengua y labios, que por ellos   5
muestra los blancos y menudos dientes,
con palabras tan graves y prudentes
que es gloria oíllas si es descanso vellos;

    con vivo ingenio y tono regalado,
con clara voz y pocas veces mucha,   10
con poco afecto y con serena calma,

    con un descuido en el mayor cuidado
habla Lucinda . . . ¡Triste del que escucha,
pues no le puede responder con alma!

CXXVI

To fall in faint, to dare, be furious,
Ungracious, giving, scornful, sensitive,
Vivacious, mortal, active, not to live,
Courageous, cowardly, true, traitorous;

To lose the core outside the virtuous,   5
To be sad, joyful, meek, insensitive,
Consumed by anger, valiant, fugitive,
Self-satisfied, offended, dubious;

To have face flee to clear disillusionment,
To drink a poison as sweet muscatel,   10
Ignore advantage, love a detriment;

To think a heaven fits into a hell,
To give life, soul to disillusionment:
All this is love: he who's tried it knows well.

CXXVII

With laughter in those eyes fair as a gem
Sufficient to assuage the accidents
Of those four heterogeneous elements
When she displays that soulful love in them:

With tender tongue and lips, for it's through them 5
Her teeth snow-white and perfect she presents,
With words of gravity and of good sense:
It's glory to hear these, rest to see them.

With pleasant tone and lively wit with flair,
With voice that's crystal clear and rarely much,   10
With little emotion and with calm control,

With touch of carelessness in greatest care
Lucinda speaks . . . Sad he who listens to such,
For he cannot respond to her with soul!

CXXXIII

Ya no quiero más bien que sólo amaros,
ni más vida, Lucinda, que ofreceros
la que me dais, cuando merezco veros,
ni ver más luz que vuestros ojos claros.

Para vivir me basta desearos,   5
para ser venturoso, conoceros;
para admirar el mundo, engrandeceros,
y para ser Eróstrato, abrasaros.

La pluma y lengua, respondiendo a coros,
quieren al cielo espléndido subiros,   10
donde están los espíritus más puros;

que entre tales riquezas y tesoros,
mis lágrimas, mis versos, mis suspiros
de olvido y tiempo vivirán seguros.

CXXXV

Cuando digo a Lucinda que me mata
y que me hiela y juntamente enciende,
libre responde que mi mal no entiende,
como quien ya de no pagarme trata.

¡Ay de mi amor satisfacción ingrata,   5
pues lo que un monte un árbol comprehende,
niega Lucinda, que mi mal pretende
y la esperanza de mi bien dilata!

Montes que de mi mal testigos fuistes,
piedras donde lloré, corrientes ríos   10
que con mis tiernas lágrimas crecistes,

decidle mis confusos desvaríos,
declaradle mi mal, paredes tristes,
pues alma os dieron los suspiros míos.

CXXXIII

I want no other good than loving you,
Lucinda, no other life than offering you
That life you give when I rate seeing you,
No other light than seeing your eyes blue.

To live it is enough desiring you,   5
To be adventurous, just knowing you;
To stun the world in magnifying you,
To be Herostratos in burning you.

The pen and tongue in chorus answering
Would to the splendid heavens have you rise,   10
Where dwell the spirits ever more than pure,

For among such wealth and treasure flourishing,
My flowing tears, my verses, and my sighs
From time and oblivion will live secure.

CXXXV

When I Lucinda tell that she me slays,
And that she freezes me and yet flame lends,
She says my ill she never comprehends,
Like him who owes me, yet who never pays.

Sad is my love, whose satisfaction strays,   5
For what a tree, a hillock comprehends,
Denies Lucinda she my ill pretends,
And every hope of my great good delays.

Hills that to my long ill were witnesses,
Stones where I wept, deep-flowing rivers there,   10
Which grew in current with my tears benign,

Tell her of my tormented caprices;
Let wistful walls my ill to her declare,
For spirit gave to you these sighs of mine.

CXXXVII
A la noche

Noche, fabricadora de embelecos,
loca, imaginativa, quimerista,
que muestras al que en ti su bien conquista
los montes llanos y los mares secos;

habitadora de celebros huecos,   5
mecánica, filósofa, alquimista,
encubridora vil, lince sin vista,
espantadiza de tus mismos ecos:

la sombra, el miedo, el mal se te atribuya,
solícita, poeta, enferma, fría,   10
manos del bravo y pies del fugitivo.

Que vele o duerma, media vida es tuya:
si velo, te lo pago con el día,
y si duermo, no siento lo que vivo.

CXLII

Hermosa Babilonia en que he nacido
para fábula tuya [ha] tantos años,
sepultura de propios y de extraños,
centro apacible, dulce y patrio nido;

cárcel de la razón y del sentido,   5
escuela de lisonjas y de engaños,
campo de alarbes con diversos paños,
Elisio entre las aguas del olvido;

cueva de la ignorancia y de la ira,
de la murmuración y de la injuria,   10
donde es la lengua espada de la ira.

A lavarme de ti me parto al Turia:
que reír el loco lo que al sabio admira,
mi ofendida paciencia vuelve en furia.

CXXXVII
To Night

O night, as fabricator who all feigns,
Imaginative, insane, chimerical,
Who shows him who attains dreams magical
In you the seas as dry, the hills as plains;

Inhabitant of hollow human brains,   5
Wise lady, alchemist, mechanical,
Lynx without sight, concealer cynical,
Affrighted by your own echoing strains;

The shadow, evil, fear that are called yours,
Concerned, unhealthy, poet, cold as ice,   10
Hands of the brave and feet of fugitive.

Sleep I or watch, the half of life is yours:
If I stand watch, I pay by day the price,
And if I sleep, I don't feel what I live.

CXLII

Enticing Babylon, in which I fear
I years ago was born your talk to be,
Tomb of both native and of refugee,
Calm center, native home so dear;

Jail of both sentiment and reason clear,   5
School of deception and of flattery,
Ground of crude Moors in varied drapery,
Elysium in oblivion's waters drear;

Cave of crass ignorance as well as rage,
Of buzzing gossip and of injury,   10
And where the tongue is sword of that same rage.

I wash my hands of you, to Turia flee:
The madman laughs at what astounds the sage;
In fury my strained patience burns in me.

CXLIX

Cadenas desherradas, eslabones,
tablas rotas del mar en sus riberas,
tronchadas astas de alabardas fieras,
reventados mosquetes y cañones;

    ruinas de combatidos torreones,   5
a cuya vista forma blancas eras
el labrador, jirones de banderas,
abollados sangrientos morrïones;

    jarcias, grillos, reliquias de estandartes,
cárcel, mar, guerra, Argel, campaña y vientos   10
muestran en tierra o templo suspendidos.

    Y así mis versos en diversas partes,
mi amor cautivo, el mar de mis tormentos
y la guerra mortal de mis sentidos.

CL

    Rota barquilla mía, que (arrojada
de tanta envidia y amistad fingida,
de mi paciencia por el mal regida
con remos de mi pluma y de mi espada,

    una sin corte y otra mal cortada)   5
conservaste las fuerzas de la vida,
entre los puertos del favor rompida
y entre las esperanzas quebrantada;

    sigue tu estrella en tantos desengaños;
que quien no los creyó sin duda es loco,   10
ni hay enemigo vil ni amigo cierto.

    Pues has pasado los mejores años,
ya para lo que queda, pues es poco,
ni temas a la mar ni esperes puerto.

CXLIX

Unshackled irons, with connecting links beside,
The shattered shafts of halberds foes deplore,
Old driftwood from the sea along the shore,
Long muskets and siege-guns burst open wide,

Ruins of assaulted towers fortified,   5
Near where the laborer white threshing-floor
Creates, in tatters what were flags before,
Deep-dented helmets with caked blood half-dried,

Ship-rigging, fetters, relics of banners there,
Sea, jail, combat, Argel, winds and campaigns   10
On earth, in temple, show suspended life.

And thus my verses scattered everywhere,
The sea of my torments, my love in chains,
And in my feelings mortal war and strife.

CL

My little bark all broken, that (betrayed
By so much envy and by friendship feigned,
My patience used, by wrong on course constrained
With oars made of my pen and of my blade,

One choppy, dull, the other chopped, dull made)   5
The vital forces of my life retained,
Among the ports of favor spirit drained,
Among all future hopes, still disarrayed,

Pursue your star in great disillusionment,
For he is mad who didn't believe in such;   10
There's no vile foe or friend of good report.

For you the best years of your life have spent,
And, as for what remains, in truth not much,
Don't fear the sea or hope to reach a port.

CLI
Al Contador Gaspar de Barrionuevo

Gaspar, si enfermo está mi bien, decilde
que yo tengo de amor el alma enferma,
y en esta soledad desierta y yerma
lo que sabéis que paso persuadilde.

Y para que el rigor temple, advertilde   5
que el médico también tal vez enferma,
y que segura de mi ausencia duerma:
que soy leal cuanto presente humilde.

Y advertilde también, si el mal porfía,
que trueque mi salud y su acidente: 10
que la que tengo el alma se la envía,

Decilde que del trueco se contente;
mas ¿para qué le ofrezco salud mía?
Que no tiene salud quien está ausente.

CLX

Esto de imaginar si está en su casa,
si salió, si la hablaron, si fue vista;
temer que se componga, adorne y vista,
andar siempre mirando lo que pasa;

temblar del otro que de amor se abrasa   5
y con hacienda y alma la conquista,
querer que al oro y al amor resista,
morirme si se ausenta o si se casa;

celar todo galán rico y mancebo,
pensar que piensa en otro si en mí piensa,   10
rondar la noche y contemplar el día,

obliga, Marcio, enamorar de nuevo;
pero saber como pasó la ofensa,
no sólo desobliga, mas enfría.

CLI
To the Auditor Gaspar de Barrionuevo

Gaspar, if sick my precious is, tell her
That sick with love my very soul have I,
And in this solitude, a wasteland dry,
To what you know I'm suffering win her.

So that she harshness temper, stress to her   5
That even the doctor may in sickness lie;
May she sleep trusting me who absence sigh,
For I, there humble, here am trustier.

And warn her also, if the illness stays,
That she my health change for her accident,   10
For all I have my soul to her relays,

And tell her with the exchange she be content;
But why this offer of my health now raise?
For he who's absent has his health all spent.

CLX

This thing of if she's home imagining,
If she went out, they talked to her, if she was seen;
To fear that she get dressed and primp and preen,
To amble seeing all that's happening;

To shake if another feels love's burning sting   5
And with estate and soul makes her his queen;
To wish that she both gold and love demean,
To die if she's away or marrying;

To spy on every rich, young gallant swain,
To think she thinks of others—not the case,   10
To muse by day, to spend night at the grilles,

Obliges one to conquer hearts again,
But, Marcio, knowing how the wrong took place
Not only disobliges, but him chills.

CLXI

Cual engañado niño que, contento,
pintado pajarillo tiene atado
y le deja en la cuerda, confiado,
tender las alas por el manso viento,

y cuando más en esta gloria atento,   5
quebrándose el cordel, quedó burlado,
siguiéndole, en sus lágrimas bañado,
con los ojos y el triste pensamiento,

contigo he sido, Amor: que mi memoria
dejé llevar de pensamientos vanos,   10
colgados de la fuerza de un cabello;

llevóse el viento el pájaro y mi gloria,
y dejóme el cordel entre las manos,
que habrá por fuerza de servirme al cuello.

CLXII

Ya vengo con el voto y la cadena,
desengaño santísimo, a tu casa,
porque de la mayor coluna y basa
cuelgue, de horror y de escarmiento llena.

Aquí la vela y la rompida entena   5
pondrá mi amor, que el mar del mundo pasa,
y no con alma ingrata y mano escasa,
la nueva imagen de mi antigua pena.

Pero aguárdame un poco, desengaño;
que se me olvidan en la rota nave   10
ciertos papeles, prendas y despojos.

Mas no me aguardes, que serás engaño;
que si Lucinda a lo que vuelvo sabe,
tendráme un siglo con sus dulces ojos.

CLXI

Much like a child deluded, who, content,
A brightly-colored little bird keeps tied,
And lets it, trusting in the string untried,
Take wing upon the breezes gently sent,

And while in glory such as this intent,   5
The cord then breaking, he was sorely tried,
And bathed in tears, to follow it he tried,
Both with his eyes and wistful sentiment;

Thus, Love, I've been with you: my memory
I let be seized by my thoughts vainly grand,   10
Thoughts hanging by the strength of single hair.

The wind both bird and glory took from me,
And left me with the cord here in my hand,
Which I perforce around my neck should wear.

CLXII

I come to your house with the vow and chain
Today, most blesséd disillusionment,
To hang it from the great stone pediment,
Filled with heart-warnings and with horrid strain.

Here broken yardarm and the ragged main   5
Will place my love, that spans sea prominent,
And not with soul ungrateful and hand spent,
The reborn image of my ancient pain.

But, disillusionment, please wait for me,
For certain papers, keepsakes, spoils hard-earned   10
Have slipped my mind in ship that battered lies.

But no, don't wait, deception you will be,
For if Lucinda learns why I've returned
She'll keep me centuries with her sweet eyes.

CLXX

No tiene tanta miel Atica hermosa,
algas la orilla de la mar, ni encierra
tantas encinas la montaña y sierra,
flores la primavera deleitosa,

lluvias el triste invierno, y la copiosa   5
mano del seco otoño por la tierra
graves racimos, ni en la fiera guerra
más flechas Media, en arcos belicosa;

ni con más ojos mira el firmamento
cuando la noche calla más serena,   10
ni más olas levanta el Oceano,

peces sustenta el mar, aves el viento,
ni en Libia hay granos de menuda arena,
que doy suspiros por Lucinda en vano.

CLXXI

Llamas y huyes, quieres y aborreces,
y cuando estás más cerca te retiras;
no quieres que te miren, Silvia, y miras,
Duermes y sientes, guardaste y pareces.

Vuelas y no te vas, niegas y ofreces,   5
disfrazas las verdades en mentiras;
ciegas y ves, desdeñas y suspiras,
y siendo claro sol, menguas y creces.

Contigo a solas estas cosas mide,
que de tu estrecha condición me espanto,   10
en quererse vestir amor tan justo.

Silvia, o te agrado o no, si no despide;
si agrado, no consultes mi amor tanto,
que amor no es encomienda, sino gusto.

CLXX

Not so much honey has Attica beauteous,
The seashore algae, nor has such a stand
Of lasting oaks the range of mountains grand,
So many flowers Spring harmonious,

Such rains sad winter, and the copious   5
Hand of dry autumn come upon the land
Such clusters grave, nor does fierce war command
More darts in Media's bows predaceous,

Nor does the firmament with more eyes see
When it makes night much more serene and mute,   10
Nor does the Ocean more great waves sustain,

More birds the wind, more teeming fish the sea,
In Libya more grains of sand minute,
Than for Lucinda I breathe sighs in vain.

CLXXI

You call, and run away, despise, hold dear;
You, Sylvia, retire when closest by;
You want I see you not, yet me you eye;
You sleep, and feel, held back, and then appear.

You give, deny, you soar, don't disappear;   5
You cover up the simple truth with lie;
You blind, you see, you scorn, and then you sigh;
You wax and wane, sun being bright and clear.

When you are all alone these things weigh well;
At your condition narrow I shock know,   10
Since this just love should deck itself in treasure.

If I don't please you, Sylvia, say farewell,
And if I do, don't ponder my love so,
For love is not a weighty charge, but pleasure.

CLXXIV

Daba sustento a un pajarillo un día
Lucinda, y por los hierros del portillo
fuésele de la jaula el pajarillo
al libre viento, en que vivir solía.

Con un suspiro a la ocasión tardía   5
tendió la mano, y no pudiendo asillo,
dijo (y de las mejillas amarillo
volvió el clavel, que entre su nieve ardía):

«¿Adónde vas, por despreciar el nido,
al peligro de ligas y de balas,   10
y el dueño huyes, que tu pico adora?»

Oyóla el pajarillo enternecido,
y a la antigua prisión volvió las alas:
que tanto puede una mujer que llora.

CLXXIX

Angel divino, que en humano y tierno
velo te goza el mundo, ¡oh!, no consuma
el mar del tiempo, ni su blanca espuma
cubra tu frente en su nevado invierno;

beldad que del artífice superno   5
imagen pura fuiste en cifra y suma,
sujeto de mi lengua y de mi pluma,
cuya hermosura me ha de hacer eterno;

centro del alma, venturosa mía,
en quien el armonía y compostura   10
del mundo superior contemplo y veo.

Alba, Lucinda, cielo, sol, luz, día,
para siempre al altar de tu hermosura
ofrece su memoria mi deseo.

CLXXIV

Lucinda to a pet songbird one day
Was giving food, and through the opening
Of his barred cage the little bird took wing
Into free air, in which he used to stay.

She with a sigh him seeing get away   5
Stretched out her hand, and him not fastening
She said (and yellow from her cheeks did bring
Carnation that in snow cast burning ray):

"Where will you go, your home with scorn to see,
To danger of both snares and stones from slings,   10
Your master fleeing, who your song does prize?"

The little bird heard her compassionately,
And to the ancient prison took his wings:
So much can do a woman when she cries.

CLXXIX

Angel blest, in veil almost maternal
Loved by the world, may sea of time consume
You not, and may the whitely frothing spume
Your brow not cover with its snows hibernal;

And pulchritude of artificer supernal   5
The image pure you wholly did assume;
The subject which my tongue and pen made bloom,
Whose beauty will one day make me eternal;

Fair center of my soul, sweet chance of mine,
In whom the structure and accord declare   10
The greater world I contemplate and see.

Lucinda, morning, sky, daylight, sunshine,
Upon the altar of your beauty fair
This my desire extends its memory.

CLXXXI
De doña Inés de Castro

Con pálido color, ardiendo en ira,
en los brazos de Avero y de Alencastro,
de la difunta doña Inés de Castro
el bravo portugués el rostro mira.

Tierno se allega, airado se retira   5
(trágico fin de amor, infeliz astro),
y abrazado a su imagen de alabastro,
con este llanto y voz habla y suspira:

—Si ves el alma, Nise de mis ojos,
desde el cielo en que pisas palma y cedro,   10
más que en este laurel y fe constante,

verás que soy, honrando tus despojos,
portugués en amor, en rigor Pedro,
rey en poder, y en la venganza amante.

CLXXXIII

Fugitivo cristal, el curso enfrena,
en tanto que te cuento mis pesares;
pero ¿cómo te digo que te pares
si lloro y creces por la blanda arena?

Ya de la sierra, que de nieves llena   5
te da principio, humilde Manzanares,
por dar luz al que tienen tantos mares
mi sol hizo su ocaso en la Morena.

Ya del Betis la orilla verde adorna,
en otro bosque de árboles desnudos,   10
que en agua dan por fruto plata en barras.

Yo triste, en tanto que a tu margen torna,
de aquestos olmos, a mis quejas mudos,
nidos deshago, y desenlazo parras.

CLXXXI
Of Doña Inés de Castro

Of palest hue, in raging anger's fires,
With Doña Inés de Castro lying dead
In Avero's, Alencastro's arms outspread,
The daring Portuguese her face admires.

He tender then draws near, irate retires   5
(This tragic end of love, star of joy fled),
And to her alabaster image wed,
With weeping and with voice he speaks, suspires:

"If you my soul see, Nise of my veins,
From heaven, where you palm and cedar prove,   10
More than this laurel and devotion cover,

You'll see I am, in honoring your remains,
A Pedro harsh, a Portuguese in love,
Monarch in might, and in revenge a lover."

CLXXXIII

Clear crystal fugitive, your course refrain
While I tell you about my pain and woe;
But how can I tell you to stop your flow
If when I weep you grow and soft sand stain?

Now from the mountain peaks, which snows sustain,   5
Poor Manzanares, where you start to grow,
To light sun that so many seas can show,
My sun set in the Morena in south Spain.

Now she green banks of Betis does adorn,
In different forest where the trees are bare,   10
Which give in water silver bars for fruit.

The while I to your shores return forlorn,
And in these elms, of my plaints unaware,
Bird nests I tear apart, grapevines uproot.

CLXXXVIII

Suelta mi manso, mayoral extraño,
pues otro tienes de tu igual decoro;
deja la prenda que en el alma adoro,
perdida por tu bien y por mi daño.

Ponle su esquila de labrado estaño,   5
y no le engañen tus collares de oro;
toma en albricias este blanco toro,
que a las primeras hierbas cumple un año.

Si pides señas, tiene el vellocino
pardo encrespado, y los ojuelos tiene   10
como durmiendo en regalado sueño.

Si piensas que no soy su dueño, Alcino,
suelta, y verásle si a mi choza viene:
que aun tienen sal las manos de su dueño.

CLXXXIX

Querido manso mío, que venistes
por sal mil veces junto aquella roca,
y en mi grosera mano vuestra boca
y vuestra lengua de clavel pusistes,

¿por qué montañas ásperas subistes   5
que tal selvatiquez el alma os toca?
¿Qué furia os hizo condición tan loca
que la memoria y la razón perdistes?

Paced la anacardina porque os vuelva
de ese cruel y interesable sueño   10
y no bebáis del agua del olvido.

Aquí está vuestra vega, monte y selva;
yo soy vuestro pastor y vos mi dueño;
vos mi ganado, y yo vuestro perdido.

CLXXXVIII

Let my bellwether go, head shepherd strange,
For you have more of your same origin;
Release the heart my very soul would win,
Lost for your good, yet my life to derange.

On it your false gold collars interchange   5
For simple sheepbell made of figured tin;
Take this white bull, who when the grass comes in
Completes a year, as prize for this exchange.

As for its markings, it a fleece has fine
Of brown with curls, and eyes has frolicsome,   10
As if a sweet dream-sleep does it enfold.

Should you, Alcino, think that sheep's not mine,
Let go, and watch it to my cabin come,
For these its master's hands some salt still hold.

CLXXXIX

My dearly loved bellwether, who appeared
For salt a thousand times by rocky stand,
And you your mouth placed in my vulgar hand
And tongue like red carnation persevered,

What treacherous mountains have you domineered   5
That such fierce wildness does your soul command?
What rage let madness get the upper hand,
Your memory and your reason disappeared?

On Anacardium graze to firm your will
To shun that cruel, self-centered dream you knew,   10
And don't be in oblivion's waters tossed.

Here is your woods, your vega, and your hill;
I am your shepherd, and my master you,
You flock of one, and I your poor soul lost.

CXCI

Es la mujer del hombre lo más bueno,
y locura decir que lo más malo,
su vida suele ser y su regalo,
su muerte suele ser y su veneno.

Cielo a los ojos cándido y sereno,   5
que muchas veces al infierno igualo,
por raro al mundo su valor señalo,
por falso al hombre su rigor condeno.

Ella nos da su sangre, ella nos cría,
no ha hecho el cielo cosa más ingrata;   10
es un ángel, y a veces una arpía.

Quiere, aborrece, trata bien, maltrata,
y es la mujer, al fin, como sangría,
que a veces da salud y a veces mata.

CXCIX
A la Muerte

La muerte para aquél será terrible
con cuya vida acaba su memoria,
no para aquel cuya alabanza y gloria
con la muerte morir es imposible.

Sueño es müerte, y paso irremisible,   5
que en nuestra universal humana historia
pasó con felicísima vitoria
un hombre que fue Dios incorruptible.

Nunca de suyo fue mala y culpable
la muerte, a quien la vida no resiste: 10
al malo, aborrecible; al bueno, amable.

No la miseria en el morir consiste;
sólo el camino es triste y miserable,
y si es vivir, la vida sola es triste.

CXCI

The woman is the best thing that man knows,
And it is foolishness to say the worst;
She is his joy and she his life has nursed;
She as his death and as his poison shows.

A heaven to my eyes, pure, in repose,   5
That many times I see as hell accursed;
I praise her value to the world as first;
As false to man her harshness I oppose.

She gives to us her blood, she raises us;
No more ungrateful thing could heaven see;   10
She's angel, yet a harpy in her ways.

She loves, despises, flatters, mistreats us,
And like bloodletting woman is, for she
At times gives health, and other times she slays.

CXCIX
To Death

Death for that person will be terrible
With whose own life will end his memory,
But for that one who praise and dignity
Enjoys, with death to die is impossible.

Dream-sleep is death, step irremisible,   5
Which in our common human history
A man with most felicitous victory
Endured who was God incorruptible.

Death never evil was and culpable
Inherently, death life does not resist: 10
To good man, kind; to bad, detestable.

In dying misery does not consist;
The way alone is sad and miserable;
In living, life is sadly to exist.

Vireno, aquel mi manso regalado
del collarejo azul; aquel hermoso
que con balido ronco y amoroso
llevaba por los montes mi ganado;

aquel del vellocino ensortijado,   5
de alegres ojos y mirar gracioso,
por quien yo de ninguno fui envidioso
siendo de mil pastores envidiado;

aquel me hurtaron ya, Vireno hermano;
ya retoza otro dueño y le provoca;   10
toda la noche vela y duerme el día.

Ya come blanca sal en otra mano;
ya come ajena mano con la boca
de cuya lengua se abrasó la mía.

Silvio a una blanca corderilla suya,
de celos de un pastor, tiró el cayado,
con ser la más hermosa del ganado;
oh amor, ¿qué no podrá la fuerza tuya?

Huyó quejosa, que es razón que huya,   5
habiéndola sin culpa castigado;
lloró el pastor buscando el monte y prado,
que es justo que quien debe restituya.

Hallóla una pastora en esta afrenta,
y al fin la trajo al dueño, aunque tirano,   10
de verle arrepentido enternecida.

Dióle sal el pastor y ella, contenta,
la tomó de la misma injusta mano:
que un firme amor cualquier agravio olvida.

That one, Vireno, my bellwether kind
With collar blue; that one so beauteous
Who with a bleating hoarse and amorous
My flock there in the grazing lands combined;

That distant one with curly fleece refined,   5
Of joyful eyes and look felicitous,
For whom I was of no one envious,
I by a thousand shepherds envied blind;

That one they stole from me, Vireno brother;
That sheep new master quickens, impudent,   10
Now keeps watch nights and does by day retire.

That sheep now licks white salt from hand of another,
Now licks an alien hand with mouth intent
And with whose tongue my own was set afire.

From *Flor nueva del "Fénix,"* edited by
Joaquín de Entrambasaguas (Madrid, 1942)

Silvio threw his staff in jealousy
Of another shepherd at his lamb snow-white,
Her of the flock the prettiest one in sight—
Oh love, what will your might not guarantee?

She fled complaining, and it's right she flee,   5
He having punished her without the right;
He weeping searched both hill and dale 'til night:
It's justice to repay what debts there be.

A lass then found her after the event,
And brought her to her master, tyrant still,   10
Her truly touched to see him with regrets.

The shepherd gave her salt and she, content,
From unjust hand took it without ill-will:
For lasting love whatever wrong forgets.

From *La Arcadia*

Rimas Sacras

Sacred Rhymes

Soneto Primero

Cuando me paro a contemplar mi estado,
y a ver los pasos por donde he venido,
me espanto de que un hombre tan perdido
a conocer su error haya llegado.

Cuando miro los años que he pasado,   5
la divina razón puesta en olvido,
conozco que piedad del cielo ha sido
no haberme en tanto mal precipitado.

Entré por laberinto tan extraño,
fiando al débil hilo de la vida   10
el tarde conocido desengaño;

mas de tu luz mi escuridad vencida,
el monstro muerto de mi ciego engaño,
vuelve a la patria la razón perdida.

II

Pasos de mi primera edad que fuistes
por el camino fácil de la muerte,
hasta llegarme al tránsito más fuerte,
que por la senda de mi error pudistes.

¿Qué basilisco entre las flores vistes,   5
que de su engaño a la razón advierte?
Volved atrás porque el temor concierte
las breves horas de mis años tristes.

O pasos esparcidos vanamente,
¿qué furia os incitó, que habéis seguido   10
la senda vil de la ignorante gente?

Mas ya que es hecho, que volváis os pido,
que quien de lo perdido se arrepiente
aun no puede decir que lo ha perdido.

First Sonnet

When I sit down to contemplate my plight
And view the steps upon the paths I've crossed,
I marvel that a man so wholly lost
The error of his ways now knows aright.

When I look at my years now in full flight,   5
With reason divine into oblivion tossed,
I know that it has heaven mercy cost,
Not casting me into worse harm forthright.

I entered through a labyrinth's strange domain,
Entrusting to the thread of life so slight   10
Late apprehended disillusionment:

My darkness, though, quite vanquished by your light,
The monster of my blind deception slain,
Lost reason to its home returns content.

II

Steps of my early age that zealously
Pursued the easy road of death close by,
Me bringing to fierce transit where I die,
For you along an errant path took me.

What basilisk in flowers did you see   5
That from deceit it reason notify?
Go back so that your fears may unify
The fleeting hours of those sad years for me.

Oh steps far scattered, insignificant,
What fury incited you that you have crossed   10
The common path of people ignorant?

I ask that you return, forget past cost,
For if all that is lost one can recant,
It hardly can be said it has been lost.

III

Entro en mí mismo para verme, y dentro
hallo, ¡ay de mí!, con la razón postrada
una loca república alterada,
tanto que apenas los umbrales entro.

Al apetito sensitivo encuentro,   5
de quien la voluntad mal respetada
se queja al cielo, y de su fuerza armada
conduce el alma al verdadero centro.

La virtud, como el arte, hallarse suele
cerca de lo difícil, y así pienso   10
que el cuerpo en el castigo se desvele.

Muera el ardor del apetito intenso,
porque la voluntad al centro vuele,
capaz potencia de su bien inmenso.

IV

Si desde que nací, cuanto he pensado,
cuanto he solicitado y pretendido
ha sido vanidad, y sombra ha sido,
de locas esperanzas engañado;

si no tengo de todo lo pasado   5
presente más que el tiempo que he perdido,
vanamente he cansado mi sentido,
y torres en el viento fabricado.

¡Cuán engañada el alma presumía
que su capacidad pudiera hartarse   10
con lo que el bien mortal le prometía!

Era su esfera Dios para quietarse,
y como fuera dél lo pretendía,
no pudo hasta tenerle sosegarse.

III

 I go inside myself my self to know
And find within—poor me!—my reason harmed,
A changed republic by a madness charmed,
As soon as I beyond the threshold go.

 The sensitive appetite I come to know,   5
Of which the will with reputation harmed
To heaven wails, and by its powers armed
The soul toward its true center takes in tow.

 Now Virtue, as with Art, will likely vie
Near what is difficult, and I think thence   10
The body in chastisement should watch try.

 Let die the fire of appetite intense
So that the will may to the center fly,
Effective power of its good immense.

IV

 If since I came to birth all I've perceived,
All I have sought and tried for in between
Has been but vanity, and shadow been,
By hopes bereft of reason then deceived;

 If I have not of all the past received   5
More than the time I've wasted to be seen,
I've vainly wearied all my senses keen,
And only towers in the wind achieved.

 How terribly deceived the soul presumed
That its capacity might be attained   10
With that which mortal good with promise blessed.

 God was its sphere where peace could be consumed,
And since outside of him the soul peace feigned,
It couldn't until having him find rest.

V

    ¿Qué ceguedad me trujo a tantos daños?
¿Por dónde me llevaron desvaríos,
que no traté mis años como míos,
y traté como propios sus engaños?

    ¡Oh puerto de mis blancos desengaños,   5
por donde ya mis juveniles bríos
pasaron como el curso de los ríos,
que no los vuel[v]e atrás el de los años!

    Hicieron fin mis locos pensamientos,
acomodóse al tiempo la edad mía,   10
por ventura en ajenos escarmientos.

    Que no temer el fin no es valentía,
donde acaban los gustos en tormentos,
y el curso de los años en un día.

X

    ¿Será bien aguardar, cuerpo indiscreto,
al tiempo que, perdidos los sentidos,
escuchen, y no entiendan, los oídos,
por la flaqueza extrema del sujeto?

    ¿Será bien aguardar a tanto aprieto,   5
que ya los tenga el final hielo asidos,
o en la vana esperanza divertidos,
que no siendo virtud no tiene efeto?

    ¿Querrá el jüez entonces ser piadoso?
¿Admitirá la apelación, si tiene   10
tan justas quejas, y es tan poderoso?

    Oh vida, no aguardéis que el curso enfrene
el paso de la muerte riguroso:
que no es consejo el que tan tarde viene.

V

What blindness brought me all these hurts intense?
What caprices swept me away so fast:
As if they were not mine my years I classed,
And treated as if mine their fraudulence?

Oh, port of my blank disillusionments,   5
Through which my youthful spirits too soon passed,
The way the course of rivers flows on past,
Which can't bring back those with the years gone hence!

My foolish thoughts eventually were spent;
My years adjusted to time granted me,   10
By fortune with soul-warnings others sent.

For not to fear the end isn't bravery,
Where pleasures always vanish in torment,
And course of all the years a day will be.

X

Will it be good, my body indiscreet,
To await the time that, with the senses bruised,
The ears may listen but remain confused,
Since frailty extreme the subject does maltreat?

Will it be good such tightening to greet,   5
For now the final ice has them abused,
Or by vain hope, diverted and amused,
That not being virtue can no aim complete?

Then will the judge want to be merciful?
Will he admit the appeal if it contain   10
Such just complaints, he being so powerful?

Oh life, don't wait to have your course refrain
The rigorous step of death implacable:
For it's not counsel that comes late in vain.

XII

Si es el instante fin de lo presente,
y principio también de lo futuro,
y en un instante al riguroso y duro
golpe tengo de ver la vida ausente,

¿adónde voy con paso diligente?   5
¿Qué intento? ¿Qué pretendo? ¿Qué procuro?
¿Sobre qué privilegios aseguro
esto que ha de vivir eternamente?

No es bien decir que el tiempo que ha pasado
es el mejor, que la opinión condeno   10
de aquellos ciegos de quien es culpado.

Ya queda el que pasó por tiempo ajeno,
haciéndole dichoso o desdichado,
los vicios malo, y las virtudes bueno.

XIV

Pastor que con tus silbos amorosos
me despertaste del profundo sueño:
Tú, que hiciste cayado de ese leño
en que tiendes los brazos poderosos,

vuelve los ojos a mi fe piadosos,   5
pues te confieso por mi amor y dueño
y la palabra de seguirte empeño,
tus dulces silbos y tus pies hermosos.

Oye, Pastor, pues por amores mueres,
no te espante el rigor de mis pecados,   10
pues tan amigo de rendidos eres.

Espera, pues, y escucha mis cuidados . . . ;
pero ¿cómo te digo que me esperes
si estás para esperar los pies clavados?

XII

If the instant, of the present, end can be,
And beginning of the future time also,
And in an instant, at severe, hard blow
I my own life will absent have to see,

    With step so diligent, where do I flee?   5
What do I wish for, try for, seek to show?
Upon what privileges can I foreknow
This which is bound to live eternally?

    It is not good to say time which has passed
Is best, for I the opinion castigate   10
Of those blind ones who have misunderstood.

    Now stays that which as alien time was classed,
It making happy or unfortunate,
The vices evil, and the virtues good.

XIV

    Shepherd who with amorous whistles sweet
From my profound dream-sleep awakened me;
You who a staff did fashion from that tree
From which you now with mighty arms entreat;

    May your eyes tender see my faith complete,   5
For I would have you lord and master be;
To follow you I give my guarantee,
Your sweet-voiced whistles and your precious feet.

    Hark, Shepherd, you who die for love affairs,
Be not affrighted with my sins' degree,   10
Since you are friend to those who suffer loss.

    Await, therefore, and listen to my cares:
Yet how can I tell you to wait for me
If you await your feet nailed to the cross?

XV

¡Cuántas veces, Señor, me habéis llamado,
y cuántas con vergüenza he respondido,
desnudo como Adán, aunque vestido
de las hojas del árbol del pecado!

Seguí mil veces vuestro pie sagrado,   5
fácil de asir, en una cruz asido,
y atrás volví otras tantas atrevido,
al mismo precio que me habéis comprado.

Besos de paz os di para ofenderos,
pero si fugitivos de su dueño   10
yerran cuando los hallan los esclavos,

hoy que vuelvo con lágrimas a veros,
clavadme vos a vos en vuestro leño
y tendréisme seguro con tres clavos.

XVI

Muere la vida, y vivo yo sin vida,
ofendiendo la vida de mi muerte.
Sangre divina de las venas vierte,
y mi diamante su dureza olvida.

Está la majestad de Dios tendida   5
en una dura cruz, y yo de suerte
que soy de sus dolores el más fuerte,
y de su cuerpo la mayor herida.

¡Oh duro corazón de mármol frío!,
¿tiene tu Dios abierto el lado izquierdo,   10
y no te vuelves un copioso río?

Morir por él será divino acuerdo;
mas eres tú mi vida, Cristo mío,
y como no la tengo, no la pierdo.

XV

How many times, O Lord, you've called to me;
How many I've made response, with shame distressed,
As naked as an Adam, although dressed
With only leaves that grow upon sin's tree!

A thousand times your holy foot I'd see,   5
Not difficult to press, upon Cross pressed;
A thousand turned away with pride obsessed,
At equal price with which you have bought me.

Kisses of peace I gave offending you,
But if they from their master wandering free   10
In error go 'til found by slave details,

Now that today I return in tears to you,
Then you nail me to you upon your tree,
And you'll have me secure with those three nails.

XVI

Life dying is, and without life I live,
Offending life with my death now begun;
Blood sacred from my veins does freely run;
My diamond's hardness now turns fugitive.

Stretched out is God the King's prerogative   5
Upon harsh cross, and I by chance undone
Am of his sorrows much the strongest one,
And of his body wound superlative.

O stubborn heart of marble icy-cold!
Can you your God's left side agape behold   10
And still from you no copious river spews?

To die for him will be divine accord;
But you are all my life, O Christ my Lord,
And since I have it not, it cannot lose.

XVIII

¿Qué tengo yo, que mi amistad procuras?
¿Qué interés se te sigue, Jesús mío,
que a mi puerta cubierto de rocío
pasas las noches del invierno escuras?

¡Oh cuánto fueron mis entrañas duras,   5
pues no te abrí! ¡Qué estraño desvarío,
si de mi ingratitud el hielo frío
secó las llagas de tus plantas puras!

¡Cuántas veces el Ángel me decía:
«Alma, asómate agora a la ventana,   10
verás con cuánto amor llamar porfía!»

¡Y cuántas, hermosura soberana,
«Mañana le abriremos», respondía,
para lo mismo responder mañana!

XX

La lengua del amor, a quien no sabe
lo que es amor, ¡qué bárbara parece!;
pues como por instantes enmudece,
tiene pausas de música süave.

Tal vez suspensa, tal aguda y grave,   5
rotos conceptos al amante ofrece;
aguarda los compases que padece,
porque la causa su destreza alabe.

¡Oh dulcísimo bien, que al bien me guía!,
¿con qué lengua os diré mi sentimiento,   10
ya que tengo de hablaros osadía?

Mas si es de los conceptos instrumento,
¿qué importa que calléis, oh lengua mía,
pues que vos penetráis mi pensamiento?

XVIII

What do I have, that you my friendship seek?
What interest, Jesus mine, do you pursue
That near my door, all wet with evening dew,
You spend the nights of winter darkly bleak?

How much my deepest heart showed hardened streak,   5
I failed to let you in! What error, too,
If ice through my ingratitude to you
Did dry the wounds on your pure feet so weak!

How many times my Angel said to me:
"Dear soul, look out the window where nearby   10
With how much love he calls and calls you'll see!"

How many, Sovereign Beauty, did I cry,
"We'll let him in tomorrow certainly,"
Then tomorrow always gave the same reply!

XX

The tongue of love, to him who does not know
What love can be, how barbarous it seems!
For as in moments it as silence teems,
It pauses has of music soft and low.

Perhaps suspended, sharp, or grave and slow,   5
With its threadbare conceits the lover dreams;
It waits for measure that in suffering streams,
So that upon its skill cause praise bestow.

Oh most sweet good, that to the good guides me!,
With what tongue tell I you my sentiment,   10
Since I hold speaking to you as gallantry?

But if it's of conceits the instrument,
What means it, oh my tongue, that you quiet be,
For you do penetrate my thought's ferment?

XXII

Yo dormiré en el polvo, y si mañana
me buscares, Señor, será posible
no hallar en el estado convenible
para tu forma la materia humana.

Imprime agora, ¡oh fuerza soberana!,   5
tus efetos en mí, que es imposible
conservarse mi ser incorruptible,
viento, humo, polvo y esperanza vana.

Bien sé que he de vestirme el postrer día
otra vez estos huesos, y que verte   10
mis ojos tienen y esta carne mía.

Esta esperanza vive en mí tan fuerte,
que con ella no más tengo alegría
en las tristes memorias de la muerte.

XXIX

Luz de mis ojos, yo juré que había
de celebrar una mortal belleza,
que de mi verde edad la fortaleza
como enlazada yedra consumía.

Si me ha pesado, y si llorar querría   5
lo que canté con inmortal tristeza,
y si la que tenéis en la cabeza
corona agora de laurel la mía,

Vos lo sabéis, a quien está presente
el más oculto pensamiento humano,   10
y que desde hoy, con nuevo celo ardiente,

cantaré vuestro nombre soberano,
que a la hermosura vuestra eternamente
consagro pluma y voz, ingenio y mano.

XXII

I'll sleep in dust, and if you search for me
Tomorrow, Lord, it will be possible
That you not find in state agreeable
This human matter with your form to be.

Oh Sovereign Power, now imprint in me 5
Your good effects, for it's impossible
To keep my being incorruptible,
Wind, smoke, and dust, and hope all vanity.

How well I know that I again must dress
These bones that latter day, and must you please 10
As these my eyes, this flesh, then you address.

This living hope does me so strongly seize
That with it only I find happiness
In death with its distressing memories.

XXIX

Light of my eyes, I made a promise strong
A mortal beauty of this earth to sing,
That which the fortress of my years' green spring
Like ivy was consuming all along.

If with long sadness what I sang as song 5
Has weighed on me, and would me weeping bring,
And if that which upon your head does cling
As crown with laurel does to me belong,

You know it well, to whom is present sign
The human thought that bursts most secretly, 10
And from this day, with new zeal like firebrand,

I'll sing out loud your name of king divine,
And to your beauty fair eternally
I consecrate pen, talent, voice, and hand.

XXXI

Yo me muero de amor—que no sabía,
aunque diestro en amar cosas del suelo—;
que no pensaba yo que amor del cielo
con tal rigor las almas encendía.

Si llama la mortal filosofía   5
deseo de hermosura a amor, recelo
que con mayores ansias me desvelo,
cuanto es más alta la belleza mía.

Amé en la tierra vil, ¡qué necio amante!
¡Oh luz del alma, habiendo de buscaros,   10
qué tiempo que perdí como ignorante!

Mas yo os prometo agora de pagaros
con mil siglos de amor cualquiera instante
que, por amarme a mí, dejé de amaros.

XXXIII

Llamé mi luz a la tiniebla oscura,
gloria a mi pena, a mi dolor consuelo,
provecho al daño, y al infierno cielo,
¡qué ciego error! ¡qué bárbara locura!

Ay, luz divina, sobre todas pura,   5
¿cuántas vivieron el humano velo,
o el intelectual de ardiente celo,
quién conociera entonces tu hermosura?

Origen de la luz, luz poderosa,
luz que ilumina el sol, las once esferas,   10
luz, ¿quién es luz, si no tu luz hermosa?

Ay, loca ceguedad, cual me pusieras,
Si fiado de luz tan mentierosa,
Eterna noche de mis ojos fueras.

XXXI

Of love I'm dying—which I did not know,
Although with skill in loving earthly things;
Yet I knew not love which from heaven springs
With such severity caused souls to glow.

If our philosophy calls here below   5
Desire for beauty love, to me fear clings
And I keep watch in anxious questionings,
As higher goes this beauty I now know.

I—foolish lover!—loved on this vile earth.
Light of my soul, not seeking my love to prove,   10
What time I lost like ignoramus true!

But now I vow to pay you all you're worth,
Each moment a thousand centuries to love,
For I to love myself stopped loving you.

XXXIII

I called my light what was a mist obscure;
Grief, glory; consolation, all my pain;
Hell, heaven; benefit, what was hurt plain—
What madness wild, what error blind, unsure!

Ay, light divine, above all others pure,   5
The human veil did lesser lights constrain,
Or intellectual with seeking brain,
Who of your beauty could therefore be sure?

Source of the light, of light all-powerful,
Light that lights up the eleven spheres, the sun,   10
Light, what is light, but your light beautiful?

Ay, blindness mad, that you spread earlier,
If my trust could by such false light be won,
Eternal night of these my eyes you were.

XXXVIII

Adonde quiera que su luz aplican,
hallan, Señor, mis ojos tu grandeza:
si miran de los cielos la belleza,
con voz eterna tu deidad publican;

si a la tierra se bajan, y se implican   5
en tanta variedad, Naturaleza
les muestra tu poder con la destreza
que sus diversidades significan;

si al mar, Señor, o al aire, meditando
aves y peces, todo está diciendo   10
que es Dios su autor, a quien está adorando.

Ni hay tan bárbaro antípoda que, viendo
tanta belleza, no te esté alabando:
yo solo, conociéndola, te ofendo.

XLIII
A una calavera

Esta cabeza, cuando viva, tuvo
sobre la arquitectura destos huesos
carne y cabellos, por quien fueron presos
los ojos que, mirándola, detuvo.

Aquí la rosa de la boca estuvo,   5
marchita ya con tan helados besos;
aquí los ojos de esmeralda impresos,
color que tantas almas entretuvo.

Aquí la estimativa en que tenía
el principio de todo el movimiento,   10
aquí de las potencias la armonía.

¡Oh hermosura mortal, cometa al viento!,
¿donde tan alta presunción vivía
desprecian los gusanos aposento?

XXXVIII

In every place my eyes their light apply,
They ever find, my Lord, your majesty:
If they the beauty of the heavens see,
They with long voice your godhead magnify.

If down to earth they then descend and try   5
To be involved in such variety,
Your power Nature shows in dexterity
That her diversities do signify.

If, Lord, the birds and fishes meditating
In sea and air, all beings cries are raising   10
That God their author is, their praise extending,

There's no wild antipode who, contemplating
Your beauty pure, will then not you be praising:
I only, viewing it, you keep offending.

XLII
To a Skull

This head, that time it was alive, retained
Upon the architecture of this bone
Both flesh and hair, in which imprisoned shone
The eyes that, on it looking, it detained.

Right here the rose that formed the mouth remained,   5
Now with so many frozen kisses flown;
Right here the eyes etched emerald in tone,
A color countless souls once entertained.

Here was the moral estimate in which it held
Beginnings of all motion positive,   10
Here of the potencies the harmony.

Oh mortal beauty, kite by winds impelled!
Where such a bold presumption used to live,
Do worms this lodging place scorn utterly?

XLIV

Cuando lo que he de ser me considero,
¿cómo de mi bajeza me levanto?
Y si de imaginarme tal me espanto,
¿por qué me desvanezco y me prefiero?

¿Qué solicito, qué pretendo y quiero,   5
siendo guerra el vivir y el nacer llanto?
¿Por qué este polvo vil estimo en tanto,
si dél tan presto dividirme espero?

Si en casa que se deja, nadie gasta,
pues pierde lo que en ella se reparte,   10
¿qué loco engaño mi quietud contrasta?

Vida breve y mortal, dejad el arte:
que a quien se ha de partir tan presto, basta
lo necesario, en tanto que se parte.

XLVI

No sabe qué es amor quien no te ama,
celestial hermosura, esposo bello;
tu cabeza es de oro, y tu cabello
como el cogollo que la palma enrama.

Tu boca como lirio que derrama   5
licor al alba; de marfil tu cuello;
tu mano el torno y en su palma el sello
que el alma por disfraz jacintos llama.

¡Ay Dios!, ¿en qué pensé cuando, dejando
tanta belleza y las mortales viendo,   10
perdí lo que pudiera estar gozando?

Mas si del tiempo que perdí me ofendo,
tal prisa me daré, que un hora amando
venza los años que pasé fingiendo.

XLIV

When I consider what I am to be,
How can I raise myself from baseness low?
And if I imagine such and stupor show,
Why do I boast and flaunt my vanity?

What do I ask for, want, intend for me,   5
War being living and my birth but woe?
Why do I this vile dust keep praising so,
If from it I must very soon break free?

If on a house but fit to leave none spends,
For lost is what to it one may impart,   10
What mad deception my composure rends?

Life mortal and so brief, let go of art:
For one who soon is to depart depends
Upon the essential, getting set to part.

XLVI

He who does not love you no love has borne,
Celestial beauty and spouse fair to see;
Your head is golden, and your hair streams free,
Like budding tendrils by the palm tree worn.

Your mouth, much like the lily that at morn   5
Sweet liquor spills; your neck of ivory;
Fine tool your hand, and whose palm seal can be,
Though soul say hyacinths the palm adorn.

Ay, Lord! What was I thinking of in leaving
Such beauty, and mere mortal beauties proving;   10
I lost what could have been a joy unending.

But if for time I lost I must be grieving
I'll be so urgent that an hour loving
Can conquer all the years I spent pretending.

XLVIII

Hombre mortal mis padres me engendraron,
aire común y luz los cielos dieron,
y mi primera voz lágrimas fueron,
que así los reyes en el mundo entraron.

La tierra y la miseria me abrazaron,   5
paños, no piel o pluma, me envolvieron;
por huésped de la vida me escribieron
y las horas y pasos me contaron.

Así voy prosiguiendo la jornada,
a la inmortalidad el alma asida: 10
que el cuerpo es nada, y no pretende nada.

Un principio y un fin tiene la vida;
porque de todos es igual la entrada,
y conforme a la entrada la salida.

XLIX

En señal de la paz que Dios hacía
con el hombre, templando sus rigores
los cielos dividió con tres colores
el arco hermoso que a la tierra envía:

lo rojo señalaba la alegría,   5
lo verde paz y lo dorado amores;
secó las aguas, y esmaltaron flores
el pardo limo que su faz cubría.

Vos sois en esa cruz, cordero tierno,
arco de sangre y paz, que satisfizo   10
los enojos del Padre sempiterno;

vos sois, mi buen Jesús, quien los deshizo;
ya no teman los nombres el infierno,
pues sois el arco que las paces hizo.

XLVIII

As mortal man my parents me begot;
The heavens common air and light gave free,
And my first utterance tears came to be,
For thus the kings all entered this sad spot.

The earth and its misfortunes were my lot,   5
And clothes, not hide or plume, enveloped me;
As guest here in this life they wrote to me;
For hours and footsteps, they gave me the plot.

Thus I upon my journey ever wend,   10
My soul in grasp of immortality:
The body nothing is, claims not a thing.

Life has a mere beginning and an end,
Because all make their entrance equally,
And exit is much like the entering.

XLIX

In sign of peace that God would make amends
To man, his harshness seeing mollified,
The skies into three hues he did divide,
And lovely rainbow to the earth he sends.

The red was sign that happiness intends,   5
The green was peace, the gold loves signified;
He dried the deeps, and flowers beautified
The grayish slime that over its face extends.

You are upon that Cross, o Lamb divine,
Rainbow of blood and peace who satisfied   10
The wrath of our eternal Father and Lord.

You are the one who dissolved it, Jesus mine;
Let man by hell no more be horrified;
You are the rainbow who brought us accord.

LI

Descalzo el pie sobre la arena ardiente,
ceñida la cabeza de espadañas,
con una caña, entre las verdes cañas
que al Tajo adornan la famosa frente,

tiende sobre el cristal de su corriente   5
su cuerda el pescador, y por hazañas
tiene el sufrir que el sol por las montañas
se derribe a las aguas del Occidente.

Sale a su cebo el pez en tal distancia,
Mas, o gran Pescador Cristo, ceñido   10
de espinas que en la caña de tu afrenta

sacas del mar del mundo mi ignorancia,
el pie en la Cruz, ribera de mi olvido,
para que el cebo de tu sangre sienta.

LXI
A un hueso de San Laurencio

Poned la limpia mesa a Christo y coma,
espíritus divinos, del Cordero,
de cuyo sacrificio verdadero
el humo sube en oloroso aroma;

color de rosa en las parrillas toma,   5
sazón le ha dado amor, servidle entero,
vuele a mejor Arabia y Hemisferio
de este Fénix la cándida paloma.

Está sin corazón, asóse presto,
y que le vuelvan de otro lado avisa   10
para llevar mejor el fuego impreso:

Angeles, si la mesa le habéis puesto,
decidle que la carne coma aprisa,
que el más Cristiano Rey espera un hueso.

LI

Barefooted in the burning sands, intent,
His head with leafy rushes crowned as screen,
With his long cane among the canes of green
That famous brow of Tagus ornament,

The fisherman upon the clear extent   5
Of current casts his line, and as routine
He suffers sun that from the mountains seen
Subdues the waters of the Occident.

The distant fish does toward the bait advance,
But, Christ great Fisherman, crowned evermore   10
With thorns that with the cane of your affront

You fish from this world's sea my ignorance,
Foot on the Cross, and my oblivion's shore,
That I the bait that is your blood confront.

LXI
To a Bone of St. Lawrence

Come set a table clean and let Christ eat
Of this good lamb, you spirits heavenly,
From whose true sacrifice one can well see
The smoke now rising as sweet-smelling treat;

Upon the grills takes pinkish tone the meat;   5
Love gives it flavor, whole it should served be;
To better Hemisphere and Araby
Dove candid of this Phoenix should retreat.

It has no heart, it roasted in a trice;
That it should be turned over them entreat,   10
So that the fire's imprint be better shown.

Thus, Angels, if you've set a table nice,
Tell him to come and quickly eat the meat,
For this most Christian King awaits a bone.

LXII
A San Sebastián

Tiraban Dios y el hombre al blanco un día
flechas de amor, y de crueldad tirana
por ver quien de los dos el premio gana,
que atado a un árbol el rigor tenía,

Dios que del blanco lo que Dios sabía   5
tiraba con destreza soberana;
erraba el hombre con malicia humana,
porque la mira contra Dios ponía.

Era de emtrambos Sebastián el cierto
blanco en un tronco, donde ramas hechas   10
las flechas le dejaron tan cubierto:

Que puesto que a matarle iban derechas
quedó de Dios y no del hombre muerto,
que en las flechas de Dios rompió sus flechas.

LXXIII
A Cristo en la Cruz

O vida de mi vida, Cristo santo,
¿a dónde voy de tu hermosura huyendo?
¿Cómo es posible que tu rostro ofendo
que me mira bañado en sangre y llanto?

A mí mismo me doy confuso espanto   5
de ver que me conozco, y no me enmiendo;
ya el Angel de mi guarda está diciendo
que me avergüence de ofenderte tanto.

Detén con esas manos mis perdidos
pasos, mi dulce amor, ¿mas de que fuerte   10
las pide, quien las clava con las suyas?

Ay, Dios, ¿adónde estaban mis sentidos
que las espaldas pude yo volverte,
mirando en una Cruz por mí las tuyas?

LXII
To St. Sebastian

At marks were shooting God and man one day
Love darts, and in tyrannic cruelty
Who of the two the prize may win to see
(For rigor had it tied to tree to stay),

God who at target shooting could hold sway   5
Was shooting with a sovereign mastery;
With human malice man shot erringly,
Because toward God his aim kept going astray.

Sebastian of them both was certainly
Sure target on a trunk, where branches made   10
The darts which left him covered at a stroke.

Since they to kill him flew unerringly,
His death to God and not to man was laid,
For on God's arrows he his arrows broke.

LXIII
To Christ on the Cross

O Life that is my life, Christ holy light,
Your beauty fleeing, where is it I wend?
How can it be that I your face offend
That bathed in blood and tears holds me in sight?

I even bring myself bewildered fright   5
To know myself and yet my ways not mend;
That I should be ashamed you so to offend
My Angel of the Guard says day and night.

Detain with those your hands my gone astray
Footsteps, sweet love, but with what strongpoint true   10
Can one seek them, who nails them with his own?

Dear God, where did my good sense go away
That I could ever turn my back on you,
Yours looking out for me on Cross alone?

LXXXV

Dulce Señor, mis vanos pensamientos
fundados en el viento me acometen,
pero por más que mi quietud inquieten
no podrán derribar tus fundamentos.

No porque de mi parte mis intentos   5
seguridad alguna me prometen
para que mi flaqueza no sujeten,
ligera más que los mudables vientos:

Mas porque si a mi voz, Señor, se inclina
tu defensa y piedad, ¿qué humana guerra   10
contra lo que tú amparas será fuerte?

Ponme a la sombra de tu Cruz divina,
y vengan contra mí fuego, aire, tierra,
mar, yerro, engaño, envidia, infierno y muerte.

LXII
De Raquel y Jacob

Bajaba con sus cándidas ovejas
por el valle de Aram Raquel hermosa,
el oro puro y la purpúrea rosa
mezclando las mejillas y guedejas,

ellas lamiendo a la canal las tejas   5
y ella mirando el pozo cuidadosa;
anticipóse a levantar la losa
el que fue mayorazgo por lentejas.

Bebió el ganado caluroso, y luego
dióla beso de paz, y por despojos   10
lágrimas que lloró perdido y ciego.

Muy tierno sois, Jacob, ¿tan presto enojos?
Si que en llegando al corazón el fuego
lo que tiene de humor sale a los ojos.

LXXXV

Sweet Lord, my vain and good for nothing thought
Upon the wind sustained beleaguers me,
But though it shatter my tranquillity
It won't bring your foundations down to naught.

    And not because on my part what I've sought   5
Security of any kind can promise me,
So that my weakness not subjected be,
More frivolous than wind with changes fraught:

    But Lord, because if to my voice incline
Your mercy and defense, what war of men   10
Will strength display against your mighty breath?

    Place me in shadow of your Cross divine,
And let against me come fire, air, earth then,
Sea, error, pitfall, envy, hell, and death.

XCII
Of Rachel and Jacob

With all her snow-white sheep down Haran's plain
The comely Rachel slowly made her way,
Her cheeks and long locks mixing in display
The purplish rose and gold of purest strain.

    Upon the well she lets her eyes remain,   5
They licking at the tiles where waters play;
Then Jacob rushed to lift the stone away,
Who for some pottage did the birthright gain.

    The heated flock drank deep; and later he
Gave her the kiss of peace, and spoils apart,   10
He, blind, uncertain, felt his tears arise.

    So tender, Jacob, cares so rapidly?
For certain when the fire gets to the heart
What it of humors has fills up the eyes.

A la despedida de Cristo, Nuestro Bien, de su Madre Santisima

Los dos más dulces esposos,
los dos más tiernos amantes,
los mejores madre e hijo,
porque son Cristo y su Madre,
tiernamente se despiden,   5
tanto, que solo en mirarse
parece que entre los dos
se están repartiendo el cáliz.
«Hijo—le dice la Virgen—,
¡ay, si pudiera excusarse   10
esta llorosa partida,
que las entrañas me parte!
A morir vas, hijo mío,
por el hombre que criaste:
que ofensas hechas a Dios,   15
solo Dios las satsiface.
No se dirá por el hombre
quien tal hace que tal pague,
pues que vos pagáis por él
al precio de vuestra sangre.   20
Dejadme, dulce Jesús,
que mil veces os abrace,
porque me deis fortaleza
que a tantos dolores baste.
Para llevaros a Egipto   25
hubo quien me acompañase,
mas para quedar sin vos,
¿quién dejáis que me acompañe?
Aunque un ángel me dejéis,
no es posible consolarme: 30
que ausencia de un hijo Dios
no puede suplirla un ángel.
Ya siento vuestros azotes
herir vuestra tierna carne;
como es hecha de la mía,   35
hace que también me alcance.

On the Farewell to Christ Our Blessing
by His Most Holy Mother:
(Ballad)

The sweetest spouses are these two,
        The sweethearts tenderest,
Because they Christ, his Mother are,
        As mother and son the best.

They tenderly a farewell say,   5
        Each at the other staring,
So that it seems between the two
        The Chalice they are sharing.

"Son," the Virgin says to him,
        "If I could you relieve   10
Of this farewell that tears my heart,
        And causes me to grieve!

"You're on your way to die, my son,
        For man you did create;
Offenses done against our God   15
        God only can placate.

"'He who such does, such pays' will not
        Of mortal man be said,
For you are going to pay for him
        The price of your blood red.   20

"Leave me, sweet Jesus; a thousand times
        Let me your form embrace,
Because you give me fortitude
        So many pains to face.

"When I to Egypt carried you   25
        Someone accompanied me,
But with you gone, whom will you leave
        Me to accompany?

"Though you an angel leave with me,
        My grief he cannot still,   30
For absence of a Son of God,
        An angel cannot fill.

"Your lashes I again now feel,
        Because your tender flesh
Since it is really made of mine   35
        I must feel them afresh.

Vuestra cruz llevo en mis hombros,
y no hay pasar adelante,
porque os imagino en ella,
y, aunque soy vuestra, soy madre.»					40
Mirando Cristo a María
las lágrimas venerables,
a la emperatriz del cielo
responde palabras tales:
«Dulcísima madre mía,					45
vos y yo dolor tan grande
dos veces le padecemos,
porque le tenemos antes.
Con vos quedo, aunque me voy:
que no es posible apartarse					50
por muerte ni por ausencia
tan verdaderos amantes.
Ya siento más que mi muerte
el ver que el dolor os mate:
que el sentir y el padecer					55
se llaman penas iguales.
Madre, yo voy a morir
porque ya mi Eterno Padre
tiene dada la sentencia
contra mí, que soy su imagen.					60
Por el más errado esclavo
que ha visto el mundo ni sabe,
quiere que muera su Hijo;
obedecerle es amarle.
Para morir he nacido:					65
El me mandó que bajase
de sus entrañas paternas
a las vuestras virginales.
Con humildad y obediencia
hasta la muerte ha de hallarme.					70
La cruz me espera, Señora.
Consuéleos Dios: abrazadme.»
Contempla a Cristo y María,
alma, en tantas soledades,
que ella se queda sin hijo,					75
y que El sin madre se parte.

"Your Cross I upon my shoulders bear,
    Which does my movement smother,
Since I imagine you on it
    And though I'm yours, I'm mother."   40

In Mary Christ beholding then
    Her tears so venerable,
To Heaven's Empress he responds
    In these words memorable:

"O sweetest mother mine, this pain   45
    That makes us both heartsore,
We suffer, you and I, two times,
    For we know it before.

"With you I stay, although I go,
    For it's not possible   50
That death or absence separate
    Sweethearts so worshipful.

"More than my death I now must feel
    The pain that's killing you;
That suffering and feeling are   55
    Woes similar is true.

"Mother, I'm on my way to die;
    My eternal Father indeed
Against me, who his image am,
    This sentence has decreed.   60

"Although the world's most erring slave
    Knows not his time is nigh,
To obey him is to love him when
    He wills his Son to die.

"I have been born on earth to die;   65
    He willed that I come down,
His bowels paternal leaving thus,
    Your virgin womb to crown.

"With trust and with humility,
    Death will encounter me;   70
The Cross me calls, may God bless you,
    My Lady, cuddle me."

Now Christ and Mary contemplate,
    My soul, alone their hearts;
For she remains without a son,   75
    He without mother parts.

Llega, y dile: «Virgen pura,
¿queréis que yo os acompañe?»
Que si te quedas con ella,
el cielo podrá envidiarte.   80

Al ponerle en la Cruz
Romance

En tanto que el hoyo cavan,
a donde la cruz asienten,
en que el Cordero levanten
figurado por la sierpe,
     aquella ropa inconsútil,   5
que de Nazareth ausente
labró la hermosa María
después de su parto, alegre,
     de sus delicadas carnes
quitan con manos aleves   10
los camareros que tuvo
Cristo al tiempo de su muerte.
     No bajan a desnudarle
los espíritus celestes,
sino soldados, que luego   15
sobre su ropa echan suertes.
     Quitáronle la corona,
y abriéronse tantas fuentes,
que todo el cuerpo divino
cubre la sangre que vierten.   20
     Al despegarle la ropa
las heridas reverdecen,
pedazos de carne y sangre
salieron entre los pliegues.
     Alma pegada en tus vicios,   25
si no puedes, o no quieres
despegarte tus costumbres,
piensa en esta ropa, y puede.

Come near and tell her, "Virgin pure,
    Shall I accompany you?"
For if you can remain with her
    Then heaven will envy you.   80

On Putting Him on the Cross
(Ballad)

While they are digging out the hole
    Where the Cross is to be placed,
On which the Lamb will then be raised,
    By serpent figure traced,

Those garments fine without a seam   5
    That Mary beautiful,
From Nazareth absent, after the birth
    Embroidered with heart full,

From his flesh delicate and fair
    With hands vile take away   10
The stewards that attended Christ
    When he met death that day.

Celestial spirits don't come down
    His nudeness to expose,
But soldiers there who afterward   15
    Cast lots for all his clothes.

So many fountains rushed to flow
    When they removed his crown,
That covers all his form divine
    The blood that's streaming down.   20

As they his clothing strip away,
    His wounds re-bloom afresh,
And there among the folds appeared
    Chunks of his bloody flesh.

Soul in your vices firmly stuck,   25
    If you cannot, don't plan
To rid yourself of them, think on
    These garments, and you can.

A la sangrienta cabeza
la dura corona vuelven,   30
que para mayor dolor
le coronaron dos veces.
 Asió la soga un soldado,
tirando a Cristo de suerte,
que donde va por su gusto,   35
quiere que por fuerza llegue.
 Dio Cristo en la cruz de ojos
arrojado de la gente,
que primero que la abrace,
quieren también que la bese.   40
 ¡Qué cama os está esperando,
mi Jesús, bien de mis bienes,
para que el cuerpo cansado
siquiera a morir se acueste!
 ¡Oh, qué almohada de rosas   45
las espinas os prometen!
¡Qué corredores dorados
los duros clavos crueles!
 Dormid en ella, mi amor,
para que el hombre despierte,   50
aunque más dura se os haga
que en Belén entre la nieve.
 Que en fin aquella tendría
abrigo de las paredes,
las tocas de vuestra Madre,   55
y el heno de aquellos bueyes.
 ¡Qué vergüenza la daría
al Cordero santo el verse,
siendo tan honesto y casto,
desnudo entre tanta gente!   60
 ¡Ay divina Madre suya!,
si agora llegáis a verle
en tan miserable estado,
¿quién ha de haber que os consuele?
 Mirad, Reina de los cielos,   65
si el mismo Señor es éste,
cuyas carnes parecían
de azucenas y claveles.

The crown so heavy they replace
    Upon his bloody head;   30
Thus they crowned him two times and he
    Has greater pain to dread.

A soldier grabbed hold of the rope,
    Christ pulling in such way,
That where it's his own choice to go,   35
    The man would have him stay.

Christ came upon the Cross, he whom
    The people see as foe;
They want, before he embrace the Cross,
    That he kiss it also.   40

My Jesus, good that is my good,
    What a bed awaits you nigh,
So that at least your body tired
    Can go to bed to die!

O what a bed of roses soft   45
    The thorns will you reward!
What corridors of finest gold
    The nails so cruel and hard!

Sleep tight in it, my precious love,
    That Man awake may go,   50
Although it harder seem for you
    Than Bethlehem in snow.

For finally that one would have
    A shelter in its walls,
The hay on which the oxen feed,   55
    And near your Mother's shawls.

What shame 'twould give the holy Lamb
    To see himself as nude,
His being so honest and so chaste,
    Among such people rude.   60

Ay, Mother divine of such a son,
    If you arrive here late,
Who could you consolation give
    In such a wretched state?

Queen of the heavens, look to see,   65
    Is this Lord of the Nations,
Whose body seemed to be before
    Of lilies and carnations?

Mas, ¡ay Madre de piedad!,
que sobre la cruz le tienden,   70
para tomar la medida
por donde los clavos entren.
        ¡Oh terrible desatino!,
medir el inmenso quieren,
pero bien cabrá en la cruz   75
el que cupo en el pesebre.
        Ya Jesús está de espaldas,
y tantas penas padece,
que con ser la cruz tan dura,
ya por descanso la tiene.   80
        Alma de pórfido y mármol,
mientras en tus vicios duermes,
dura cama tiene Cristo:
no te despierte la muerte.

A la muerte de Carlos Félix

Este de mis entrañas dulce fruto,
con vuestra bendición, oh Rey eterno,
ofrezco humildemente a vuestras aras;
que si es de todos el mejor tributo
un puro corazón humilde y tierno,   5
y el más precioso de las prendas caras,
no las aromas raras
entre olores fenicios
y licores sabeos,
os rinden mis deseos,   10
por menos olorosos sacrificios,
sino mi corazón, que Carlos era;
que en el que me quedó, menos os diera.

        Diréis, Señor, que en daros lo que es vuestro
ninguna cosa os doy, y que querría   15
hacer virtud necesidad tan fuerte,
y que no es lo que siento lo que muestro,
pues anima su cuerpo el alma mía,
y se divide entre los dos la muerte.

But they stretch him upon the Cross—
    Ay, Mother who mercy show!—   70
So they can take the measurements
    Where all the nails will go.

Oh ghastly deed! To measurement
    These men the vast submit,
But well will fit upon the Cross   75
    He who in manger fit.

Now Jesus is upon his back
    And he such sorrows bears
That though the Cross so hard now is
    He thinks he's without cares.   80

Soul of cold marble, porphyry,
    While you in vices sleep,
Christ has the hardest kind of bed:
    May death leave you asleep.

On the Death of Carlos Félix

    This of my very bowels tender fruit,
With your firm blessing—Oh Eternal King!—
With downcast eyes I offer at your shrine,
For if this is of all the best tribute,
A spotless heart, now tender, faltering,   5
And that most precious of all treasures fine,
Not heady smell of wine
Among Phoenician scents,
And strong Sabaean brew,
My wants thus yield to you   10
For sacrifices of less redolence,
But my own heart, which Carlos was for me,
For that one left to give you, less would be.

    You'll say, my Lord, that giving you what's yours
I give you nothing, that I'd like to make   15
A virtue of a hard necessity,
And that my heart feels not what it assures,
For my soul does his body bring awake,
And between us two death does division find.

Confieso que de suerte   20
vive a la suya asida,
que cuanto a la vil tierra,
que el ser mortal encierra,
tuviera más contento de su vida;
mas cuanto al alma, ¿qué mayor consuelo   25
que lo que pierdo yo me gane el cielo?

    Póstrese nuestra vil naturaleza
a vuestra voluntad, imperio sumo,
autor de nuestro límite, Dios santo;
no repugne jamás nuestra bajeza,   30
sueño de sombra, polvo, viento y humo,
a lo que vos queréis, que podéis tanto;
afréntese del llanto
injusto, aunque forzoso,
aquella inferior parte   35
que a la sangre reparte
materia de dolor tan lastimoso,
porque donde es inmensa la distancia,
como no hay proporción, no hay repugnancia.

    Quiera yo lo que vos, pues no es posible   40
no ser lo que queréis, que no queriendo,
saco mi daño a vuestra ofensa junto.
Justísimo sois vos: es imposible
dejar de ser error lo que pretendo,
pues es mi nada indivisible punto.   45
Si a los cielos pregunto
vuestra circunferencia
immensa, incircunscrita,
pues que sólo os limita
con margen de piedad vuestra clemencia,   50
¡oh guarda de los hombres!, yo ¿qué puedo
adonde tiembla el serafín de miedo?

    Y vos, dichoso niño, que en siete años
que tuvistes de vida, no tuvistes
con vuestro padre inobediencia alguna,   55
corred con vuestro ejemplo mis engaños,
serenad mis paternos ojos tristes,
pues ya sois sol, donde pisáis la luna;
de la primera cuna
a la postrera cama   60
no distes sola un hora
de disgusto, y agora
parece que le dais, si así se llama
lo que es pena y dolor de parte nuestra,
pues no es la culpa, aunque es la causa, vuestra.   65

I admit it's fortune kind   20
My soul to his is seized;
As for vile earth that holds
All mortals in her folds,
She with his life here would be better pleased;
As for my soul, what greater balm than this: 25
With what I lose I thus gain heaven's bliss?

    Let our vile human nature bend the knee
Before your holy will, empire supreme,
The author of our limits, Holy One;
Let not our loneliness repugnant be,   30
Of shadow, dust, of wind, of smoke and dream,
To what you will, whose strength is never outdone;
For unjust weeping done,
Though unavoidable,
Let that inferior part   35
Shame suffer to impart
To blood the matter of pain formidable,
For where the distance really is immense,
There's no repugnance with such difference.

    Your will show me, since it's not possible   40
To not be what you will; not loving you
I'm for my hurt, your wounds, responsible.
Extremely just are you; it's impossible
Not to be error what I try to do:
My nothingness is point indivisible.   45
If I heaven merciful
Ask your circumference,
Immense, uncircumscribed,
For only is circumscribed
With mercy's margin your benevolence,   50
Oh keeper of all men, how weak am I,
While seraphim of fear atremble cry! . . .

    And you, child blest, who in the seven years
You had of life, in that time never had
A disobedient act mean-spirited,   55
With your example chase my frauds and sneers;
Bring calm to my paternal eyes so sad,
For you are sun where upon the moon you tread.
Even when on your death-bed,
As in your cradle small,   60
You never gave a day
Of worry, and today
It seems you do give it, if such we call
What now is pain and sorrow on my part;
Though you're the cause, blame is a thing apart. . . .   65

Yo para vos los pajarillos nuevos,
diversos en el canto y las colores,
encerraba, gozoso de alegraros;
yo plantaba los fértiles renuevos
de los árboles verdes, yo las flores,   70
en quien mejor pudiera contemplaros,
pues a los aires claros
del alba hermosa apenas
salistes, Carlos mío,
bañado de rocío,   75
cuando, marchitas las doradas venas,
el blanco lirio convertido en hielo,
cayó en la tierra, aunque traspuesto al cielo.

¡Oh qué divinos pájaros agora,
Carlos, gozáis, que con pintadas alas   80
discurren por los campos celestiales
en el jardín eterno, que atesora
por cuadros ricos de doradas salas
más hermosos jacintos orientales,
adonde a los mortales   85
ojos la luz excede!
¡Dichoso yo, que os veo
donde está mi deseo
y donde no tocó pesar, ni puede;
que sólo con el bien de tal memoria   90
toda la pena me trocáis en gloria!

La inteligencia que los orbes mueve
a la celeste máquina divina
dará mil tornos con su hermosa mano,
fuego el León, el Sagitario nieve;   95
y vos, mirando aquella esencia trina,
ni pasaréis invierno ni verano,
y desde el soberano
lugar que os ha cabido,
los bellísimos ojos,   100
paces de mis enojos,
humillaréis a vuestro patrio nido;
y si mi llanto vuestra luz divisa,
los dos claveles bañaréis en risa.

Y os di la mejor patria que yo pude   105
para nacer, y agora, en vuestra muerte,
entre santos dichosa sepultura;
resta que vos roguéis a Dios que mude
mi sentimiento en gozo, de tal suerte,
que a pesar de la sangre que procura   110

I then those different little birds for you,
Diverse both in their color and their song,
In cages kept, to please you, fortunate;
I planted many fertile shoots that grew
Upon the trees, and flowers all along   70
In which I better you could contemplate,
For in air delicate,
My Carlos, with first day
You briefly came to view,
Bathed in the morning dew,   75
When, golden veins then withering away,
The snow-white lily now of ice composed
Fell to the earth, although to heaven transposed.

     Oh Carlos, what divine birds there today
You glory in, who with their colored wings   80
Now roam about the fields celestial
In that eternal garden, which stores away
In art in rooms with golden furnishings
Oriental hyacinths most beautiful,
And where light powerful   85
Exceeds mere mortal eyes!
Blest I, who you admire
From here with my desire,
Which there did never weigh, nor tries;
For only with the good of memory   90
In glory you change all my grief for me. . . .

     The intelligence that all the orbs makes go
Of that celestial machine divine
Will give a thousand turns with its hand fair,
The Lion as fire, Sagittarius as snow;   95
And you, as you behold that essence trine,
Will spend no summer and no winter there,
And in that sovereign air
Where you have found your place,
Your eyes so fair repose,   100
Peace for my angry woes,
You will humiliate your own birth-place;
And if your light descry my lamentations,
In laughter you will bathe your two carnations.

     I gave to you the best home that I could   105
For your birth here, and in your death, today
Among the saints in happy burial place;
Now left to you ask God if change he would
My sorrow into joy, in such a way
That in spite of the blood that would erase   110

cubrir de noche escura
la luz de esta memoria,
viváis vos en la mía;
que espero que algún día
la que me da dolor me dará gloria,   115
viendo al partir de aquesta tierra ajena,
que no quedáis adonde todo es pena.

Dios, centro del alma

Si fuera de mi amor verdad el fuego,
él caminara a tu divina esfera;
pero es cometa que corrió ligera
con resplandor que se deshizo luego.

¡Qué deseoso de tus brazos llego   5
cuando el temor mis culpas considera!
Mas si mi amor en ti no persevera,
¿en qué centro mortal tendrá sosiego?

Voy a buscarte, y cuanto más te encuentro,
menos reparo en ti, Cordero manso,   10
aunque me buscas tú del alma adentro.

Pero dime, Señor: si hallar descanso
no puede el alma fuera de su centro,
y estoy fuera de ti, ¿cómo descanso?

And with dark night replace
Light of this memory,
May you in mine ever stay;
For I hope that some day
Instead of pain it glory will give me,   115
When I no more on alien earth remain,
For you do not abide where all is pain.

God, Center of the Soul

If of my love the flame burned truthfully,
Then it would journey to your sacred sphere;
It comet is that flashed in brief career
With splendid gleam that vanished suddenly.

How to your arms I come in necessity   5
When my deep faults are pondered by my fear!
Yet can my love in you not persevere,
What mortal center grants serenity?

I go in search of you, Lamb ever meek:
You meeting more, less is my interest,   10
Though you inside my very soul do seek.

Tell me, however, Lord: if to find rest
The soul outside its center knows hope bleak,
If I am outside you, how can I rest?

From *Triunfos divinos*

Selecciones de Varios Libros y de
las Comedias de Lope de Vega

Selections from Various Books and from
the Plays of Lope de Vega

Castitas Res Est

La calidad elementar resiste
mi amor, que a la virtud celeste aspira,
y en las mentes angélicas se mira,
donde la idea del calor consiste.

No ya como elemento el fuego viste   5
el alma, cuyo vuelo al sol admira,
que de inferiores mundos se retira,
adonde el querubín ardiendo asiste.

No puede elementar fuego abrasarme;
la virtud celestial, que vivifica,   10
envidia el verme a la suprema alzarme.

Que donde el fuego angélico me aplica,
¿cómo podrá mortal poder tocarme?
Que eterno y fin contradición implica.

Amor con tan honesto pensamiento
arde en mi pecho, y con tan dulce pena,
que haciendo grave honor de la cadena,
para cantar me sirve de instrumento.

No al fuego humano, al celestial atento;   5
en alabanza de *Amarilis* suena
con esta voz, que el curso el agua enfrena,
mueve la selva y enamora el viento.

La luz primera del primero día,
luego que el sol nació, toda la encierra   10
círculo ardiente de su lumbre pura:

Y así también, cuando tu sol nacía,
todas las hermosuras de la tierra
remitieron su luz a tu hermosura.

Castitas Res Est

My love the basic quality resists,
Love that to virtue heavenly aspires,
And in the minds of angels one admires,
There where idea of warmth and heat consists.

Not now as element the fire persists   5
Around the soul, whose flight the sun admires,
Which from worlds far inferior retires,
To where the burning cherubin assists.

The elemental fire cannot burn me;
Celestial virtue, that which vivifies,   10
My rising envies toward supremacy.

Thus where angelic fire to me applies,
How can a merely mortal force touch me?
For end-eternal contradiction implies.

From *La Filomena*

Love with such honest thought beneficent
Burns in my breast, and with such tender pains,
That doing gravest honor to the chains,
To sing they can serve me as instrument.

With heavenly, not human, fire intent;   5
In praise of Amaryllis sound the strains
Of this my voice, which water's course restrains,
The forest moves, and charms winds violent.

The initial light of that first day at morn,
The sun's birth new, with its pure fire aglow   10
All is enclosed in circle burning bright.

And thus too, when your soul was being born,
All of the beauties of the earth below
Then yielded to your beauty their own light.

From *La Circe*

Soneto

Quien dice que es amor cuerpo visible,
¡qué poco del amor perfeto sabe!
Que es el honesto amor llama süave
a los humanos ojos invisible.

Es su divina esfera inacesible   5
a materia mortal, a cuerpo grave;
no hay fin que su inmortal principio acabe,
como acabarse el alma es imposible.

Tú, Persio, como tienes a tu lado
un cuerpo igual al tuyo, no imaginas   10
que hay limpio amor en noble amor fundado.

Yo, que soy alma todo, en peregrinas
regiones voy de un genio acompañado
que me enseña de amor ciencias divinas.

Soneto

De la beldad divina incomprehensible
a las mentes angélicas deciende
la pura luz, que desde allí trasciende
el alma deste punto indivisible.

A la materia corporal visible   5
da vida y movimiento, el sol enciende,
conserva el fuego, el aire, el agua extiende,
la tierra viste amena y apacible.

Enseña nuestro humano entendimiento
de un grado en otro a contemplar la cumbre   10
de donde viene tanta gloria al suelo.

Y entre los ecos de tu claro acento,
halla mi honesto amor tan alta lumbre,
que en oyendo tu voz penetra el cielo.

Sonnet

He who says love is body visible,
How little of the perfect love he knows!
For honest love is flame that softly glows,
Flame to our human eyes invisible.

Its sphere divine is inaccessible   5
To mortal matter, body that pain knows;
No aim can this great principle depose,
Since ending for the soul is impossible.

You, Persius, as you have at your side
A body much like yours, don't even dream   10
That pure love can be based on noble love.

For I, who am all soul, in regions wide
Go about accompanied by force supreme
That teaches me the science divine of love.

From *La Circe*

From beauty divine incomprehensible
Down to the minds angelical descends
The purest light, which enters and amends
The soul from this point indivisible.

To matter corporal and visible   5
It life and motion gives, the sun flame lends,
Conserves the fire, the air, the water extends,
The earth decks out as mild and affable.

It thus our human understanding trains
By slow degrees to contemplate the crests   10
Where glory for earth's regions emanates.

And in the echoes of your lucid strains
My honest love such lofty glow attests
That hearing your voice it heaven penetrates.

From *La Circe*

Soneto

Beautus qui invenit amicum verum.

Eccl., cap. 35.

Yo dije siempre, y lo diré, y lo digo,
que es la amistad el bien mayor humano;
mas ¿qué español, qué griego, qué romano
nos ha de dar este perfeto amigo?

Alabo, reverencio, amo, bendigo   5
aquél a quien el cielo soberano
dio un amigo perfeto, y no es en vano;
que fue, confieso, liberal conmigo.

Tener un grande amigo y obligalle
es el último bien, y, por querelle,   10
el alma, el bien y el mal comunicalle;

mas yo quiero vivir sin conocelle;
que no quiero la gloria de ganalle
por no tener el miedo de perdelle.

Temores en el Favor

Cuando en mis manos, rey eterno, os miro,
y la cándida víctima levanto,
de mi atrevida indignidad me espanto
y la piedad de vuestro pecho admiro.

Tal vez el alma con temor retiro,   5
tal vez la doy al amoroso llanto,
que arrepentido de ofenderos tanto
con ansias temo y con dolor suspiro.

Volved los ojos a mirarme humanos
que por las sendas de mi error siniestras   10
me despeñaron pensamientos vanos;

Sonnet

Beatus qui invenit amicum verum.

Eccl., Ch. 35.

I always said, I say, and I will say
That friendship does our greatest good remain;
What Greek, what Roman, or what man from Spain
Can in himself that perfect friend display?

I praise, revere, care for, and blessings pray   5
For him whom heaven that does sovereign reign
Did give a perfect friend, and not in vain;
It liberal was with me, I have to say.

To have and to oblige this noble friend
Would be the finest good, and loving him,   10
The soul the good, the bad to him commend.

But I prefer to live not meeting him,
For I don't want the gift of such a friend,
So as not to have the fear of losing him.

From *La Circe*

Fears Concerning His Favor

When in my hands I see you, eternal sire,
And I raise up the victim innocent,
I shudder at my baseness truculent,
And I the mercy of your breast admire.

Perchance the soul with terror I retire,   5
Perchance give it to amorous lament,
For I of much offending you repent;
With pain I sigh and fretfulness acquire.

Your human eyes please fix again on me,
For on gross paths of needed reprimands   10
My foolish thoughts cast me down steep incline;

no sean tantas las miserias nuestras
que a quien os tuvo en sus indignas manos
vos le dejéis de las divinas vuestras.

Boscán, tarde llegamos—. ¿Hay posada?
—Llamad desde la posta, Garcilaso.
—¿Quiés es? —Dos caballeros del Parnaso.
—No hay donde nocturnar palestra armada.

—No entiendo lo que dice la criada.   5
Madona, ¿qué decís? —Que afecten paso,
que obstenta limbos el mentido ocaso
y el sol depingen la porción rosada.

—¿Estás en ti, mujer? —Negóse el tino
el ambulante huésped—. ¡Que en tan poco   10
tiempo tal lengua entre cristianos haya!

Boscán, perdido habemos el camino,
preguntad por Castilla, que estoy loco
o no habemos salido de Vizcaya.

Canta, cisne andaluz, que el verde coro
del Tajo escucha tu divino acento,
si, ingrato, el Betis no responde atento
al aplauso que debe a tu decoro.

Más de tu *Soledad* el eco adoro   5
que el alma y voz de lírico portento,
pues tú solo pusiste al instrumento,
sobre trastes de plata, cuerdas de oro.

Let our misfortunes not so many be
That he who held you in unworthy hands
You him abandon far from yours divine.

From *Triunfos divinos*

"Is there still room? Boscán, we have come late."
"Call, Garcilaso, from posthouse direct."
"Who is it?" "Two Parnassian knights select."
"Palestra armed cannot here nocturnate."

"I know not what this maid wants to relate.   5
Madonna, what say you?" "Your way affect,
False sunset showy edges does project
And they depict sun's portion roseate."

"Dear woman, are you mad?" "Guest ambulant
Has lost insight." "Strange that in such brief span   10
Of time such language Christian folk can spill!"

"Boscán, that we have lost our way I grant;
Ask for Castile, for I'm a crazy man
Or we indeed are in Basque country still."

From *El Laurel de Apolo*

Sing, Andalusian swan, for this green choir
Of Tagus harks to your divine accent,
If Betis, harsh, does not respond intent
With just applause your honor should inspire.

More of your *Solitudes* I echo admire   5
Than soul and voice of lyrical portent,
For you alone made into instrument
Of silver frets and golden strings your lyre.

Huya con pies de nieve Galatea,
gigante del Parnaso, que en tu llama,   10
sacra ninfa inmortal, arder desea.

Que como si la envidia te desama,
en ondas de cristal la lira orfea,
en círculos de sol irá tu fama.

A mis soledades voy . . .

A mis soledades voy,
de mis soledades vengo,
porque para andar conmigo
me bastan mis pensamientos.
    No sé qué tiene el aldea   5
donde vivo, y donde muero,
que con venir de mí mismo,
no puedo venir más lejos.
    Ni estoy bien ni mal conmigo;
mas dice mi entendimiento   10
que un hombre que todo es alma
está cautivo en su cuerpo.
    Entiendo lo que me basta,
y solamente no entiendo
cómo se sufre a sí mismo   15
un ignorante soberbio.
    De cuantas cosas me cansan,
fácilmente me defiendo;
pero no puedo guardarme
de los peligros de un necio.   20
    Él dirá que yo lo soy,
pero con falso argumento;
que humildad y necedad
no caben en un sujeto.

Let Galatea flee with feet of snow,
Parnassian giant you, for in your flame   10
Immortal sacred nymph desires to glow.

For in case envy comes to hate your name,
In crystal waves the Orphic lyre will go,
In circles of bright sun your lasting fame.

From *La Filomena*

Back from my solitudes I come . . .

Back from my solitudes I come,
    To solitudes I go,
Because when I walk by myself
    Sufficient my thoughts grow.

This village I know not where I   5
    Do live and die each day,
For coming from inside myself,
    I come from far away.

My moods are neither good nor bad
    But my clear mind is sure   10
That captive to the body is
    A man who is soul pure.

I know all that I need to know,
    I just don't understand
How some conceited simpleton   15
    In truth himself can stand.

I easily protect myself
    From things that me offend,
But from the onslaughts of a fool
    Myself I can't defend.   20

He'll say that I'm the fool and thus
    False argument submit,
For humbleness and foolishness
    Can't in one subject fit.

La diferencia conozco,   25
porque en él y en mí contemplo
su locura en su arrogancia,
mi humildad en mi desprecio.
    O sabe naturaleza
más que supo en este tiempo,   30
o tantos que nacen sabios
es porque lo dicen ellos.
    «Sólo sé que no sé nada»,
dijo un filósofo, haciendo
la cuenta con su humildad,   35
adonde lo más es menos.
    No me precio de entendido,
de desdichado me precio;
que los que no son dichosos,
¿cómo pueden ser discretos?   40
    No puede durar el mundo,
porque dicen, y lo creo,
que suena a vidro quebrado
y que ha de romperse presto.
    Señales son del jüicio   45
ver que todos le perdemos,
unos por carta de más,
otros por carta de menos.
    Dijeron que antiguamente
se fue la verdad al cielo: 50
tal la pusieron los hombres,
que desde entonces no ha vuelto.
    En dos edades vivimos
los propios y los ajenos:
la de plata los extraños,   55
y la de cobre los nuestros.
    ¿A quién no dará cuidado,
si es español verdadero,
ver los hombres a lo antiguo,
y el valor a lo moderno?   60
    Todos andan bien vestidos,
y quéjanse de los precios,
de medio arriba romanos,
de medio abajo romeros.

I know the difference, since in him,   25
    In me I can see born
His madness in his arrogance,
    My meekness in my scorn.

Either Nature different from before
    Is wiser in our day,   30
Or many of our brilliant wits
    Are wise since they such say.

"I only know I nothing know,"
    A philosopher did stress,
Thus seeing with humility   35
    Where more is always less.

I make no boast of what I know,
    Misfortune is my boast;
For those estranged from happiness,
    Can wit be uppermost?   40

The world can't last, because they say,
    And my mind this admits,
It rings like weakened glass that soon
    Will shatter into bits.

Some signs there are of Judgment Day,   45
    Since we are losing ours,
Some for their acting overbold,
    And some who waste their powers.

They said that in the ancient days
    To heaven truth adjourned;   50
Since then attacked on every hand
    It never has returned.

We live in different ages now,
    Ourselves and those outside,
They in a silver age, but we   55
    In copper age abide.

How can a Spaniard tried and true
    Not really worried be,
To see men as they were of old,
    And valor modern see?   60

Now all come forth dressed lavishly
    And urge that prices fall,
From waist up Romans in their pride,
    From waist down roamers all!

Dijo Dios que comería   65
su pan el hombre primero
en el sudor de su cara
por quebrar su mandamiento;
    y algunos, inobedientes
a la vergüenza y al miedo,   70
con las prendas de su honor
han trocado los efetos.
    Virtud y filosofía
peregrinan como ciegos;
el uno se lleva al otro,   75
llorando van y pidiendo.
    Dos polos tiene la tierra,
universal movimiento:
la mejor vida, el favor
la mejor sangre, el dinero.   80
    Oigo tañer las campanas,
y no me espanto, aunque puedo,
que en lugar de tantas cruces
haya tantos hombres muertos.
    Mirando estoy los sepulcros,   85
cuyos mármoles eternos
están diciendo sin lengua
que no lo fueron sus dueños.
    ¡Oh! ¡Bien haya quien los hizo,
porque solamente en ellos   90
de los poderosos grandes
se vengaron los pequeños!
    Fea pintan a la envidia;
yo confieso que la tengo
de unos hombres que no saben   95
quién vive pared en medio.
    Sin libros y sin papeles,
sin tratos, cuentas ni cuentos,
cuando quieren escribir,
piden prestado el tintero.   100
    Sin ser pobres ni ser ricos,
tienen chimenea y huerto;
no los despiertan cuidados,
ni pretensiones ni pleitos,

The Lord told Adam he must eat   65
    His bread by toil and sweat,
As penalty for turning from
    Commandment by God set,

And some, now disobedient
    Who shame and fear forget,   70
Have sense of honor cast aside
    And left things all upset.

Now Virtue and Philosophy,
    Blind pilgrims on their way,
The one the other carrying   75
    They weep and beg away.

Two poles there are upon the earth
    In eternal movement bold:
Where favor means the better life,
    The best blue blood is gold.   80

I hear the ringing of the bells,
    And barely escape from dread:
Instead of many crosses there,
    So many men lie dead.

I'm staring at the sepulchers   85
    Of eternal marble made,
That voiceless say their owners proud
    Were not, they soon to fade.

Blest be the maker of the tombs,
    For he did thus create   90
A place where all the poor could lie
    As equal with the great!

As ugly hag they envy paint,
    And I admit the same
For those few men who never know   95
    Their next-door-neighbor's name.

Without books, paper, and accounts,
    Relations, tales to tell,
Whenever they desire to write
    They even beg inkwell.   100

Thus being neither poor nor rich
    They hearth and garden keep:
Pretensions, lawsuits they don't have,
    Or cares to rob their sleep.

ni murmuraron del grande,   105
ni ofendieron al pequeño;
nunca, como yo, firmaron
parabién, ni Pascuas dieron.
    Con esta envidia que digo,
y lo que paso en silencio,   110
a mis soledades voy,
de mis soledades vengo.

Pobre barquilla mía . . .

    Pobre barquilla mía,
entre peñascos rota,
sin velas desvelada,
y entre las olas sola;
        ¿adónde vas perdida?   5
¿adónde, di, te engolfas?
que no hay deseos cuerdos
con esperanzas locas.
        Como las altas naves,
te apartas animosa   10
de la vecina tierra,
y al fiero mar te arrojas.
    Igual en las fortunas,
mayor en las congojas,
pequeño en las defensas,   15
incitas a las ondas,
    advierte que te llevan
a dar entre las rocas
de la soberbia envidia,
naufragio de las honras.   20
    Cuando por las riberas
andabas costa a costa,
nunca del mar temiste
las iras procelosas.

They never gossiped of the great,   105
    Or little folk maligned,
Like me, they gave no Easter gifts
    Or ceremonies signed.

With this the envy thus confessed,
    And more that I forego,
Back from my solitudes I come,
    To solitudes I go.

From *La Dorotea*

Poor little bark of mine . . .

    Poor little bark of mine,
Upon the reefs now thrown,
Without sails vigilant
Among the waves alone!

    Where are you bound, so lost,   5
Where, heading out to sea?
There are no sane desires
With mad hope running free.

    Like lofty galleon
You set forth spiritedly;   10
From friendly coast to sail
Upon the wild, wild sea,

    In fortune all the same,
In anguishes much worse,
And smaller in defense,   15
You challenge waves adverse.

    Be warned, for they'll cast you
Upon the rocky reef
Of envy proud where wrecked
All honor comes to grief.

    When you then sailed the coasts   20
With landmarks obvious,
You never feared the sea
In rage tempestuous.

     Segura navegabas;
que por la tierra propia   25
nunca el peligro es mucho
adonde el agua es poca.
     Verdad es que en la patria
no es la virtud dichosa,
ni se estimó la perla   30
hasta dejar la concha.
     Dirás que muchas barcas
con el favor en popa,
saliendo desdichadas,
volvieron venturosas.   35
     No mires los ejemplos
de las que van y tornan;
que a muchas ha perdido
la dicha de las otras.
     Para los altos mares   40
no llevas cautelosa,
ni velas de mentiras,
ni remos de lisonjas.
     ¿Quién te engañó, barquilla?
Vuelve, vuelve la proa,   45
que presumir de nave
fortunas ocasiona.
     ¿Qué jarcias te entretejen?
¿Qué ricas banderolas
azote son del viento   50
y de las aguas sombra?
     ¿En qué gabia descubres,
del árbol alta copa,
la tierra en perspectiva
del mar incultas orlas?   55
     ¿En qué celajes fundas
que es bien echar la sonda,
cuando, perdido el rumbo,
erraste la derrota?
     Si te sepulta arena,   60
¿qué sirve fama heroica?
Que nunca desdichados
sus pensamientos logran.

In confidence you sailed,
With native shores nearby,   25
For danger is never much
Where shallow waters lie.

It's true in our own land
That Virtue fares not well;
The pearl was never esteemed   30
Until it left the shell.

You'll say that many ships
With favoring winds behind,
Outgoing miserable,
Returning triumph did find.   35

Don't those examples choose
That have the waters crossed,
For those who had success
Have many others lost.

On high seas venturing,   40
You neither cunning know,
Nor oars of flattery,
Nor sails that falsehoods show.

Who tricked you, little bark?
Turn back, turn back the prow;   45
To strive like galleon
Will trouble bring you now.

What riggings you bedeck,
What pennants bright displayed
Are whipping in the wind   50
And do the waters shade?

From what crow's nest do you
Spy crown of lofty tree,
Earth in perspective sharp,
Rough fringes of the sea?   55

What cloudglow serves as base,
That you a sounding force,
When you your bearings lost,
Strayed from your chosen course?

How can bright fame serve you,   60
You buried in the sand?
Those who misfortune know
Their goals cannot command.

¿Qué importa que te ciñan
ramas verdes o rojas,   65
que en selvas de corales
salado césped brota?
    Laureles de la orilla
solamente coronan
navíos de alto bordo   70
que jarcias de oro adornan.
    No quieras que yo sea
por tu soberbia pompa
Faetonte de barqueros,
que los laureles lloran.   75
    Pasaron ya los tiempos,
cuando lamiendo rosas
el céfiro bullía
y suspiraba aromas.
    Ya fieros huracanes   80
tan arrogantes soplan,
que, salpicando estrellas,
del Sol la frente mojan.
    Ya los valientes rayos
de la vulcana forja,   85
en vez de torres altas,
abrasan pobres chozas.
    Contenta con tus redes,
a la playa arenosa
mojado me sacabas;   90
pero vivo, ¿qué importa?
    Cuando de rojo nácar
se afeitaba la aurora,
más peces te llenaban
que ella lloraba aljófar.   95
    Al bello sol que adoro,
enjuta ya la ropa,
nos daba una cabaña
la cama de sus hojas.
    Esposo me llamaba,   100
yo la llamaba esposa,
parándose de envidia
la celestial antorcha.

What good if you are crowned
With branches red or green,   65
Where in a coral wood,
The salt-dipped grass is seen.

Bay trees along the shore
A special crown withold
For those high-riding ships   70
Whose rigging gleams in gold.

You in your prideful pomp
Will not desire that I
Phaethon of boatmen be,
Those whom the laurels cry.   75

The times are now no more
When zephyr breeze was streaming
And licking roses red,
Aromas gently teeming.

Ferocious hurricanes   80
Blow arrogantly now,
The stars bespattering,
And wetting great sun's brow.

Now from old Vulcan's forge
The flashing bolts and rays,   85
Instead of towers high,
Poor huts and hovels raze.

Content with all your nets,
Up to a sandy spot
You brought me, fully drenched,   90
But still alive—then what?

When dawn with mother-of-pearl
In rouge her face was steeping,
Your hold would have more fish
Than pearls that she was weeping.   95

In fair sun I adore,
My clothes now fully dry,
A bower gave to us
Its bed of leaves nearby.

Her husband she called me,   100
And I called her my bride,
While torch celestial
Its envy could not hide.

Sin pleito, sin disgusto,
la muerte nos divorcia: 105
¡ay de la pobre barca
que en lágrimas se ahoga!
    Quedad sobre la arena,
inútiles escotas;
que no ha menester velas   110
quien a su bien no torna.
    Si con eternas plantas
las fijas luces doras,
¡oh dueño de mi barca!,
y en dulce paz reposas,   115
    merezca que le pidas
al bien que eterno gozas,
que adonde estás me lleve
más pura y más hermosa.
    Mi honesto amor te obligue;   120
que no es digna vitoria
para quejas humanas
ser las deidades sordas.
    Mas ¡ay que no me escuchas!
Pero la vida es corta: 125
viviendo, todo falta;
muriendo, todo sobra.

Without trial or disgust,
Death now casts us apart;   105
Ay, pity this poor bark,
Where tears now flood the heart!

Remain there, useless sails,
Upon the sandy shore,
For he does not need sails   110
Who'll see his love no more.

If you the fixed stars gild
With your eternal feet,
O mistress of my bark,
Who rest in peace so sweet,   115

May I beg you ask him
In whom you joy forever,
That he take me to you,
More pure and fair than ever.

May my true love you sway;   120
For gods who can deaf be
To man's plaints won't enjoy
A worthy victory.

Ay, you're not hearing me!
However, brief is life: 125
While living, all is scarce,
In dying, things are rife.

From *La Dorotea*

Que de noche le mataron
al caballero,
la gala de Medina,
la flor de Olmedo.

Sombras le avisaron   5
que no saliese,
y le aconsejaron
que no se fuese
el caballero,
la gala de Medina,   10
la flor de Olmedo.

Trébole, ¡ay Jesús, cómo huele!
Trébole, ¡ay Jesús, qué olor!

Trébole de la casada
que a su esposo quiere bien;
de la doncella también,
entre paredes guardada,
que fácilmente engañada,   5
sigue su primero amor.
    Trébole, ¡ay Jesús, cómo huele!
Trébole, ¡ay Jesús, qué olor!

Trébole de la soltera,
que tantos amores muda;   10
trébole de la vïuda
que otra vez casarse espera,
tocas blancas por defuera
y el faldellín de color.
    Trébole, ¡ay Jesús, cómo huele!   15
Trébole, ¡ay Jesús, qué olor!

So they struck down this knight
    At darkest hour,
Medina's pride and joy,
    Olmedo's flower.

Shadows cautioned him   5
    Not to depart,
And they admonished him
    That he not start,
    This noble knight,
Olmedo's flower fair,   10
    Medina's light.

    Sweet clover, Lord, oh how it smells!
Sweet clover, Jesus, what a scent!

    Sweet clover of the woman wed
Who truly loves her husband well;
And of the maiden lass as well
In her own house unvisited,
For although easily misled   5
She follows her first love intent.
    Sweet clover, Lord, oh how it smells!
Sweet clover, Jesus, what a scent!

    Sweet clover of the lass still free
Who sheds so many loves not true;   10
Sweet clover of the widow too,
Who once more married hopes to be,
Outside, a head-dress white wears she,
Inside, bright colors lend accent.
    Sweet clover, Lord, oh how it smells!   15
Sweet clover, Jesus, what a scent!

Caminito toledano,
¡quién te tuviera ya andado!

Echen las mañanas
después del rocío
en espadas verdes
guarnición de lirios.

¡Cómo retumban los remos,
madre, en el agua,
con el fresco viento
de la mañana!

Manzanares claro,
río pequeño,
por faltarle el agua
corre con fuego.

Linda molinera,
moler os vi yo,
y era la harina
carbón junto a vos.

Road going down Toledo way,
Would that your miles behind me lay!

Let mornings then send forth
    In dewy sheen
A jewel of irises
    In swords of green.

How in the water, mother,
    Resound the oars,
As in the early morning
    Fresh breeze now soars!

Small Manzanares River
    Its clearness shows;
Since it has little water
    With fire it flows.

I watched you, miller lass,
    Your milling do;
The flour then became
    Coal next to you.

Río de Sevilla,
¡cuán bien pareces,
con galeras blancas
y ramos verdes!

En el Grao de Valencia,
noche de San Juan,
todo el fuego que tengo
truje de la mar.

Verdes tienes los ojos,
niña, los jueves,
que si fueran azules
no fueran verdes.

No corráis, vientecillos,
con tanta prisa,
porque al son de las aguas
duerme la niña.

Apacibles prados
creced las hierbas,
que ganado de oro
pasa por ellas.

River of Seville,
  O sparkling scene,
With snow-white caravels
  And garlands green!

On St. John's night in June
Along Valencia's coast,
I brought back from the sea
All of this fire I boast.

Sweet lass, on Thursdays green
  Your eyes are seen;
If only they were blue,
  They'd not be green.

Don't run so, little winds,
  And rush to pass,
For to the waters' sound
  Now sleeps the lass.

Sweet meadows mild,
Your grasses grow;
My golden flock
Through them must go.

Un soneto me manda hacer Violante,
que en mi vida me he visto en tanto aprieto;
catorce versos dicen que es soneto;
burla burlando van los tres delante.

Yo pensé que no hallara consonante,   5
y estoy a la mitad de otro cuarteto;
mas si me veo en el primer terceto,
no hay cosa en los cuartetos que me espante.

Por el primer terceto voy entrando,
y parece que entré con pie derecho,   10
pues fin con este verso le voy dando.

Ya estoy en el segundo, y aun sospecho
que voy los trece versos acabando;
contad si son catorce, y está hecho.

¡Qué pas gozara el mundo si no hubiera
nacido amor ni su furor mostrara!
Troya estuviera en pie, Grecia reinara,
ociosa y sin valor la guerra fuera.

Ni tortolilla en álamo gimiera,   5
ni toro en bosque de dolor bramara,
ni su cama el celoso ensangrentara,
ni el mar tranquilo arar su campos viera.

No tuviera las almas el profundo
que le dieron Briseida, Elena y Cava,   10
Cava española y el Sinón segundo.

Pero perdona, amor, que me olvidaba
de que por ti se ha conservado el mundo,
pues más engendras que la muerte acaba.

crea ...
carta a tu amigo Herna...
hace (presente).

Antes

Ahora

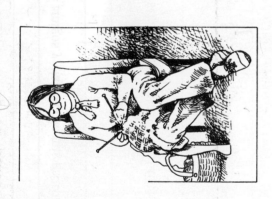

Panamá, 10 de enero

Querido Hernando:

No lo vas a creer; acabo de ver a Paulina Mateos. ¿La recuerdas?

Recuerdas que era una poca gorda con anteojos y pelo largo.
Ella trabajaba en su casa. Estaba muy triste.

_____
_____ .

Pues ahora ella está delgada con con tactivos y pelo
corto. Ella trabaja en la oficina y estaba muy contenta
con su trabajo.

_____
_____
_____ .

_____

Un abrazo,

Graciela

_____

Actividad 16: ¡Cómo cambiamos! Paulina asistió a la universidad contigo. La viste ayer y qué... cómo está... parece una persona totalmente diferente. Mira estas dos fotos (imperfecto), y cómo es Paulina hoy y qué... cómo es Paulina diferente. Describe cómo era y qué hacía Paulina (imperfecto).

La viste ayer y escríbele hoy y qué puedes escribirle una...

M

D   _____ en adultos.

_____ hoy los niños de la escuela donde enseño en los Estados Unidos   ¿verbo?
                                                                                 que

_____ sus padres.

_____ de amigos

_____ familia

MARISEL   Son como pequeños adultos; casi no tienen infancia.

DIANA   Pero eso no es todo; también _la habilidad de controlar a sus estudiantes._ _ningunos de los maestros tienen_

MAR   ¡Es una lástima!

alcohol es muy malo.

no olvide de usar
la "a" "personal"

Amanda Menendez
Gulay

Viola bids that I a sonnet make,
And such a fix I've never seen as yet;
A sonnet's fourteen lines they say are set;
Here are three now and I'm just half-awake.

I thought my rhymes I'd simply have to fake,   5
And here I'm halfway through this new quartet,
But if I can to that first tercet get,
In two quartets still nothing makes me quake.

Into first tercet I'm now entering,
And it appears I entered set to run,   10
For with this verse its end I'm rendering.

I even suspect, now in the second one,
That thirteen verses I am finishing:
If there fourteen are count, and it is done.

If love had not been born, what peace would see
The world, love's furor never on display!
Troy would be standing, Greece would still hold sway;
As useless, without value war would be.

No turtledove would wail in poplar tree,   5
Nor fighting bull in forest roar away,
Nor jealous one his bed with blood would spray,
Nor see fresh-plowed its fields the tranquil sea.

Souls would not have the hellish gravity
Which Helen and Briseis and Cava served,   10
The Spanish Cava, other Sinon's friend.

But, love, I was forgetting, pardon me:
Through you alone the world has been preserved,
For you engender more than death can end.

Rimas Humanas y Divinas
del Licenciado Tomé de Burguillos

Rhymes Human and Divine
of the Licentiate Tomé de Burgillos

El Conde Claros al Licenciado
Tomé de Burguillos

España de Poetas que te honoran,
Garcilaso es el Príncipe, el segundo
Camoes, tan heroico, tan fecundo,
que en repetido Sol su nombre adoran;

Figueroa y Herrera te decoran,   5
los dos Lupercios, y admirando el mundo
Borja, de cuyo ingenio alto y profundo
la pura lengua y Arte se mejoran.

Sin éstos, o provectos o noveles
que a número no puedo reducillos: 10
pero entre tantas plumas y pinceles,

Viva Vuestra Merced, señor Burguillos,
que más quiere aceitunas que laureles,
y siempre se corona de tomillos.

1
Desconfianza de sus versos

Los que en sonoro verso y dulce rima
hacéis conceto de escuchar poeta
versificante en forma de estafeta,
que a toda dirección número imprima:

oíd de un Caos la materia prima,   5
no culta como cifras de receta,
que en lengua pura, fácil, limpia y neta
yo invento, Amor escribe, el tiempo lima.

Estas, en fin, reliquias de la llama
dulce que me abrasó, si de provecho   10
no fueren a la venta, ni a la fama,

sea mi dicha tal, que a su despecho
me traiga en el cartón quien me defama,
que basta por laurel su hermoso pecho.

Count Claros to the Licentiate
Tomé de Burguillos

Oh Spain of poets who your honor sing
(The Prince is Garcilaso, second reigns
Camöens, with his rich, heroic strains,
Whose name in Sun repeated they make ring);

Herrera, Figueroa you honor bring,   5
The two Lupercios, and the world sustains
That Borja, from whose wit of high, deep veins
The language pure and Art are profiting.

Not counting these, the new, the seasoned grow
In numbers such as I cannot set down: 10
Among so many pens and brushes though,

Burguillos, may Your Grace live in renown,
Who more than laurel love your olives so,
And always of wild thyme you wear a crown.

1
Distrust in His Verses

You who in sonorous verse and dulcet rhyme
Do make conceit of hearing poetry
Of versifiers who like couriers flee
In all directions making measures chime:

Hear from a Chaos deep the matter prime   5
(Not euphuistic like a recipe),
That in a language pure, clear, simple, free,
I can invent, Love writes, and smoothens time.

These, in a word, these relics of the flame
So sweet that set me aglow, if at the best   10
They do not sell, or fail to bring me fame,

Be such my luck, that with her spite obsessed
May she a copy wear who brands my name:
Enough of laurel is her lovely breast.

2
Propone lo que ha de cantar en fe de
los méritos del sujeto

Celebró de Amarilis la hermosura
Virgilio en su Bucólica divina,
Propercio de su Cintia, y de Corina
Ovidio en oro, en rosa, en nieve pura.

Catulo de su Lesbia la escultura   5
a la inmortalidad pórfido inclina;
Petrarca por el mundo peregrina
Constituyó de Laura la figura.

Yo, pues, amor me manda que presuma
de la humilde prisión de tus cabellos,   10
Poeta Montañés, con ruda pluma;

Juana, celebraré tus ojos bellos,
que vale más de tu jabón la espuma,
que todas ellas, y que todos ellos.

7
No se atreve a pintar su dama muy hermosa
por no mentir que es mucho para poeta

Bien puedo yo pintar una hermosura,
y de otras cinco retratar a Elena,
pues a Filis también, siendo morena,
ángel, Lope llamó, de nieve pura.

Bien puedo yo fingir una escultura,   5
que disculpe mi amor, y en dulce vena
convertir a Filene en Filomena,
brillando claros en la sombra escura.

Mas puede ser que algún letor extrañe
estas musas de Amor hiperboleas,   10
y viéndola después se desengañe.

Pues si ha de hallar algunas partes feas,
Juana, no quiera Dios que a nadie engañe:
basta que para mí tan linda seas.

2
He proposes what he is to sing
in light of the merits of the subject

The beauty of Amaryllis Vergil told
In song, in his Bucolics near-divine;
Propertius, Cynthia's; and Ovid fine
Corinne's in rose, in purest snow, in gold;

    Catullus of his Lesbia in sculpture bold   5
Does porphyry to everness incline;
And Petrarch too the figure peregrine
Of Laura for the wider world extolled.

    Thus I, since Love commands I do likewise,
Held in the humble prison of your hair,   10
A mountain poet, with unlettered pen,

    I, Jane, will celebrate your lovely eyes,
For your soapbubbles greater worth declare
Than all these ladies, and than all these men.

7
He doesn't dare to paint his Lady very beautiful
so as not to lie, which is much for a poet

I well can paint a beauty with touch sure,
And Helen from another five portray;
For Phyllis, too, though she dark skin display,
Once Lope called her angel of snow pure.

    I well can feign a sculpture to endure   5
That may my love excuse, and in sweet way
To Philomela change Philene one day,
Light-facets gleaming in the shadow obscure.

    It may be that some reader see as rude
These hyperbolic muses of such Love,   10
And seeing her then disenchanted be.

    If he is bound to find some features crude,
My Jane (for none does God deceit approve),
Enough it is you pretty be for me.

9
Dice el mes en que se enamoró

Érase el mes de más hermosos días,
y por quien más los campos entretienen,
señora, cuando os vi, para que penen
tantas necias de Amor filaterías.

Imposibles esperan mis porfías,   5
que como los favores se detienen,
vos triunfaréis cruel, pues a ser vienen
las glorias vuestras, y las penas mías.

No salió malo este versillo octavo,
ninguna de las musas se alborote   10
si antes del fin el sonetazo alabo.

Ya saco la sentencia del cogote;
pero si, como pienso, no le acabo,
echaréle después un estrambote.

10
Describe un monte, sin qué
ni para qué

Caen de un monte a un valle entre pizarras,
guarnecidas de frágiles helechos,
a su margen carámbanos deshechos,
que cercan olmos y silvestres parras.

Nadan en su cristal ninfas bizarras,   5
compitiendo con él cándidos pechos,
dulces naves de amor, en más estrechos
que las que salen de españolas barras.

Tiene este monte por vasallo a un prado,
que para tantas flores le importuna   10
sangre las venas de su pecho helado;

y en este monte y líquida laguna,
para decir verdad como hombre honrado,
jamás me sucedió cosa ninguna.

9

He tells the month in which he fell in love

It was the month of days most beautiful,
And for which month the fields most entertain,
When, Lady, I saw you, so that in pain
Of love came much fast talking fanciful.

My fierce persistence waits impossible: 5
Because your precious favors you detain
You'll triumph over us, and will remain
The glories yours and my pains at the full.

This eighth verse didn't turn out bad at all;
Let no one of the muses throw a fit   10
If ere the end I praise this sonnet-stroke.

Now I the message from my noggin call;
But, as I guess, if I can't finish it,
I'll later to it an extra tercet yoke.

10

He describes a mount, without rhyme
or reason

Between shale walls from mount down to a vale,
With fragile ferns in fancy trimming dressed,
Fall shattered icicles and borders test,
Where lofty elms and wild grape arbors veil.

Nymphs splendid in the crystal pool prevail,   5
And with the crystal candid breasts contest,
Sweet barks of love, there in more straits hard-pressed,
Than those which from the Spanish sandbanks sail.

The mount for vassal has a meadow strewn
With such rich flowers that it does cajole   10
Blood for the veins of its breast shivering.

And in the mount and liquid-filled lagoon,
To tell the truth, as should an honest soul,
To me there never happened anything.

12
Satisfaciones de celos

Si entré, si vi, si hablé, señora mía,
ni tuve pensamiento de mudarme,
máteme un necio a puro visitarme,
y escuche malos versos todo un día.

Cuando de hacerlos tenga fantasía,   5
dispuesto el genio, para no faltarme
cerca de donde suelo retirarme,
un menestril se enseñe a chirimía.

Cerquen los ojos, que os están mirando,
legiones de poéticos mochuelos,   10
de aquellos que murmuran imitando.

¡Oh si os mudasen de rigor los cielos!
Porque no puede ser (o fue burlando)
que quien no tiene amor pidiese celos.

14
A la ira con que una noche
le cerró la puerta

¿Qué estrella saturnal, tirana hermosa,
se opuso, en vez de Venus, a la luna,
que me respondes grave e importuna,
siendo con todos fácil y amorosa?

Cerrásteme la puerta rigurosa,   5
donde me viste sin piedad alguna,
hasta que a Febo en su dorada cuna,
llamó la aurora en la primera rosa.

¿Qué fuerza imaginó tu desatino,
aunque fueras de vidrio de Venecia,   10
tan fácil, delicado y cristalino?

O me tienes por loco, o eres necia;
que ni soberbio soy para Tarquino,
ni tú romana para ser Lucrecia.

12
Satisfactions of jealousy

If I, my Lady, came, saw, talked away,
And never had a thought of change to see,
May some fool's visits be the death of me,
And may I hear bad verses one whole day.

When I to write them fantasy display,   5
Disposed my talent, let not lacking be
Near where I settle customarily
A minstrel who for me can hornpipe play.

Your eyes bring near, their staring has begun,
Those legions of night-owls of poetry,   10
Who imitate, with gossip overdone.

Oh, would the Lord you from your harshness free!
For it can't be (or he did jest) that one
Who has no love would ask for jealousy.

14
On the anger with which she closed the door
to him one night

What star of Saturn, tyrant beauteous,
Instead of Venus did oppose the moon,
That you to me respond, grave, importune,
Your being free with all and amorous?

You closed the door against me rigorous,   5
Where you saw me to mercy then immune,
'Til Phoebus' golden cradle did festoon
The dawn in that first rose victorious.

What power did your tactlessness invent,
Although you might be made of Venice glass,   10
A yielding, crystalline, and fragile piece?

You're foolish, or you think my reason spent:
I'm not so proud that I as Tarquin pass,
Nor you so Roman as to be Lucrece.

15
A un peine, que no sabía el poeta
si era di boj u de marfil

Sulca del mar de Amor las rubias ondas
barco de Barcelona y por los bellos
lazos navega altivo, aunque por ellos,
tal vez te muestres y tal vez te escondas.

Ya no flechas, Amor; doradas ondas   5
teje de sus espléndidos cabellos;
tú con los dientes no le quites dellos,
para que a tanta dicha correspondas.

Desenvuelve los rizos con decoro,
los paralelos de mi sol desata,   10
boj o colmillo de elefante moro,

y en tanto que, esparcidos, los dilata,
forma por la madeja sendas de oro,
antes que el tiempo los convierta en plata.

19
Dice como se engendra Amor,
hablando como Filósofo

Espíritus sanguíneos vaporosoa
suben del corazón a la cabeza,
y saliendo a los ojos su pureza
pasan a los que miran amorosos.

El corazón opuesto los fogosos   5
rayos, sintiendo en la sutil belleza,
como de ajena son naturaleza
inquietase en ardores congojosos.

Eso puros espíritus que envía
tu corazón al mío, por extraños   10
me inquietan como cosa que no es mía.

Mira, Juana, ¡qué amor, mira qué engaños,
pues hablo en natural filosofía
a quien me escucha jabonando paños!

15
To a comb, the poet not knowing
if it was of boxwood or of ivory

Cleaves bark from Barcelona Love's sea wide
Of blonde-gold waves, and through fair diadem
Of ties sails haughtily, although through them
At times you show yourself, at times you hide.

Not arrows now, let Love gold waves provide   5
By weaving from her splendid locks a gem;
You with your teeth don't take away from them,
So that you so much bliss can share with pride.

Unravel all the curls decorously,
The parallels that are my sun untie,   10
Boxwood or tusk of Moorish elephant,

And while, spread out, you comb them lovingly,
Form golden trails that will the skein supply,
Before to silver changes them Time adamant.

19
He tells how love is engendered,
speaking like a Philosopher

Sanguineous the spirits vaporous
Up to the head out of the heart arise;
Their purity upwelling to the eyes
They pass to those whose look is amorous.

The heart, contrary to those igneous   5
Firebolts, a subtle beauty feeling rise,
How with an alien sound all nature wise
Might restless show in ardors dolorous.

Those spotless spirits that sends readily
Your heart to mine, astonishment disclose,   10
And like some thing not mine they ruffle me.

Look, Jane, what love, look what deceitful pose:
I'm speaking Natural Philosophy
To one who's hearing me while soaping clothes!

28
Cortando la pluma, hablan los dos

—Pluma, las musas, de mi genio autoras,
versos me piden hoy. ¡Alto; a escribillos!
—Yo solo escribiré, señor Burguillos,
estas que me dictó rimas sonoras.

    —¿A Góngora me acota a tales horas?   5
Arrojaré tijeras y cuchillos,
pues en queriendo hacer versos sencillos
arrímese dos musas cantimploras.

    Dejemos la campaña, el monte, el valle,
y alabemos señores. —No le entiendo.   10
¿Morir quiere de hambre? —Escriba y calle.

    —A mi ganso me vuelvo en prosiguiendo,
que es desdicha, después de no premialle,
nacer volando y acabar mintiendo.

39
Desgarro de una panza un día de toros.
Habla el rocín

Yo, Bragadoro, valenzuela en raza,
diestro como galán de entrambas sillas,
en la barbada, naguas amarillas,
aciago, un martes, perfumé la plaza.

    Del balcón al toril, con linda traza,   5
daba por los toritos carrerillas,
y andábame después, por las orillas,
como suelen los príncipes, a caza.

    Pero mi dueño, la baqueta alzada,
a un hosco acometió con valentía,   10
a pagar de mi panza desdichada.

    Porque todos, al tiempo que corría,
dijeron que era nada, y fue cornada.
¡Malhaya el hombre que de cuernos fía!

28
He trimming his pen, the two speak

"The muses, Pen, who gave me wit sublime
Ask me for poems today. Let's write forthright!"
"My dear Burguillos, I will only write
This, that dictated muse, sonorous rhyme."

"You bring me Góngora at such a time?   5
I'll knives and scissors throw away in spite,
Two muses of the water jar hold tight,
In writing simple verse with easy rhyme.

"Let's leave the hill, the vale, the land in Spring
And praise great lords." "This I don't comprehend.   10
Is it you want to starve?" "Write, stop complaining."

"Back to my goose I'll go, continuing,
For it is sad, with no prize at the end,
To be born flying, and to end up feigning."

39
Ripping of a belly one bullfight day
(The nag speaks.)

I, Goldipants, Arabian by race,
Like gallant who all saddles rides, adept,
With yellow petticoats at jawbone kept,
Ill-starred, one Tuesday, I perfumed the place.

From stands to bull pen gate with pretty pace   5
Out toward the bovines dancingly I stepped,
And afterward along the margins crept,
As princes often do, before the chase.

But my good master, with true gallantry,
Attacked a Fierce One with his cane outthrust,   10
And my poor belly paid unfortunately.

Because they all while I was raising dust
Called nothing what a goring was to me,
Cursed be the man who puts in horns his trust!

40
Encarece su amor para obligar a su dama
a que lo premie

Juana, mi amor me tiene en tal estado,
que no os puedo mirar, cuando no os veo;
ni escribo ni manduco ni paseo,
entretanto que duermo sin cuidado.

Por no tener dineros no he comprado   5
(¡oh Amor cruel!) ni manta, ni manteo;
tan vivo me derrienga mi deseo
en la concha de Venus amarrado.

De Garcilaso es este verso Juana:
todos hurtan, paciencia, yo os le ofrezco.   10
Mas volviendo a mi amor, dulce tirana,

tanto en morir y en esperar merezco,
que siento más el verme sin sotana
que cuanto fiero mal por vos padezco.

41
A una dama que salió revuelta
una mañana

Hermoso desaliño, en quien se fía
cuanto después abrasa y enamora,
cual suele amanecer turbada aurora,
para matar de sol al mediodía.

Solimán natural, que desconfía   5
el resplandor con que los cielos dora;
dejad la arquilla, no os toquéis, señora,
tóquese la vejez de vuestra tía.

Mejor luce el jazmín, mejor la rosa
por el revuelto pelo en la nevada   10
columna de marfil, garganta hermosa.

Para la noche estáis mejor tocada;
que no anocheceréis tan aliñosa
como hoy amanecéis desaliñada.

40
He extols his love so as to oblige
his lady to reward him

Dear Jane, my love has me so overwrought
That I can't look at you, you out of sight;
I neither cram, nor go for walk, nor write,
The while I sleep without disturbing thought.

Not having any funds I have not bought   5
(Cruel Love!) a blanket or a cloak outright;
My fierce desire racks me both day and night
Inside the shell of Venus tied up taut.

From Garcilaso is this verse, my Jane:
So people filch, have patience, it's for you.   10
But, tyrant sweet, back to my love again,

So much in dying, hoping I am due
That I regret more being without soutane
Than all the rabid ill I bear for you.

41
To a lady who came out untidy
one morning

Disorder beautiful, in whose trust stay
Those charms which later fire and love provide,
Much like a dawn, when murky clouds abide,
Which at high noon the sun will burn away.

Inborn cosmetic can distrust display   5
Of gilded glow that is the heavens' pride;
Don't make up, Lady, lay your kit aside,
And let your aging aunt with make-up play.

The rose, the jasmine both shine forth more bright
With that free-flowing hair at column straight   10
Of snow-touched ivory, throat beautiful.

You are arranged much better for the night,
For you will not as tidy night await
As you dawn in disorder wonderful.

44
A una dama que, llamando a su puerta, le dijo
desde la ventana: «Dios le provea»

Señora, aunque soy pobre, no venía
a pediros limosna; que buscaba
un cierto licenciado que posaba
en estas casas, cuando Dios quería.

Extraña siempre fue la estrella mía;   5
que a un pobre parecí desde la aldaba,
pues ya que a la ventana os obligaba,
trujiste desde allá la fantasía.

No porque culpa vuestro engaño sea,
que a tal *Dios le provea* no replican   10
mis hábitos, que son de ataracea.

No mis letras, mis penas significan;
pero ¿cómo queréis que me provea,
si tales como vos se lo suplican?

46
Consuela a Tamayo de que todos
le maldigan sin culpa

—Aquí del rey, señores. ¿Por ventura
fui yo Caín de mi inocente hermano?
¿Maté yo al rey don Sancho el castellano,
o sin alma signé falsa escritura?

¿Púsome acaso en la tablilla el cura?   5
¿No soy hidalgo y montañés cristiano?
¿Por qué razón, con maldecirme en vano,
no tengo vida ni ocasión segura?

De oír decir a todos me desmayo,
sin que haya lluvia o trueno resonante,   10
«que vaya a dar en casa de Tamayo».

—Vuesamerced, rey mío, no se espante,
ni tenga pena que le mate el rayo:
que sólo va a buscar su consonante.

44
To a lady who, his calling at her door, said to him from the window: "God Provide for Your Grace"

Lady, though I'm poor, I did not show
Up here for alms, but I was looking for
The lodgings of a certain counsellor
Who here resided when God willed it so.

Forever strange this star of mine did glow;   5
You from door-knocker saw poor visitor;
Since I obliged you from the exterior,
From there you let your imagination grow.

Thus for your error you need not blamed be,
For such a "God provide" can't intimate   10
My garments, much inlaid with finery.

They, not my letters, troubles indicate;
But why ask you that God provide for me
If people like yourself such supplicate?

46
He consoles Tamayo that everyone curses him without reason

"The King provides, good gentlemen. Perchance
Was I Cain to my brother innocent?
Did I depose a statement fraudulent?
Caused I King Sancho of Castile's death-dance?

"Did priest put me on that marked list by chance?   5
Am I not Christian, noble in descent?
Their cursing me, upon what argument
Have I no life, no trusted circumstance?

"From hearing all speak ill of me I faint,
And really to Tamayo's house should go,   10
Without much rain or thunder resonant."

"Your Grace, my Sovereign, don't lose all restraint,
Or fear that lightning bolt should lay him low,
He's just in search of rhyming consonant."

47
A la muerte de una dama, representanta única

Yacen en este mármol la blandura,
la tierna voz, la enamorada ira,
que vistió de verdades la mentira
en toda acción de personal figura;

la grave del coturno compostura,   5
que ya de celos, ya de amor suspira,
y con donaire, que, imitado, admira
del tosco traje la inocencia pura.

Fingió toda figura de tal suerte,
que, muriéndose, apenas fue creída   10
en los singultos de su trance fuerte.

Porque como tan bien fingió en la vida,
lo mismo imaginaron en la muerte,
porque aun la muerte pareció fingida.

49
A la sepultura de Marramaquiz, gato famoso en lengua culta, que es en la que ellos se entienden

Este, si bien sarcófago, no duro
pórfido, aquel cadáver bravo observa,
por quien de mures tímida caterva
recóndita cubrió terrestre muro.

La Parca, que ni al joven ni al maturo   5
su destinado límite reserva,
ministrándole pólvora superba,
mentido rayo disparó seguro.

Ploren tu muerte Henares, Tajo, Tormes,
que el patrio Manzanares, que eternizas,   10
lágrimas mestas libará conformes.

Y no le faltarán a tus cenizas;
pues viven tantos gatos multiformes
de lenguas largas y de manos mizas.

47
On the death of a lady, unique actress

In marble lie soft voice of eloquence,
The gentleness, the rage with love inspired,
Which with bright truths falsehood attired
In every move with personal accents.

The serious, composed grandiloquence   5
That now with envy, now with love suspired,
And with a flair which, copied, much admired
Of her rough dress the purest innocence.

She played each character in such a way
That with her dying it hardly was believed   10
As she gasps of the final trance sustained.

Since she in life so well her parts did play,
Then everyone the same her death conceived,
For even death itself it seemed was feigned.

49
At the burial of Tom-in-Heat, cat famous in
cultish language, the one they understand

This, while sarcophagus, not to endure
In porphyry, cadaver fierce observes,
For whom of mice the timidest reserves
Recondite covered earthly wall secure.

The Parca, who for young or for mature   5
From set of destined limits never swerves,
Administering gunpowder from reserves
Pretended lightning bolt projected sure.

Weep Tagus, Tormes, Henares your demise;
Your Manzanares that you eternalize   10
Will pour confluent tears without a pause.

And be assured your ashes will survive;
For countless filching cats remain alive,
With lengthy tongues as well as feline paws.

51
Al mismo sujeto de la dama que
le dijo: «Dios le provea»

Vuesamercé se puso a la ventana,
y luego conoció que era poeta;
que la pobreza nunca fue secreta,
sin duda se lo dijo mi sotana.

Si bien no a todos fiera e inhumana   5
estrella sigue y saturnal cometa,
a muchos dio carroza, a mí carreta;
para otros Venus, para mí sultana.

Soy en pedir tan poco venturoso,
que sea por la pluma o por la espada,   10
todos me dicen con rigor piadoso:

«Dios le provea», y nunca me dan nada;
tanto, que ya parezco virtuoso,
pues nunca la virtud se vio premiada.

61
A un secreto muy secreto

¡Oh, qué secreto, damas; oh galanes,
qué secreto de amor; oh, qué secreto,
qué ilustre idea, qué sutil conceto!
¡Por Dios que es hoja de me fecit Ioanes!

Hoy cesan los melindres y ademanes,   5
todo interés, todo celoso efeto;
de hoy más Amor será firme y perfeto,
sin ver jardines, ni escalar desvanes.

No es esto filosófica fatiga,
trasmutación sutil o alquimia vana,   10
sino esencia real, que al tacto obliga.

Va de secreto, pero cosa es llana,
que quiere el buen letor que se le diga:
pues váyase con Dios hasta mañana.

51
To the same subject, the lady who told him,
"May God provide for Your Grace"

Your Grace there from your window looked secure,
And then you learned that I a poet must be,
For never secret was deep poverty,
My cassock said it all to you for sure.

Although not everybody must endure   5
Inhuman star, Saturnian comet flee,
Fate gave some carriage, but a cart to me,
For others Venus, me a sultry Moor.

In begging I'm so little prosperous
That whether I my pen or sword regard   10
They all tell me with rigor ponderous:

"May God provide," and me they naught award
To such a point that I seem virtuous,
For Virtue never saw a just reward.

61
To a secret very secret

Oh, what a secret, ladies, lords displayed,
What secret, oh, love secret in effect,
Oh, what a deep conceit, idea select!
Dear Lord, it is *me fecit Ioanes* blade!

Today broad hint and prudery are stayed,   5
All self-concern, all envious effect;
From now Love will be firm, without defect,
Will see no gardens, no closed lofts invade.

This is not philosophic weariness,
Or subtle change, or alchemy quite vain,   10
But essence real, which sense of touch will press.

It goes as secret, yet it is so plain,
Which some good Reader wants me to express;
So long, then, and may God with you remain.

68
Describe un lindo deste tiempo

Galán Sansón tenéis, señora Arminda;
toda la fuerza tiene en las guedejas;
bravas salieron hoy las dos madejas;
llore Anaxarte, Dafne se le rinda.

    ¿Qué manutisa, qué clavel, qué guinda   5
en púrpura con él corrió parejas?
Y más con los bigotes a las cejas,
que en buena fe, que no sois vos tan linda.

    ¡Qué bravo, qué galán, qué airoso viene!
Pero ya vuestro amor en los luceros   10
de la risa dormida se previene.

    Mas es forzoso lástima teneros;
porque sabed que tanto amor se tiene,
que no le ha de sobrar para quereros.

73
Que en este tiempo muchos saben griego
sin haberlo estudiado

A don Francisco López de Aguilar

Das en decir, Francisco, y yo lo niego,
que nadie sabe griego en toda España,
pues cuantos Helicón poetas baña
todos escriben, en España, en griego.

    Para entender al Venusino ciego,   5
querrás decir, por imposible hazaña,
si a las lenguas la ciencia no acompaña,
lo mismo es saber griego que gallego.

    Cierto poeta de mayor esfera,
cuyo dicipulado dificulto,   10
de los libros de Italia fama espera.

    Mas, porque no conozcan por insulto
los hurtos de Estillani y del Cabrera,
escribe en griego, disfrazado en culto.

68
It describes a pretty boy of today

Bold Samson, Lady Arminda, you possess;
In his long locks all of his strength remains;
Today they flowered forth in his two skeins:
Weep Anaxarete, Daphne acquiesce.

What pinks, carnations, cherries in spring dress   5
Can thus with him compete in purple stains?
And more, with mustache that toward eyebrows strains,
That you are not as pretty I confess.

How brave, how gallant, how in triumph he nears!
But now your love fixed on the stars above   10
Should be forewarned of sleeping laughter due.

But for you pity without fail appears;
For know that for himself he has such love
That he can none have left for loving you.

73
Thus in these times many know Greek
without having studied it

To don Francisco López de Aguilar

You stress, Francisco, and I counter speak,
That not a man knows Greek in all of Spain;
For all the Helicon bathes poets vain,
When they all write in Spain they write in Greek.

The blind Venusian's meaning thus to seek,   5
You mean to say, result looked for in vain,
If science and languages go not in train
They're all the same: Galician or Greek.

A certain poet, of the greater sphere,
To be whose pupil I find difficult,   10
With books Italian furthers his career.

But that such not be taken as insult,
From Stigliani and Chiabrera filchings clear,
He writes in Greek, in euphuistic cult.

75
Da la razón el poeta de que la boca
de Juana fuese rosa

Tiraba rosas el Amor un día
desde una peña a un líquido arroyuelo,
que de un espino trasladó a su velo,
en la sazón que abril las producía.

Las rosas mansamente conducía   5
de risco en risco el agua al verde suelo,
cuando Juana llegó y, al puro hielo,
puso los labios, de la fuente fría.

Las rosas, entre perlas y cristales,
pegáronse a los labios, tan hermosas,   10
que afrentaban claveles y corales.

¡Oh pinturas del cielo milagrosas!
¿Quién vio jamás transformaciones tales:
beber cristales y volverse rosas?

76
Cánsase el poeta de la dilación
de su esperanza

¡Tanto mañana, y nunca ser mañana!
Amor se ha vuelto cuervo, o se me antoja.
¿En qué región el sol su carro aloja
desta imposible aurora tramontana?

Sígueme inútil la esperanza vana,   5
como nave zorrera o mula coja;
porque no me tratara Barbarroja
de la manera que me tratas, Juana.

Juntos Amor y yo buscando vamos
esta mañana. ¡Oh dulces desvaríos!   10
Siempre mañana, y nunca mañanamos.

Pues si vencer no puedo tus desvíos,
sáquente cuervos destos verdes ramos
los ojos. Pero no, ¡que son los míos!

75
The poet reasons how Jane's mouth
might be a rose

The Love god throwing roses was one day
From nearby cliff into a liquid rill,
Which from a rosebush he his mask did fill,
The April time them making for display.

The water then was wafting roses gay   5
From crag to crag toward meadow green downhill,
When Jane appeared, and to the icy chill,
She put her lips, of frigid water-way.

The roses, mixing pearls and crystallizations,
Stuck to her lips, so very beauteous,   10
That gave offense to corals and carnations.

Oh paintings sent from heaven, marvelous!
Who ever came to view such transformations:
To crystals drink, and turn to roses thus?

76
The poet grows weary of the delay
of his hope

So much tomorrow, tomorrow never again!
Love now is cawing crow, or teases me.
In what place will the sun's car lodging see
For this impossible hope tramontane?

There follows useless after me hope vain,   5
Like old lame mule, or ship that lugs at sea;
For Barbarossa himself would not treat me
In this cruel way that you abuse me, Jane.

Joined Love and I (Oh sweet inconstancy!)
A search for this tomorrow we pursue.   10
Always tomorrow, tomorrow not to be.

If I your fierce disdain cannot subdue
Let crows pluck from the boughs of greenery
Your eyes. But no, that they are mine is true!

77
Lo que han de hacer los ingenios grandes
cuando los murmuran

Un lebrel irlandés de hermoso talle,
bayo, entre negro, de la frente al anca,
labrada en bronce y ante la carlanca,
pasaba por la margen de una calle.

Salió confuso ejército a ladralle,   5
chusma de gozques, negra, roja y blanca,
como de aldea furibunda arranca
para seguir al lobo en monte o valle.

Y como escriben que la diosa trina,
globo de plata en el celeste raso,   10
los perros de los montes desatina,

este hidalgo lebrel, sin hacer caso,
alzó la pierna, remojó la esquina,
y por medio se fue su paso a paso.

78
Que el amor verdadero no le olvidan el tempo
ni la muerte

Escribe en serio

Resuelta en polvo ya, mas siempre hermosa,
sin dejarme vivir, vive serena
aquella luz que fue mi gloria y pena,
y me hace guerra cuando en paz reposa.

Tan vivo está el jazmín, la pura rosa,   5
que blandamente ardiendo en azucena,
me abrasa el alma, de memorias llena,
ceniza de su fénix amorosa.

¡Oh memoria cruel de mis enojos!,
¿qué honor te puede dar mi sentimiento,   10
en polvo convertidos sus despojos?

Permíteme callar solo un momento:
que ya no tienen lágrimas mis ojos
ni conceptos de amor mi pensamiento.

77
What the truly talented should do
on hearing gossip

An Irish wolfhound with bloodlines elite,
All over reddish-brown to black as night,
His elkskin collar with bronze spikes upright,
Was passing along the margin of a street.

A ragtag army came barking him to greet,   5
A pack of yappers black and red and white,
Such as from village gate the wolf do sight
And chase over hill and dale with frenzied feet.

And since the goddess trine, some certify,
All country dogs leads totally astray   10
(She globe of silver in a velvet sky),

This wolfhound noble, indifference on display,
Wet down the corner quite, his leg raised high,
And through them with firm step went on his way!

78
That true love neither time
nor death destroys

Nor turned to dust, but always beauteous,
Not letting me to live, that light serene
Lives which my glory and my pain has been,
Makes war on me in peace felicitous.

The jasmine bright, the rose harmonious   5
Which blandly burns as lily of white sheen
My soul makes glow, with memories full and keen,
The ashes of its phoenix amorous.

Oh cruel memory of my troubles bleak!
How can my sentiment your honor stress,   10
Now dust become the leavings that remain?

Permit me for a moment not to speak:
For now my eyes do not one tear possess,
Nor does my thought conceits of love retain.

79
Al baño de dos ninfas aloques

Una morena, y otra blanca dama,
siendo por sus riberas y malezas
Manzanares la tabla destas piezas,
de su breve cristal hicieron cama:

La escultura en las dos era de fama,   5
compitiendo colores y bellezas,
si bien de dos iguales gentilezas,
más la blancura se apetece y ama.

En esta clara y fácil competencia,
un galán que pasaba por la orilla   10
dijo por sosegar la diferencia:

—Buenas entrambas son a maravilla,
la una de jazmines de Valencia,
la otra de polvillos de Sevilla.

80
Encarce el poeta el amor conyugal
de este tiempo

Fugitiva Eurídice entre la amena
hierba de un valle, por la nieve herida,
del blanco pie de un áspid escondida,
pisándola clavel, cayó azucena.

Lloróla Orfeo, y a la eterna pena   5
bajó animoso, y con la voz teñida
en lágrimas, pidió su media vida;
así la lira dulcemente suena.

La gracia entonces con tremendo labio
Plutón concede al conyugal deseo   10
del marido, más músico que sabio.

En fín, sacó su esposa del Leteo;
pero en aqueste tiempo, hermano Fabio,
¿quién te parece a ti que fuera Orfeo?

79
At the bath of two nymphs red-white in hue

One lady dark, another lady fair,
Along its shores and thickets unexplored
The Manzanares for these pieces board,
Of its brief crystal they a bed made there:

The sculpture of the two was beyond compare,   5
In hue and beauties conflict underscored;
Though blondness is more sought out and adored,
In gentle breeding equal is this pair.

In this clear, easy test of influence,
A gallant who was walking by the rill   10
Spoke up to mitigate the difference:

"Now both of them provide a wondrous thrill,
The one Valencia's jasmine so intense,
The other white face powder of Seville."

80
The poet extols the conjugal love
of these times

Eurydice as fugitive, in dell
Of pleasant grass, in snow a wound sustained
Of foot by asp who had concealed remained,
She, trod upon carnation, lily fell.

Her Orpheus wept, and to eternal hell   5
Went down with spirit bold, and with voice stained
In tears, begged that her half-life be regained:
Therefore the sounds of lyre so sweetly swell.

This grace, with lip of massive size
Grants Pluto to the conjugal desire   10
Of this good spouse more musical than wise.

At last he wife from Lethe did retire;
But, brother Fabio, who do you surmise
This Orpheus might be in these times dire?

85
Que no hay remedio contra malos vecinos

Trujo un galán de noche una ballesta
al sitio en que una dama requebraba,
con que de su ventana retiraba
una vecina en escuchar molesta;

entonces ella, una caldera puesta   5
en la cabeza, volvió a ver si hablaba;
tiraba el caballero, y resonaba
en el herido cobre la respuesta.

En carros dijo el Momo peregrino
que las casas debieran fabricarse,   10
o como son portátiles al chino;

que a quien se conviniere recatarse
de lengua y ojos de un traidor vecino,
no tiene más remedio que mudarse.

86
Desdenes de Juana y quejas del poeta

Si digo a Juana (cuanto hermosa, fiera)
lo que la quiero, ingrata corresponde;
si digo que es mi vida, me responde
que se muriera porque no lo fuera.

Si la busco del soto en la ribera,   5
entre los verdes álamos se esconde;
si va a la plaza, y la pregunto adónde,
con la cesta me rompe la mollera.

Si digo que es la hermosa Policena,
dice que miento, porque no es troyana,   10
ni griega si la igualo con Helena.

Eres hircana tigre, hermosa Juana;
mas, ¡ay!, que aun para tigre no era buena,
pues siendo de Madrid, no fuera hircana.

85
There is no remedy against bad neighbors

A gallant brought a crossbow one dark night
To place where he a dame was celebrating,
So that a neighbor listening went vacating
Her window, she being bothered by the rite.

Then she, a pot upon her head placed tight,   5
Returned to see if he was still orating;
The gallant shot, the answer resonating
Upon the wounded copper kettle bright.

The houses, said this Momus peregrine,
Should be on carts constructed with great labor,   10
Or like the Chinese houses, portable be.

Because if someone really wants to screen
Himself from eye and tongue of spiteful neighbor,
Then moving is the only remedy.

86
Jane's disdain and the poet's complaints

If I tell Jane (as beautiful as beast)
How I love her, disdain she corresponds;
If I say she's my life, she then responds
To not be such she'd rather be deceased.

If in grove by the river I would feast   5
My eyes on her in poplars green she absconds;
If in the square I say she vagabonds,
She with her basket leaves my noggin creased.

If I say she's Polyxena the fair,
Since she's not Trojan, she declares I lie,   10
Nor Greek, if her as Helen I do plot.

You're, precious Jane, Hyrcanian tiger rare;
But ay! your being a tiger was awry,
Since from Madrid, Hyrcanian you are not.

88
Al corto premio de un amigo suyo
que le merecía

«Pobre y desnuda vas, Filosofía»,
dijo el Petrarca; luego siempre ha sido,
Fabio, la ciencia, en miserable olvido,
desprecio de la humana monarquía.

Llorad la vuestra, que la inútil mía,   5
ni aun el nombre merece que ha tenido;
olio, tiempo y estudio habéis perdido:
tales efectos la esperanza cría.

Dicen, cuando en los males no hay mudanza,
que la paciencia es premio de la ciencia;   10
¿qué hará quien, por ser premio, no la alcanza?

¡Aforismo cruel, cruel sentencia!
Récipe para estítica esperanza,
ayudas de silencio y de paciencia.

96
Enójase con Amor, con mucha cortesía

Vuesa merced se tiemple en darle penas,
Señor Amor, a un hombre de mi fama,
que si quiso Aristóteles su dama,
también le desterraron los de Atenas.

Malas comidas y peores cenas,   5
y como calle pasear la cama;
súfralo Amor, un toro de Jarama,
¡qué va! no es tiempo de templar Ximenas.

Mande Vuesa merced, Señor Cupido,
que Juana me respete como debe,   10
y valga el Montañés sobre raído;

Si los paños me manda que le lleve,
y alguna rosa de sus labios pido,
cuanto fuego le doy, me trueca a nieve.

88
To the scant reward of a friend
who merited more

"You poor and naked go, Philosophy,"
Said Petrarch; afterward it's been the same
With learning mired in apathy and shame,
Scorned, Fabio, by human sovereignty.

Weep yours, for useless my philosophy,   5
The one I've had does not deserve the name;
You've lost time, study, oils beyond all claim:
This kind of effects hope raises readily.

They say, when in our ills there is no change,
That patience must reward of learning be;   10
What will one do who cannot learning reach?

Cruel aphorism, sentence cruel and strange!
For stingy future hope a recipe,
You with your silence and your patience teach.

96
He becomes angry with Cupid with much Courtesy

Your Grace, ease up in bringing such distress,
Sir Cupid, to a man that boasts my fame;
Though Aristotle loved his wedded dame
The Athenians exiled him nevertheless.

Snacks terrible and meals a bigger mess,   5
And bed and street as scenes of strife the same,
Let bear it, Love, Jarama bull not tame:
It's not the times to ease the Cid's wife's stress.

So Cupid, honored Lord, command your Grace
That Jane her due respect for me should show,   10
And prize, not scruffiness, my highland race.

If I beg of her lips a rose or so,
And she have me much cloth in her hands place,
What fire I bring her she turns into snow.

97
La pulga, falsamente atribuida a Lope

Picó atrevido un átomo viviente
los blancos pechos de Leonor hermosa,
granate en perlas, arador en rosa,
breve lunar del invisible diente.

Ella dos puntas de marfil luciente,   5
con súbita inquietud, bañó quejosa,
y torciendo su vida bulliciosa,
en un castigo dos venganzas siente.

Al expirar la pulga, dijo: ¡«Ay, triste,
por tan pequeño mal, dolor tan fuerte!»   10
«¡Oh, pulga! —dije yo—, dichosa fuiste!

«Detén el alma, y a Leonor advierte
que me deje picar donde estuviste,
y trocaré mi vida con tu muerte.»

99
A una dama que le preguntó qué tiempo corre

El mismo tiempo corre que solía,
que nunca de correr se vio cansado;
deciros que es menor el que ha pasado
de más de necedad vejez sería.

O mayor o menor, ay noche y día   5
sube y declina, Filis, todo estado,
dichoso el rico, el pobre desdichado,
con que sabréis cual fue la estrella mía.

Ay pleitos, y de aquestos grandes sumas,
trampas, mohatras, hurtos, juegos, tretas,   10
flaquezas al quitar, naguas de espumas.

Nuevas, mentiras, cartas, estafetas,
lenguas, lisonjas, odios, varas, plumas,
y en cada calle cuatro mil Poetas.

97
The Flea, falsely attributed to Lope

A living atom bit intrepidly
The snow-white breasts of Leonor so fair,
In pearls deep garnet, in rose mite plowing there,
Mole miniscule with tooth one cannot see.

She those two points of lucent ivory   5
Complaining bathed with sudden anxious care;
Two avengements from one punishment does dare
By twisting life from this vivacious flea.

She said, "Ay, forlorn creature," as it dies,
"For such a tiny wrong, such pain to incur!"   10
"Oh, flea," said I, "you were so fortunate!"

"Your soul hold back, and Leonor advise
That will she let me nibble where you were
I'll for your death my life reciprocate."

99
To a lady who asked him about time flying

Time flying is the same he used to be,
For he from flying never was prostrate;
To tell you he now passed knows younger date,
More than just foolishness, old age would be.

If older or younger, night and day we see,   5
And, Phyllis, up or down goes every state;
The rich man blessed, the poor unfortunate,
So now you know what star attached to me.

There are lawsuits, which great sums realize,
Fake sales, card games, tricks, schemes, and robberies,   10
Fluffed petticoats, and weaknesses to score,

Fresh news and letters, couriers, big lies,
Hates, pens, sticks flying, babble, flatteries,
And on each street four thousand poets or more.

107
Escribe a un amigo el suceso de una jornada

Claudio, después del Rey, y los tapices
de tanto grande, y forastero incauto,
no tiene la jornada a ver el Auto,
que te pueda escribir que solemnices:

Fue todo cortesanas meretrices   5
de las que pinta en sus comedias Plauto;
anduve casto, porque ya soy cauto
en ayunarlas, o comer perdices.

Y a los ventores con el pico al norte,
andaban por las damas circunstantes,   10
que al recibír las cartas se da el porte.

Partióse el Rey, llevóse los amantes;
quedó al lugar un breve olor de Corte,
como aposento en que estuvieron guantes.

109
A un poeta rico, que parece imposible

La rueda de los orbes circunstantes
pare el veloz primero movimiento;
déjese penetrar el pensamiento;
iguálese la arena a los diamantes.

Tengan entendimiento los amantes   5
y falte a la pobreza entendimiento;
no tenga fuerza el oro, y por el viento
corran los africanos elefantes.

Blanco sea el cuervo y negros los jazmines,
rompan ciervos del mar los vidros tersos,   10
y naden por la tierra los delfines;

no sufra la virtud casos adversos,
den los señores, hagan bien los ruines,
pues hay un hombre rico haciendo versos.

107
He writes to a friend what happend at an outing

Claudio, near the King, and tapestries
Of worthies great, outsider ripe for play,
The outing's not to see a Mystery Play,
That I comment for your solemnities:

Like those that Plautus paints in comedies,   5
It was all courtesans who go for pay;
I chaste stayed, since I cautious am today
And fast with them, don't eat quail as I please.

And while to north the bird dogs noses trained,
The men went for the ladies to be seen,   10
Who, message grasping, tariff is obtained.

The King retired, the lovers left the scene,
And in the place faint scent of Court remained,
Like inner chamber where some gloves had been.

109
To a rich poet, a seeming impossibility

May wheeling of the orbs in circumstance
The swift primary movement cause to slow;
May thought prodigious penetration show;
Let sand now equal diamond's radiance.

May lovers all have understanding stance,   5
And poverty intelligence not know;
May gold no power have, and running go
Upon the breezes African elephants.

Let jasmine black become, the crow be white,
Let stags break in the sea the crystals terse,   10
And dolphins on the earth swim in delight.

Let virtue never suffer case adverse,
May lords now give, the down-and-out do right,
For here's a rich man calmly writing verse.

112
Que no es hombre el que no hace bien a nadie

Dos cosas despertaron mis antojos,
extranjeras, no al alma, a los sentidos:
Marino, gran pintor de los oídos,
y Rubens, gran poeta de los ojos.

Marino, fénix ya de sus despojos,   5
yace en Italia resistiendo olvidos;
Rubens, los héroes del pincel vencidos,
da gloria a Fla[n]des y a la envidia enojos.

Mas ni de aquél la pluma, o la destreza
déste con el pincel pintar pudieran   10
un hombre que, pudiendo, a nadie ayuda.

Porque es tan desigual naturaleza,
que cuando a retratalle se atrevieran,
ser hombre o fiera, les pusiera en duda.

113
Que amando no hay dificultad

Carbón me pide Inés, que la criada
dice que se le fue con un lacayo
medio francés, entre bermejo y bayo,
del caballero de la Ardiente Espada.

Si me pidiera lumbre, la abrasada   5
Troya del alma le prestara un rayo;
pero carbón, por Dios que me desmayo
de ir a la tienda, la sotana alzada.

Pero pedirme fuera más cuidado
qué asar con él, perdone la sotana,   10
perdone lo escolar, perdone el grado.

Todo lo puede amor, todo lo allana,
pues Hércules se puso rueca al lado,
y Júpiter las naguas de Diana.

112
He is not a man who does not do good to someone

Two things my fancies then did exercise,
While alien to the senses, to soul clear:
Marino, that great painter of the ear,
And Rubens, that great poet of the eyes.

Oblivion fighting, there in Italy lies   5
Marino, phoenix of his leavings drear;
And Rubens, with the brush without compeer,
Gives rage to envy and to Flanders prize.

But neither he with pen, nor talent full
Of him with brush could possibly project   10
A man who, capable, no one helps out.

For Nature ever is so changeable
That when to picture him they dared select,
If man or beast, they would be cast in doubt.

113
Loving, there is no problem

Inez asks me for coal, her maid unfazed
Declaring that some groom took it away,
The groom, half-French, between bright red and bay,
Of some Knight of the Burning Sword upraised.

If she asked me for light, the by-fire-dazed   5
Troy of my soul would lend to her a ray;
But coal, dear Lord, I'm fainting in dismay
To plod off to the store, my cassock raised.

But asking me much more concern did bring
Than roasting with the coal—excuse high tone,   10
Excuse the cassock and the scholar's notes.

Love can work wonders, level everything,
For Hercules a distaff made his own,
And Jupiter Diana's petticoats.

117
Decía una dama que no hallaba
a quien querer

Entre tantas guedejas y copetes,
tantos rizos, jaulillas y bigotes;
entre tantos ilustres Lanzarotes,
reservando gualdrapas y bonetes;

entre tantos sombreros capacetes,   5
ámbares negros, rubios achïotes,
lampazo ligas, cuerpos chamelotes,
poenes de armas, de Moclín jinetes;

entre tantos que van el pico al viento,
que a que los ruegue por lindeza espera[n],   10
¿no halláis a quien querer? ¡Extraño cuento!

¿A tantos vuestros ojos vituperan?
Señora, o no tenéis entendimiento,
o vendréis a querer cuando no os quiera[n].

120
Conjura un culto, y hablan los dos
de medio soneto abajo

—Conjúrote, demonio culterano,
que salgas deste mozo miserable,
que apenas sabe hablar, caso notable,
y ya presume de Anfión tebano.

Por la lira de Apolo soberano   5
te conjuro, cultero inexorable,
que le des libertad para que hable
en su nativo idioma castellano.

—«¿Por qué me torques bárbara tan mente?
¿Qué cultiborra y brindalín tabaco   10
caractiquizan toda intonsa frente?

—«Habla cristiano, perro. —Soy polaco.
—Tenelde, que se va. —No me ates, tente.
Suéltame. —Aquí de Apolo. —Aquí de Baco.»

117
A lady kept saying she couldn't find
anyone to love

Among such pompadours and manes with sheen,
Among curls, nets, mustaches vigorous;
Among such Lancelots illustrious,
Concealing bonnets, trappings not too clean;

Among so many hats like helmets seen,   5
Black ambers, blonds with tint rubineous,
Forms camel's hair, and garters verdurous,
Foot soldiers, cowboys local from Moclín;

Among such hosts beak in the wind who go,
Who for someone to note their cuteness wait,   10
You find no one to love? Can this be true!

So many do your eyes vituperate?
You, Lady, either no understanding show
Or you'll be loving when they don't love you.

120
He exorcizes a euphuist, and the two talk
in the last half of the sonnet

"You demon euphuist, I conjure you
That you come out of this lad miserable,
For he can barely talk, case notable,
And Theban swears to be, Amphion new.

By sovereign Apollo's lyre, I conjure you   5
As Gongoristicate inexorable,
That you free him to speak in syllable
Of his own native tongue, Castilian true."

"Why are you torquing me barbaric-so-ly?
What wiped-out cult, tobacco toast tiptop   10
Charactecatechize each unshorn brow?"

"Speak Christian language, dog." "I Polack be."
"Hold him, he's getting away." "Don't tie me, stop.
Let go." "Apollo, Bacchus, help us now!"

124
Intentó el poeta ausentarse para olvidar
y no le aprovechó el remedio, con que parece
que habla de veras

En la Troya interior de mi sentido,
metió un caballo Amor con gran secreto,
parto de más soldados, sólo a efeto
de verme en salamandra convertido.

Salen a media noche, y al rüido   5
despierta el alma al corazón inquieto,
y fugitivo yo, de tanto aprieto,
entre la viva llama, emprendo olvido.

Mi padre al hombro (que es mi ingenio) intento
buscar algún remedio a tanto estrago,   10
embarcado en mi propio pensamiento.

Pero poco mis daños satisfago,
pues con mudar de patria y de elemento,
me vuelvo a Troya porque no hay Cartago.

125
Había duende en una casa y amaneció preñada
una doncella

Siete meses, Filena, son cumplidos
que este espíritu malo se defiende;
no vos del mismo a vos, por más que enmiende
el cuidado a los ojos los vestidos.

Dispútase por hombres entendidos   5
si fue de los caídos este duende
o vos la que cayó, si no se entiende
que sois los dos espíritus caídos.

Entre tantos conjuros he notado
que espíritu sin carne no podía   10
seros tangible a vos, si os ha tocado.

No le conjuren más, Filena mía,
porque aunque éste se vaya, el que ha dejado
podrá sustituir la duendería.

124
The poet tried to absent himself to forget
and the remedy didn't work, so that it
seems he speaks truly

In inner Troy that is my consciousness,
Love placed a horse with secret substantive,
Birth of more troops, with single effect to give
Of seeing me as salamander progress.

At midnight they come forth in noisiness;   5
The soul wakes up the heart inquisitive,
And I, from so much pressure, fugitive,
Among live flame attempt forgetfulness.

My father shouldered (being my wit) I try,
Embarked in my own thoughtful argument,   10
To seek some cure for what would me destroy.

But little I my havoc satisfy,
With changing homeland, changing element:
Since there's no Carthage I return to Troy.

125
There was a demon in the house
and a fair maid turned up pregnant

Now seven lingering months fulfilled, Philene,
This spirit malevolent himself defends;
Not you from him, however much emends
Your care of clothing, prying eyes to screen.

Dispute it men of understanding keen   5
If this bold imp among the fallen ends,
Or it was you who fell, if none contends
That both of you are fallen spirits mean.

Among such conjuration I have seen
That spirit without flesh could never be,   10
Though touching you, to you real and terrene.

Let them not conjure more, Phi dear to me:
Though he may go, the one left at the scene
Can substitute some diabolology.

136
Discúlpase con Lope de Vega de su estilo

Lope, yo quiero hablar con vos de veras,
y escribiros en verso numeroso,
que me dicen que estáis de mi quejoso,
porque doy en seguir Musas rateras.

Agora invocaré las verdaderas,   5
aunque os sea (que sois escrupuloso)
con tanta Metafísica enfadoso,
y tantas categóricas quimeras.

Comienzo, pues, ¡O tú que en la risueña
aurora imprimes la celeste llama,   10
que la soberbia de Faeton despeña!

Mas perdonadme, Lope, que me llama
desgreñada una musa de estameña,
celosa del tabí de vuestra fama.

137
Prosigue la misma disculpa

Señor Lope: este mundo todo es temas;
cuantos en él son fratres, son orates;
mis musas andarán con alpargates,
que los coturnos son para supremas.

Gasten espliegos, gasten alhucemas,   5
perfúmenlas con ámbar los magnates;
mi humor escriba siempre disparates,
y buen provecho os hagan los poemas.

Merlín Cocayo vio que no podía
de los latinos ser el siempre Augusto,   10
y escribió macarrónica poesía.

Lo mismo intento, no toméis disgusto:
que Juana no estudió Filosofía,
y no hay Mecenas como el propio gusto.

136
He makes apology to Lope for his style

I, Lope, want to speak the truth with you,
And write for you with verses numerous,
For they tell me that you are querulous
Because pickpocket muses I pursue.

From now on I'll invoke those tried and true,   5
Though it may be for you (as scrupulous)
With too much Metaphysics rancorous
And categorical chimaeras too.

Thus I commence: Thou who in affable
Aurora dost imprint celestial flame,   10
Which hurls down Phaëton's own pride at full!

But, Lope, pardon me, for calls my name
Disheveled muse of simple homespun wool,
Who's jealous of the rich silk of your fame.

137
The same apology continues

Sir Lope: all this world is one mad theme,
Where all as brothers, lunatics parts play;
My muses in hemp sandals make their way,
For buskins are for those who stand supreme.

May lavender both Moorish, Latin stream,   5
Let magnates them with amber perfume spray;
Let my own wit write foolishness all day,
And may your poems bring to you high esteem.

So Merlin Coccai saw he could not be
Among the Latins always the August,   10
And he wrote macaronic poetry.

I strive to do the same, don't show disgust,
For Jane has never studied Philosophy,
And as Maecenas I my own taste trust.

146
Describe el poeta su Juana en forma de sirena,
sin valerse de la fábula de Ulises

De dulces seguidillas perseguidos,
lavando Juana en la ribera amena
del río, que entre lazos de verbena,
verdes construye a los gazapos nidos,

de Ulises quise hacer mis dos sentidos,   5
pero estaba tan bella de sirena,
que viendo y escuchando hasta la arena,
los vi anegados y lloré perdidos.

Allí el deseo y el amor iguales,
linces del agua en círculos sutiles,   10
buscaban bienes aumentando males.

Yo, con los ojos como dos candiles,
«Vengad —dije— mi ardor, dulces cristales,
pues que tenéis allá sus dos marfiles.»

147
Responde a un poeta que le afeaba escribir
con claridad, siendo, como es, la mas excelente
parte del que escribe

Livio, yo siempre fui vuestro devoto,
nunca a la fe de la amistad perjuro;
vos, en amor como en los versos duro,
tenéis el lazo a consonantes roto.

Si vos imperceptible, si remoto,   5
yo blando, fácil, elegante y puro,
tan claro escribo como vos oscuro;
la vega es llana e intrincado el soto.

También soy yo del ornamento amigo;
solo en los tropos imposibles paro,   10
y deste error mis números desligo;

en la sentencia sólida reparo,
porque dejen la pluma y el castigo
oscuro el borrador y el verso claro.

146
The poet describes his Jane in form of a
siren, without using Ulysses' fable

By seguidillas sweet my senses pressed,
Jane washing clothes upon the pleasant shore
Of river with verbena ties galore,
Which for the bunnies builds of green a nest,

Ulysses I did my two senses test,   5
But she such beauty as a siren wore
That, while the sands to see, to hear implore,
I saw them drowned and wept them dispossessed.

As equal there my love and my desire,
Like lynxes of the water in circles neat,   10
Were seeking riches, with misfortune growing.

I with my eyes much like two lamps of fire,
"Avenge," said I, "my ardor, crystals sweet,
For her two ivories you have there showing."

147
He responds to a poet who attacked his writing
with clarity, this being the most excellent
quality of the writer

Livio, I've remained your advocate,
And worth of friendship never would abjure;
You, in both love and verses hard, impure,
Have broken the bonds of consonance of late.

If you, remote, too subtle to appreciate,   5
I, gentle, facile, elegant, and pure,
I write as clearly as you write obscure:
The Vega is plain, the thicket intricate.

I also am of ornament a friend;
I only halt at tropes that all deceive,   10
And of this fault my numbers I keep free.

To solid core of meaning I attend,
So that both pen and punishment may leave
My blotter dark, and clear my poetry.

149
Al retrato de una dama,
después de muerta

Duerme el sol de Belisa en noche oscura,
y Evandro, su marido, con extraño
dolor pide a Felipe de Liaño
retrate, aunque sin alma, su figura.

Felipe restituye a su hermosura   5
la muerta vida con tan raro engaño,
que pensando negar el desengaño,
la vista de los ojos se perjura.

Tú dices que mejor fuera olvidarla,
Octavio, pues ya queda helada y fría,   10
que no dejar espejo en que mirarla.

Y yo digo, con paz de tu porfía,
que tuvo muy buen gusto en retratarla
al tiempo que mejor le parecía.

152
Sentimientos de ausencia, a imitación
de Garcilaso

Señora mía, si de vos ausente
en esta vida duro y no me muero,
es porque como y duermo, y nada espero,
ni pleiteante soy ni pretendiente.

Esto se entiende en tanto que accidente   5
no siento de la falta del dinero;
que entonces se me acuerda lo que os quiero,
y estoy perjudicial y impertinente.

Sin ver las armas ni sulcar los mares,
mis pensamientos a las musas fío;   10
sus liras son mis cajas militares.

Rico en invierno y pobre en el estío,
parezco en mi fortuna a Manzanares,
que con agua o sin ella siempre es río.

149
To the portrait of a lady,
after her death

Now sleeps Belisa's sun in darkest night;
Her spouse Evander with strange misery
Of Philip de Liaño asks that he
Portray her features, now without soul's light.

Liaño brings back to her beauty bright   5
The life now gone with such rare trickery
That in her eyes the look seems perjury,
Attempting thus the normal truth to slight.

You say that to forget her better were,
Octavian, since she lies with icy breast,   10
No mirror leaving in which to look at her.

And I declare, that you in peace may rest,
That he showed proper taste in painting her
That moment when to him she looked her best.

152
Sentiments of absence, in imitation
of Garcilaso

My Lady, if from you in absence pent
In this life I endure and do not die,
It's that I eat and sleep, all hope pass by,
No office seek, no legal argument.

This can be understood the while as accident   5
The lack of money I do not decry;
For I recall the love for you I sigh,
And I am harmful and impertinent.

Without arms seeing, or the seas outdaring,
My thoughts unto the muses I confide;   10
Their lyres are my martial drums no doubt.

In winter rich, in summer poorly faring,
I like the Manzanares in my luck abide,
Which river is, with water or without.

156
A don Francisco de Quevedo Villegas, Señor
de la Villa de la Torre de Juan Abad,
Caballero de la Orden de Santiago

Para cortar la pluma, en un profundo
ideal concepto, y trasladarle en rima
hallé (peregrinando el patrio clima)
que érais vos lo más sutil del mundo.

Atento os miro, y tan valiente infundo   5
alma al ingenio, al instrumento o prima,
que a escribir, a cantar, a ser me anima
de vuestro claro Sol, Faeton segundo.

Para alabaros hoy, pedíle al coro
de Apolo (si es que tanto emprender puedo)   10
permitiese mi pluma a su tesoro,

y respondióme con respeto y miedo,
Burguillos, si queréis teñirla en oro,
bañadla en el ingenio de Quevedo.

.

158
Preguntóle un caballero si haría comedias
por el principio de una que le enviaba

¿Si harás comedias, me preguntas, Cloro;
y un acto de Penélope me envías?
¿Qué fama te engañó que en tales días
de Falaris te metes en el toro?

Después que un autorón cantante, loro,   5
con idiotismos y objeciones frías,
la exponga al vulgo, comeránte arpías
el dulce néctar del castalio coro.

Es el teatro de ámbar un escudo
en un carro de estiércol o en un coche,   10
donde habla el ganso y está el cisne mudo;

y cuando más tu ingenio se trasnoche,
veráste en una esquina con engrudo,
y no te faltará para la noche.

156
To Don Francisco Quevedo Villegas, Lord of
the Township of La Torre de Juan Abad,
Knight of the Order of St. James

To sharpen well my pen, in one profound,
Ideal conceit, and translate it in rhyme,
I found, as pilgrim in my native clime,
That you the subtlest were the world around:

    I keep you close, and I so bravely ground   5
My wit in soul, on instrument or chime,
That I am stirred to be, write, sing sublime
By your clear Sun, O Phaeton new-crowned.

    To praise you, I Apollo's chorus polled
That to its treasures it today admit   10
My pen (if I dare enterprise so bold),

    And with respect, and fear, responded it:
"If you, Burguillos, pen would tinge in gold,
Bathe it in great Quevedo's stunning wit."

158
A gentleman, asked him if he should keep writing plays
along the lines of one he was sending him

You ask me, Chlorine, if you should write plays,
And send the first act of *Penelope*?
What fame misled you that from loon you flee
And bull grab by the very horns these days?

    For after some director glib does raise   5
His cold objections with mere idiocy
And casts it to the herd, each vulture free
On nectar of Castalian Chorus preys.

    The theater of amber is escutcheon plate
On coach or on a cart of dungish waste   10
Where speaks the goose, the swan is muted quite.

    And when your talent most would shine out late,
You'll on a corner be with paper paste,
And you'll not nothing have to face the night.

161
Discúlpase el poeta del estilo humilde

Sacras luces del cielo, yo he cantado
en otra lira lo que habéis oído;
saltó la prima y el bordón lo ha sido
al nuevo estilo, si le habéis culpado.

De mí mismo se burla mi cuidado,   5
viéndome a tal estado reducido;
pero, pues no me habéis favorecido,
¿por qué disculpo lo que habéis causado?

Entre tantos estudios os admire,
y entre tantas lisonjas de señores,   10
que de necesidad tal vez suspire;

mas tengo un bien en tantos disfavores,
que no es posible que la envidia mire:
dos libros, tres pinturas, cuatro flores.

Hoy cumple trece, y merece
Antonia dos mil cumplir;
ni hubiera más que pedir
si se quedara en sus trece.

161
The poet apologizes for his humble style

O sacred lights of heaven, I my song
Have sung on another lyre that you have heard;
The treble capered, and the bass has stirred
In newer style, if you have deemed it wrong.

Against myself my cares their scorn prolong,   5
Myself thus seeing reduced to state absurd,
But since to me your favors you've deferred,
Why do I excuse what you have caused so long?

Among so many études you I bless,
Among so much of nobles' flattery,   10
That I indeed must sigh away the hours;

But I in such reproofs one good possess,
That it's not possible that envy see:
Two books, three oil paintings, and four flowers.

Today Antonia thirteen has seen
And she deserves two thousand more;
Nor would there be more to implore
If she could always be thirteen.

Index of First Lines